POVERTY ALLEVIATION THROUGH MICROFINANCE

POVERTY ALLEVIATION THROUGH MICROFINANCE

Editor

Dr. B. Ramachandra Reddy

Professor

Department of Commerce

Sri Venkateswara University

Tirupati (Andhra Pradesh)

(INDIA)

D P H

DISCOVERY PUBLISHING HOUSE PVT. LTD.

INDIA

Published by:

Namit Wasan

DISCOVERY PUBLISHING HOUSE PVT. LTD.

4383/4B, Ansari Road, Darya Ganj
New Delhi-110 002 (India)
Phone : +91-11-23279245, 43596064-65
Fax : +91-11-23253475
E-mail : discoverypublishinghouse@gmail.com
namitwasan9@gmail.com
sales@discoverypublishinggroup.com

website: www.discoverypublishinggroup.com

***First Edition:* 2017**

ISBN: 978-93-5056-865-1

Poverty Alleviation Through Microfinance

Printed at:
Infinity Imaging Systems
Delhi

Preface

In India, the history of microfinance dates back to establishment of Syndicate Bank in 1921 in private sector. During the early years, Syndicate Bank concentrated on raising micro deposits in the form of daily/weekly basis and sanctioned micro loans to its clients for shorter period of time. But microfinance came to limelight only when Dr. Yunus gave it a mass movement in Grameen Bank experiment. Microfinance can be called a novel approach to provide saving and investment facility to the poor around world. Improved access and efficient provision of savings, credit, and insurance facilities in particular can enable the poor to smoothen their consumption, manage their risks better, gradually build their asset base, develop their business, enhance their income earning capacity, and enjoy an improved quality of life. In India, microfinance mainly operates through Self-Help Group (SHGs), Non-Government Organizations (NGOs), and Credit Agencies. It provides poor people with the means to find their own way out of poverty.

One of the greatest challenges before the Indian sub-continent which accommodates more than one-third of the population is poverty. India, one of the BRIC nations with more than 1.2 billion population is seen by many developed countries as an emerging economy. India's economic growth has failed to make a significant improvement in its poverty figures with 400 million more than the total in the poorest African Nations – still stuck in poverty. Government of India with its concern started various poverty alleviation programmes but they have failed to deliver the objectives to the level which is desired. The reasons may be many such as: failure to reach the target group, loopholes in the system, developing a robust mechanism to name a few.

Lending to the poor through micro credit is not the end of the problem but beginning of a new era. If effectively handled, it can create miracle in the field of poverty alleviation. But it must be bundled with capacity building programmes. Government cannot abdicate its responsibility of social and economic development of poor and down trodden. In absence of any special skills with the clients of micro credit, the fund is being used in consumption and procurement of non-productive assets. Hence it is very important to provide skills development training programme like: handicraft, weaving, carpentry, poultry, goat rearing, masonry, bees farming, vegetable farming and many other agricultural and non-agricultural training. Government has to play proactive role in this case. People with some special skills have to be given priority in lending micro credit. These clients should also be provided with post loan technical and professional aid for success of their micro enterprises. If government and MFIs act together then micro credit can play a great role in Poverty alleviation.

The present book is the outcome of National Seminar organized by the Department of Commerce, Sri Venkateswara University, Tirupati during 27-28th February 2016. The proceedings of this seminar will definitely supports the decision-makers to examine the impact of microfinance on rural poor in different parts of the country and find out feasible and possible measures to reduce the poverty. Further, the publication proves a good reference for the Researchers, Bankers, customers, professionals and policy makers in their pursuits.

I am grateful to Prof. A. Damodaram, Vice-chancellor, Prof. M. Bhaskar, Rector, Prof. M. Devarajulu, Registrar, Prof. B. Bhagavan Reddy, Dean and Principal, SVU College of Commerce, Management and Computer Science and all the faculty members in the department of commerce for their continuous support and encouragement.

Prof. B. Ramachandra Reddy

Contents

Pages 1-7

POVERTY ALLEVIATION THROUGH MICROFINANCE
Edited by : **Dr. B. Ramachandra Reddy**
Edition : **2017**
ISBN : 978-93-5056-865-1
Published by : **Discovery Publishing House Pvt. Ltd., New Delhi (India)**

1 Microfinance A Macro Approach for Poverty Alleviation in India

Dr. V. Sampath

INTRODUCTION

Poverty is a general scarcity or the state of one who lacks a certain amount of material possession or money. It is a multifaceted concept which includes: social, economical and political elements. Poverty may be absolute or relative. Absolute poverty refers to lack of means required to meet basic needs such as: food, clothing and shelter. Relative poverty refers individual's social and economical status compared to the rest of the society.

Poverty is a universal phenomena and it exist everywhere in various amount whether it is developed or developing or under developed country. India also suffering from poverty for a very long time even from the British colonial rule. Some of the indicators for the nature of World's poverty are:

- Almost half of the world live on less than 2.50 Dollar per day.
- One in two children live in poverty, 640 million people live without adequate shelter, 400 million have no access to safe water, 270 million have no access to health services and roughly more than 25,000 children died every day due to lack of care.
- Nearly a billion people entered the 21st century without knowing to read a book or to sign their names.
- The GDP of 41 heavily indebted poor countries is less than the wealth of the world's top 7 richest countries.
- Less than one per cent of what the world spent every year on weapons was more than enough to put every child into school.

Associate Professor in Commerce, Yadava College, Madurai, Tamil Nadu.

Poverty in India

The World Bank in 2011, based on 2005 Purchasing Power Parity (PPP), estimated that 23.6 per cent of Indian population (*i.e.* 276 million people) lived with an income of less than 1.25 American Dollar per day. Another estimation of Indian poverty made under United Nation's Millennium Development Goal Programme in 2011-12 revealed that 270 million of Indians out of 1.2 billions (21.9%) lived below poverty line of 1.25 Dollar per day.

In 2014 under PPP basis World Bank estimated that the World had 872.3 million people below the new poverty line. Out of this 179.6 million lived in India. In other words, India with 17.5 per cent of total World's population had 20.6 per cent of World's poorest.

Poverty Alleviation

Poverty in any form in any part of the World under any social set-up should be eradicated to have a civilized society having faith on Government. The organizations at international level like: UNO, World Bank, IMF etc., are approaching this problem through its schemes and programmes. But still poverty eradication is a challenge for them. Poverty should be solved economically by guaranteeing a minimum daily income and socially by developing and providing reasonable social environment. Lasting peace can be achieved only by bring back large population by breaking out the boundaries of poverty. Though poverty is a socio-economic problem, economical part should be attended by which the social part can be resolved easily. A country is poor because it is poor. → Low savings → Low investment → Low income Low savings. Bringing people out of this circle by overcoming the economical poverty is very much essential to improve the living condition of World's population.

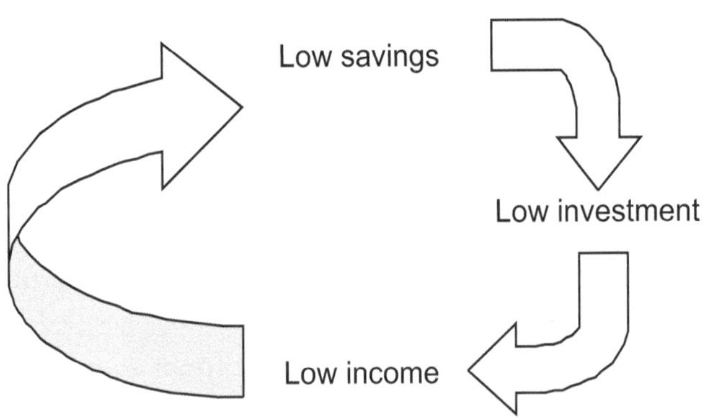

Poverty Alleviation in India

India on its part, with the support of international organizations, constantly and consistently taking measures to remove poverty. It is also succeeds in this venture considerably. India is adding more and more people to its middle class every year than any other country. Poverty reduction in India in fast and it is expected that if India is going with this much of speed in poverty eradication it will be free from the clutches of poverty by 2020.

Indian Progress in Poverty Alleviation

Year	Percentage of Population Below Poverty Line	
	Rural	Urban
2004-05	42	25.5
2009-10	33.8	20.9
2014-15	25.7	13.7

Microfinance and Poverty Alleviation

In poverty the social part should be solved by economical measures. This alone be an independent and permanent solution to poverty. But for this charity is not the answer to poverty. Taking this fact into consideration, India is approaching this problem from and through economical measures. One of the popular tools for economical development and poverty reduction is microfinance. It is a global measure also followed by many of the countries.

Prof. Muhammad Yunus, a Bangladeshi social entrepreneur, banker, economist and civil society leader, who was awarded the Nobel Prize for peace for founding Grameen Bank pioneered the concept microfinance and microcredit in 1970. This was conceptualised in his mind when a loan of 27 Dollar changed the lives of 42 families in a village in Bangladesh and also enabled them to repaid the entire loan with interest. Following this concept, the first Microfinance Community Development Bank was founded in 1974 at Chicago.

Microfinance is the provision of financial service to low income clients or solidarity lending groups including consumers and self-employed who traditionally lack access to banking and related services.

Microfinance sector grown rapidly over the past few decades all over the World. And today it has evolved into a vibrant industry with a variety of business models suitable to the requirements of various segments of poor and needy people Worldwide.

Microfinance in India exist in different form to meet out the needs of the target groups. Some of the popular forms are:

- NGO (Society/Trust).
- Section 25 companies.
- Non-Banking Financial Companies.
- Commercial Banks.
- Regional Rural Banks.
- Co-operative Societies.
- Large lenders in the form of refinance to microfinance institutions.
- Self-Help Groups.

Microfinance is not only gives micro credit to poor but also provides a wide range of financial services like: savings, insurance, remittance and non-financial services like: training, counselling, consultancy etc. A microfinance system has the following features to satisfy the needs of poor village people:

- Borrowers are from the low income group.
- Loans are of small amount.
- Loan duration in very short.
- Loans are offered without collaterals.
- High frequency of repayment.
- Loans are taken generally for income generation purposes.
- No transaction cost.
- Target people who deprived of all banking services.

Considering the achievements of microfinance institutions and to make used of their potentials to eradicate poverty, the United Nations Economic and Social Council proclaimed the year 2005 as the 'International Year of Microcredit'. The Prime objective of this proclamation was to fuel the strong entrepreneurial spirit of poor people all around the World.

In India the achievements of MFIs since their inception is marvellous in terms of geographical coverage, number of branches, client outreach, loan disbursement and loan portfolio outstanding. To understand the achievements of microfinance in India the performance of top 10 MFIs are given below as sample.

Achievements of Top 10 MFIs in India

Rank	1	2	3	4	5	6	7	8	9	10
No. of States/ UTs Covered	24	22	19	17	15	14	12	11	11	11
No. of Branches	2022	1273	784	618	423	422	407	361	270	267
Client Outreach (in Lakhs)	65	36	33	23	23	22	20	14	12	9
Loan Outstanding (Rs. in Crores)	9524	4155	3774	3570	3274	2665	2144	2141	1603	1447
Loan disbursed in 2014-15 (Rs. in Crores)	14989	6891	4328	4121	3530	2366	2129	1981	1894	1699

From the above exhibited data of the top 10 MFIs, we can very well visualise the total coverage of microfinance in India under different variables.

Apart from the supply of microfinance services by the top 10 institutions, the services supplied by the rest also considerable. In India there are 400-500 NGOs and around 20 non-profit companies engaged in the supply of microfinance. In this venture in addition to the above organizations, 200-250 microfinance institutions and nearly 50 non-banking financial companies are also functioning, All these organizations jointly contributing a lot for the upliftment of poor who are below the poverty line. The overall contributions of all microfinance institutions are given here.

Table 1.1: Overall Contributions of MFIs in India

Variables	2010-11	2011-12	2012-13
Savings of SHGs with banks (Rs. in Crores)	7016	6551	8217
Savings of Women SHG with banks (Rs. in Crores)	5299	5104	6515
Loan disbursed to SHGs (Rs. in Crores)	14548	16535	20585
Loan disbursed to Women SHGs (Rs. in Crores)	12622	14132	17854
Loan outstanding with SHGs (Rs. in Crores)	31221	36340	39375
Loan outstanding with Women SHGs (Rs. in Crores)	26124	30465	32840
Loans to MFIs by Banks (Rs. in Crores)	8449	5205	7840
Grant support to partner agencies (Rs. in Lakhs)	-	-	22650
NPA of Banks against SHG loans (Rs. in Crores)	-	-	2787
NABARD support for Training and Capacity Building (No. of persons)	-	-	3018269

From the information given in the above Table 1.1 it can be observed that the microfinance institutions functioning in India are taking constant efforts to eradicate poverty from India by promoting savings, lending loans, supporting SHGs, empowering women and developing people by training and capacity building.

Problems and Remedies

Microfinance institutions by their informal nature, rural based operations, women dominant SHGs, income generated form of lending and entrepreneurial promotion character penetrated deeply into the poor illiterate mass. The close networking of various microfinance institutions also provide easy access to more and more people to enjoy the benefits of microcredit. In spite of these advantages to beneficiaries, the microfinance institutions are facing certain problems. If such problems are overhauled, no doubt, the performance of microfinance institutions and benefits extended to individuals and group members will be still better.

1. Dropout/migration of group members indirectly affects the reaming members from getting subsequent loans. Therefore, members who want to leave or migrate to another group should be taken such decisions only in unavoidable situations that too without affecting other members from getting benefits.
2. Financial illiteracy of members is an another hindrance faced by microfinance institutions. Due to illiteracy, the rate of awareness about the schemes and operations of microfinance institutions is less among members. Therefore, steps should be taken through educational training to improve the literacy of members so as to make use of the services of microfinance institutions effectively.
3. The not - for- profit form of microfinance institutions are not allowed to raise equity fund. They depend on grants from Government, NABARD and SIDBI to increase their portfolio size to get back loans. Therefore, sanctioning bank loans to microfinance institutions on the basis of portfolio size may be relaxed in case of not - for - profit form of microfinance institutions. It will increase the lending potentiality of such MFIs.
4. The members of the SHGs may be given training on aspects like: cost reduction, mechanisation and marketing to enhance their earning potentiality. This will be very useful to strengthen the microfinance institutions as well as the group members.

5. Microfinance institutions may be asked to open new branches in areas with no or low microfinance penetration to serve outreach people and to provide an evenly distributed financial services.

Conclusion

Microfinance institutions from its inception, acting as a good substitute for banks in non-banking areas. They are extending financial services and financial products informally at the place of clients at a lower cost than what banks charged. They developed entrepreneurial culture among poor with potential, thereby enable them to generate-income. All these contribute much to eradicate poverty in a large way. Popularising the concept microfinance further with necessary charges as suggested above will help to make poverty poor and poor in the days to come.

Pages 8-15

POVERTY ALLEVIATION THROUGH MICROFINANCE
Edited by : Dr. B. Ramachandra Reddy
Edition : 2017
ISBN : 978-93-5056-865-1
Published by : Discovery Publishing House Pvt. Ltd., New Delhi (India)

2

Role of SHPIs in Promotion of Micro Enterprises in Andhra Pradesh
An Outlook

Dr. P. Saritha[1]
Dr. K. Lavanya Latha[2]

INTRODUCTION

Microfinance has been recognised and accepted as one of the new development paradigms for alleviating poverty through social and economic empowerment of the poor with special emphasis on empowering women. Microfinance, by definition, refers to the entire range of financial services rendered to the poor and including: skill upgradation, entrepreneurial development that would enable them to overcome poverty. Various SHPIs (Self-Help Promoting Institutions) and NGOs (Non-Government Organizations) have been recognised as an entity in the microfinance concept especially in providing credit plus services. NGOs, which were initially confined to the social aspects of development, were enlarged to help the poor and weaker sections of the rural society in their economic pursuits. In Andhra Pradesh, many NGOs acting as SHPIs, who had promoted and nurtured SHGs, have been permitted to open Mutually Aided Cooperative Societies (MACS) and take care of all financial pursuits of their own SHGs and also imbibe SHG members to promote different IGAs (Income Generating Activities/MEs (Micro Enterprises).

The SHPIs are agencies which help the poor to organize themselves into groups, help them in their organizational, managerial and financial matters and in upgrading their skills and in some cases, in countering

1. Assistant Professor, Department of Business Administration, Yogi Vemana University, Kadapa - 516 003.
2. Assistant Professor, Department of Management Studies, Pondicherry University, Pondicherry.

pressures from vested interests. There have been a wide variety of SHPIs in the SHG movement in the country ranging from government agencies to the NGOs, Farmers Clubs, banks and Individual Rural Volunteers (IRVs). In the State of Andhra Pradesh, the SHG movement has been mainly driven by the government agencies. About 96 per cent of the SHGs formed in the state are by the DRDA (District Rural Development Agency), IKP (Indira Kranthi Patham) and other government agencies (Table 2.1).

Table 2.1: SHPIs in Andhra Pradesh and in India

Number of SHGs Promoted by	India		Andhra Pradesh	
	No.	% to Total	No.	% to Total
Government Agencies	1312390	50.74	557105	96.09
Banks	140120	5.42	2381	0.43
NGOs	1118817	43.26	20148	3.48
Farmer Clubs	14019	0.54	114	0.0
Individual Rural Volunteer	911	0.04	-	-
Total	2586257	100	579748	100

Source: DRDA Reports.

State as an SHPI – Role of DRDA and IKP

The IKP Project and the DRDA are the major SHPIs in the State of Andhra Pradesh. The Project is managed by the SERP, an autonomous Society registered under the societies act along with DRDA. The SERP combines the authority and accountability of the government and operational flexibility of an NGO. The institutional model under the project has focused on formation and strengthening of SHGs for addressing the rural poverty. The major role played by the State Government is given in the following paragraphs. The IKP has so far promoted 1,85,446 new SHGs and strengthened 2,86,414 old SHGs covering a total of 45.35 lakh poor household. The project staff facilitates linkage of SHGs with the banks under the SBL Programme of NABARD. They also help the banks in recovery of loans.

In order to sustain the large number of SHGs formed in the State, Government of Andhra Pradesh has promoted federations of SHGs at the village level (VOs) and mandal level (MSs) under the IKP Project. A third tier, Zilla Samakhya, is also in the evolutionary process. The SHG federations are intended to take over the function of capacity building of existing SHGs, formation of new SHGs, audit, maintaining quality standards, resource support to SHGs etc. The federations are being registered under the APMACS Act, 1995.

Capacity Building and Training

In order to meet the capacity building needs of the SHGs, VOs and MSs, as also Mandal Training Centres in 729 project mandals and 22 Training and Technology Development Centres (TTDCs) in all the district headquarters have been established. So far, 2,52,687 SHGs have received first level training whereas 1,52,894 SHGs have received the subsequent series of formal training including: capacity building in health, gender and livelihood sectors. The articulate and resourceful women from SHGs are identified and are developed as Community Resource Persons, Community Activists, Livelihood activists, health activists etc. This cadre is utilised in organizing new SHGs, revival of dormant/defunct SHGs, facilitation of regular SHG meetings, savings, trainings, identify/train book keepers, prepare micro credit plans and facilitate SHGs and VOs to adopt social agenda.

The study observed that out of a total of 56 sample SHGs, 75 per cent of SHGs received one or other sorts of training. About 25 per cent of SHGs had not received any sort of training. Age-wise, older SHGs (71%) received more training on IGAs as compared to recently formed SHGs (49% for SHGs of 4-6 years old and 27 per cent of SHGs of three year old). About 81 per cent of SHGs reported that the training received by them is quite useful. Similarly, about 20 per cent of SHGs reported that training is very much useful for the day to day operations (Table 2.2).

Table 2.2: Capacity Building through Training of Sample SHGS

(Percentage)

Particulars on Training	SHG Age (Years)			Overall
	Up to 3	4-6 Years	7 and Above	
1. SHGs received training	66.0	80.3	100.0	75.0
(ii) Training on SHG orientation	48.0	31.3	28.6	55.0
(iii) Training on orientation and IGAs	27.0	49.0	71.4	20.0
2. SHGs received no training	34.0	20.7	0.0	25.0
Total (I+II)	100.0	100.0	100.0	100.0
Effectiveness of Training				
Useful	57.8	89.0	62.6	71.9
Very Useful	32.4	9.0	35.4	21.8
Not Useful	9.8	2.0	2.0	6.3
Total	100.0	100.0	100.0	100.0

Promotion of IGAs and Micro Enterprises

Under the IKP project, assistance is provided out of Community Investment Fund (CIF) to the SHGs, VOs and MSs to support a wide range of activities such as: agriculture, animal husbandry, nonfarm, commodity marketing and food security etc. Social development activities such as: health, education, nutrition, creation of infrastructure such as: drying platforms, procurement centers, weighing scales, etc., are also provided from CIF. The IGA component of CIF are provided to MSs as revolving fund and are treated as corpus of MS. Lending from MS to VO and VO to SHG carry interest rates with interest differential at each tier. The VOs are required to repay CIF amount to the MS in 100 equal monthly installments and the SHGs will repay to the VO in 50 equal monthly installments. The members will pay to the SHG in 20 monthly installments. This arrangement is expected to accumulate capital, re-lend to the members and to meet their cost of operation from interest margin. As per guidelines, 50 per cent of the funds under CIF are planned to be provided for agri-allied activities, around 25 per cent is for non-farm and 15 per cent for direct agriculture activities. CIF has played major role in improving the livelihoods of the poor. Major interventions through commodity marketing by communities - red gram procurement in Mahbubnagar and Ranga Reddy, soyabean procurement in Adilabad, NTFPs in tribal parts of the state, lac cultivation in Adilabad have been possible due to CIF.

Market Promotion through DWCRA Bazars

DRDAs have built marketing infrastructure for marketing of the products produced by SHG women in major districts of the state. The study districts had the DWCRA bazaars. The shops built in the bazaars are only given to the SHG women on a reasonable rent. Some shops are also given jointly to two or three SHGs for marketing their products together. DRDAs also organize marketing melas in state/district head quarters to facilitate the marketing of the products of SHG women. The role of various SHPIs in facilitating SHG members in taking up IGAs/MEs in different ways shows that presence of DRDA is more in all spheres compared to NGOs and other SHPIs (Table 2.3).

RRBs as SHPI

NABARD has been encouraging RRBs to take up promotion and nurturing of SHGs and has been providing part financial assistance to them for the purpose since 1999. In Andhra Pradesh, Sri Venkateswara Grameena Bank, Chittoor, Sri Saraswathi Grameena Bank, Adilabad, Sri Rama Grameena Bank, Nizamabad and Sri Anantha Grameena Bank, Anantpur district have acted as SHPIs and promoted, nurutured and provided linkage to 2,196 SHGs. Though the groups were formed by RRB, after the advent of IKP all the groups have come under the umbrella of the IKP project and the SHGs are being taken care of by IKP-DRDA.

Table 2.3: Role in Promotion of IGAS/Micro Enterprises among SHG Members

SHPIs	Role in Promotion of IGAs/Micro Enterprises among SHG Members					
	Forming SHGs	Capacity Building*	Tng. on IGAs/MEs	Promoting IGAs	Launched MFI Arms	Product Marketing
DRDA-IKP	√	√	√	√	√	√
RRB	√					
Farmers' Clubs	√					
NGOs						
PSS	√	√		√	√	
LMPSS	√	√	√	√	√	√
MARI	√	√		√	√	
RASS	√	√				
GRAM	√	√	√	√	√	√
DHAN Foundation	√	√	√	√		√

*capacity building activities include training on SHG orientation, leadership qualities, financial management, book keeping, laws of MACS and federation, preparing Business Development Plans, MIS, etc.

Farmers Clubs as SHPIs

The Farmers Clubs had also functioned as promotional agencies in forming SHGs and facilitating linkage with the banks. Farmers Clubs have promoted a total of 114 SHGs in the state. However, their role is limited to formation of SHGs after which the SHGs come under the IKP-DRDA.

NGOs as SHPIs

NGOs have played a supporting role in formation, nurturing of SHGs groups in the state. There are still a few regions in the State where NGOs are also involved in the strengthening of SHG movement in the state in addition to the DRDA-IKP. NGOs take care of SHGs through a network of village book keepers, field organizers, coordinators etc. SHG federations have been formed and have been registered as MAC societies. Some NGOs have also formed MFI arms for providing loans to SHG members by availing funds from public/private sector banks such as: Indian Bank, IOB, ICICI, HDFC, ING Vysya, etc. The individual members of SHGs are provided loans in the range of Rs. 5,000 to Rs. 50,000 with the guarantee of the SHGs. The activities of major NGOs in the districts of Chittoor, Nizamabad and Warangal districts in the areas of microfinance are given in the following paragraphs.

Pragathi Seva Samiti

Pragathi Seva Samiti (PSS), is operating in six drought prone mandals comprising 129 villages in Warangal district. It has organised 2,700 SHGs covering 48,600 women. It has also facilitated in formation of 30 MACS in its operational area covering 21,200 SHG members. It has also established the Pragathi Microfinance Institution in 2004 to provide microfinance to the MACS established by them. As claimed by PSS, more than 50 per cent of the loan from the MACS is being utilised for Micro Enterprises. PSS provides insurance services to the members by partnering with Healing Fields, Royal Sundharam, etc. In partnership with CARE for the CASHE programme, PSS has strengthened the SHGs through regular capacity building activities, leadership qualities, financial management, book keeping, laws of MACS and federation, preparing Business Development Plans, MIS, etc. Training has been provided to women on IGAs such as: tailoring, type writing, candle making, etc.

Lodi Multipurpose Social Service Society

Lodi Multipurpose Social Service Society (LMSSS) operates in 800 villages of 35 mandals of Warangal and Karimnagar districts. It has has formed 5,345 SHGs with a membership of 79,550. It has also formed 95 physically disabled groups with 570 members. The NGO has assisted 3,100 families to take up several IGAs/MEs such as: jute bag making, STD booth, bangle shop, horticulture, vermin compost, neem seed collection, tamarind collection, milch animals, etc. About 40 members have been provided training on the banana fibre extraction with financial support from NABARD. It has facilitated in formation of 20 MACS and all the MACS have been federated at mandal level and Sri Mahila Paraspara Sahayaka Sangha has been formed covering 3,360 SHG members.

Modern Architects of Rural India

Modern Architects of Rural India (MARI), implementing the CASHE of CARE, has formed 1,366 SHGs consisting of 19,313 members covering 141 villages in Warangal District. It has facilitated in formation of 14 cluster level MACS of SHGs and registered them under the APMACS Act, 1995. An apex level MACS named 'Sanghatitha Mahila MACS Federation' has been formed to provide financial services to the SHGs. The NGO has established the system of Village Book Keepers for writing the books of SHGs. It conducts training programmes for the SHG members, book keeping systems, training for the MACS leaders. MARI has also tied up with insurance companies like Royal Sundaram for providing insurance cover to its members.

Rashtriya Seva Samiti

Rashtriya Seva Samiti (RASS) in Chittoor district has its presence in over 2,000 villages in Andhra Pradesh, Orissa, Tamil Nadu and Delhi. RASS operates micro finance activities under the banner of RASS Mahila Pragati. RASS has promoted Sri Padmavathi Mahilabhydaya Sangham, a federation of women's SHGs in 1992. It has also established a Capacity Building Institute for Microfinance in partnership with CARE-CASHE for providing training in SHG concepts and management, financial management, delinquency management etc., to the stakeholders under the microfinance programme. It also implements the Support to Training and Employment Programme (STEP) in collaboration with Department of Women and Child Development (DWCD), GoI to provide technical skill to members of SHGs in dairy activity and also to organize women into small activity groups for taking up production of dairy fodder, milk collection, marketing and veterinary services.

GRAM

Gram, a registered development organization operating in Nizmabad and Adilabad districts of Andhra Pradesh, has promoted SHGs and has facilitated in formation of 15 mandal level MACS of SHGs in Nizamabad district and 5 in Adilabad district with a membership of 42,000 members. The 15 mandal level MACS in Nizamabad district have been federated at the district level and Indur MACS federation has been formed covering 2,528 SHGs with a membership of 31,626. Indur MACS Federation is accessing financial support HDFC Bank, ABN Amro Bank, BASIX, FWWB etc., for on-lending to MACS and SHGs. For enhancement of livelihood opportunities to its SHG members, the Federation has promoted 'Intideepam dairy' with an investment of Rs. 5 lakh with the technical support from NDDB.

DHAN Foundation

Development of Humane Action (DHAN) Foundation was formed on 2 October 1997 as a trust under the Indian Trust Act with a mission of 'building institutions for development innovations and upscaling for impacting the livelihoods to enable poor communities'. It has operational presence in four states of the country including three districts in Andhra Pradesh. It has promoted around 3,000 SHGs in Andhra Pradesh with 50,000 members. Under a collaborative project with DRDA, Chittoor, the foundation had taken up a project for reviving, rebuilding and strengthening of DWCRA groups in Kuppam and Gudipalli mandals of Chittoor district.

Conclusion

DRDA is the major SHPI in the State. Though in the initial stages, banks (particularly RRBs and a few DCCBs) and NGOs had acted as SHPIs, after the launch of the Velugu (presently IKP) by State Government, all the groups in the State had come under the umbrella of DRDA with the groups taken care of by various DRDA functionaries, *i.e.,* Area Coordinators/ Community Co-ordinators, MBKs, Community Activists etc. Even, under SGSY, no new groups are formed and old groups with two/three linkages are slated for financing under SGSY. The DRDA is focusing on capacity building of the SHG federations in the State. In order to meet the capacity building needs of the SHGs, VOs and MSs, as also Mandal Training Centres in 729 project mandals and 22 TTDCs have been established. Out of a total of 56 sample SHGs, 75 per cent of SHGs received one or other sorts of training. About 25 per cent of SHGs had not received any sort of training.

Under the IKP project, assistance is provided out of CIF to the SHGs, VOs and MSs to support a wide range of activities such as: agriculture, animal husbandry, nonfarm, commodity marketing and food security etc. DRDAs have built marketing infrastructure for marketing of the products produced by SHG women in major districts of the state. The study districts had the DWCRA bazaars with shops given only to the SHG women on a reasonable rent. Some shops are also given jointly to two or three SHGs for marketing their products together. DRDAs also organize marketing melas in state/district head quarters to facilitate the marketing of the products of SHG women.

Pages 16-25

POVERTY ALLEVIATION THROUGH MICROFINANCE
Edited by : **Dr. B. Ramachandra Reddy**
Edition : **2017**
ISBN : 978-93-5056-865-1
Published by : **Discovery Publishing House Pvt. Ltd., New Delhi (India)**

3 Microfinance Trends, Delivery Models and Prospects

S. Jayasree[1]
Dr. B. Ramachandra Reddy[2]

Why Microfinance

In developing countries, financing to the rural poor through formal financial services failed to meet the credit requirements of the rural poor people. The main reason of failure was absence of any recognized employment and hence absence of collateral with the poor. The high risk and the high transaction costs of banks associated with small loans and savings deposits are other factors which make them non-bankable. The lack of loans from formal institutions leaves the poor with no other option but to borrow money from local money-lenders on huge interest rates. In different countries including: India, efforts have been made by their governments to deliver formal credit to rural areas by setting up special agricultural banks/rural banks or directing commercial banks to provide loans to rural borrowers. However, these programmes have also not worked well due to various reasons. The common reasons found by many researchers are the political difficulty for governments to enforce loan repayment and the selection of relatively wealthy and influential people, rather than the poor, for bank loans (Adams *et al.* 1984; Adams and Vogel, 1986; World Bank, 1989). Women's World Banking (1995) estimated that in most developing countries, the formal financial system reaches to only top 25 per cent of the economically active population. This leaves the bottom 75 per cent without access to financial services apart from those provided by money-lenders and family. Thus, the inability of formal credit institutions to deal with the credit requirements of poor effectively has led to emergence of microfinance as an alternative credit system for the poor.

1. **Lecturer in Commerce, SPW Degree and PG College, Tirupati.**
2. **Professor, Department of Commerce, S.V. University, Tirupati.**

Microfinance scheme provides a wide range of financial services to people who have little or nothing in the way of traditional collateral. It helps them to build up assets, survive crises and to establish small business to come out of poverty. Except extending small loans (micro-credit), microfinance programme provides various other financial and non-financial services such as: savings, insurance, guidance, skill development training, capacity building and motivation to start income-generating activities to enhance the productivity of credit.

Objectives of the Study

The main aim of this paper is theoretically evaluating the origin of microfinance, how the microfinance functions and its delivery models. The objective of this paper study is to show how microfinance works, by using group lending methodology for reducing poverty and the prospects of microfinance in India.

Origin of Microfinance

The concept of providing financial services to low income people is very old. Many informal credit groups have been operating in many countries for several years like: the *susus* in Nigeria and Ghana, *chit funds* and Rotating Savings and Credit Associations (ROSCAs) in India, *tontines* in West Africa, *pasanaku* in Bolivia, *hui* in China, *arisan* in Indonesia, *paluwagan* in Philippines etc. It is believed that initially, the informal financial institutions emerged in Nigeria dating back in the fifteenth century. Such type of institutions started establishing in Europe during the eighteenth century when in 1720 the first loan fund targeting poor people was founded in Ireland (Seibel, 2005).

In 1847, some credit co-operatives were created in Germany which served 1.4 million people by 1910. In 1880s the British controlled government of Madras in South India tried to use the German experiment to address poverty in India. This effort resulted in membership of more than nine million poor to credit co-operatives by 1946. During the same time the Dutch colonial administrators constructed a co-operative rural banking system in Indonesia which eventually became Bank Rakyat Indonesia (BRI), now one of the largest Microfinance Institutions (MFIs) of the world (Schwiecker, 2004).

In the 1970s, a paradigm shift started to take place. The failure of subsidised government or donor driven institutions to meet the demand for financial services in developing countries led to several new approaches. Bank Dagan Bali (BDB), established in Indonesia in 1970, was the earliest bank to institute commercial microfinance (Schwiecker, 2004). In 1973, ACCION International, a USA based NGO, disbursed its first loan in Brazil at commercial interest rate to start a micro enterprise. One year later in 1974, the Self-Employed Women's Association of India (SEWA) started a bank to provide loans to poor women. In 1976, Muhammad Yunus, a professor of Economics at Chittagong University, Bangladesh initiated an experimental research project of providing credit to the rural poor. He gave a small loan of 856 Taka ($27) from his pocket to 42 poor bamboo weavers and found that small loans radically changed the lives of these people and they were able to pay back the loans with interest. The success of this idea led Yunus to establish Grameen Bank in 1983 in Bangladesh. This programme showed astonishing growth rates in Bangladesh, particularly during the 1980s and 1990s. It encouraged social innovators and organizations all over the world to begin experiments with different microfinance delivery methods to bring financial services to the poor. It is now adopted worldwide in the countries of different continents.

Many international NGOs, such as: Foundation for International Community Assistance (FINCA), Americans for Community Co-operation in Other Nations (ACCION), Freedom from Hunger, Opportunity International, Co-operative for Assistance and Relief Everywhere (CARE), Consultative Group for Assisting the Poor (CGAP), etc., are promoting microfinance programme for creating new businesses and combating poverty in a sustainable way. Over the past few decades, microfinance has been experimented in many developing countries. Bank Rakyat Indonesia (BRI) in Indonesia, Bancosol in Bolivia, Bank for Agriculture and Agricultural Co-operatives (BAAC) in Thailand, Grameen Bank, and Bangladesh Rural Advancement Committee (BRAC) of Bangladesh, NABARD in India, Amannah Ikhtiar Malaysia (AIM) of Malaysia, Agriculture Development Bank of Nepal (ADBN), K-Rep in Kenya and Mibanco in Peru have yielded encouraging results in alleviating poverty and empowering the poor through microfinance.

In India, the first initiative to introduce microfinance was the establishment of Self-Employed Women's Association (SEWA) in Gujarat. SEWA was registered as a trade union of self-employed women workers of the unorganised sector in 1972. This trade union established their bank known as SEWA Bank in 1974. To establish this bank four thousand union members contributed Rs. 10 each as share capital. Since then this bank is registered as a co-operative bank and has been providing banking services to poor women and has also become a viable financial venture. In the midst of the apparent inadequacies of the formal financial system to cater to the financial needs of the rural poor, the first major effort to reach these rural poor was made by NABARD in 1986-87, when it supported and funded an action research project on 'Saving and Credit Management of Self-Help Groups' of Mysore Resettlement and Development Authority (MYRADA). For this purpose, a grant of Rs. one million was provided to MYRADA. The encouraging results were yielded. In 1988-

89, NABARD undertook a survey of 43 NGOs spread over eleven states in India to study the functioning of the SHGs and possibilities of collaboration between the banks and SHGs in the mobilisation of rural savings and improving the credit delivery to the poor. Encouraged by the results of field level experiments in group based approach for lending to the poor, NABARD launched a pilot project of linking 500 SHGs with banks in 1991-92 in partnership with non-governmental organizations (NGOs) for promoting and grooming self-help groups of socio-economically homogeneous members. In order to meet their credit requirements, in July 1991 RBI issued a circular to the commercial banks to extend credit to the SHGs formed under the pilot project of NABARD. During the project period different NGOs like: Association of Sarva Seva Farms (ASSEFA), Madras; People's Rural Education Movement (PREM), Behrampur; Professional Assistance for Development Action (PRADAN), Madurai; and Community Development Society (CDS), Kerala promoted hundreds of groups. The results were very encouraging. In February 1992, the launching of pilot phase of the SHG-Bank Linkage Programme (SHG-BLP) could be considered as a landmark development in banking with the poor.

In order to further promote this programme RBI issued instructions to banks in 1996 to cover SHG financing as a mainstream activity under their priority sector-lending portfolio. The programme acquired a national priority from 1999 through Government of India budget announcements. With the support from both the government and the Reserve Bank of India, NABARD successfully spearheaded the programme through partnership with various stakeholders in the formal and informal sector. Since the time of its origin, NABARD provides policy guidance, technical and promotional support mainly for capacity building of NGOs and SHGs. Realising the potential in the field of microfinance, the government allowed various private players to provide microfinance in microfinance, the government allowed various private players to provide microfinance in the country. These private microfinance providers, commonly known as MFIs, are various NGOs, Non-banking Financial Companies (NBFCs) and other registered companies. Many state governments amended/passed their State Co-operative Acts to use co-operative societies for providing microfinance. These days many public and private commercial banks, regional-rural banks, co-operative banks, co-operative societies, registered and unregistered NBFCs, societies, trusts and NGOs are providing microfinance by using their branch network and through different microfinance delivery models.

Meaning and Function of Microfinance

Broad range of services such as: savings, deposits, loans, payment services, money transfers and insurance to poor and low income households and their micro enterprises. This definition of microfinance is not restricted to the below poverty line people but it includes low income households also. The Task Force [1] terms microfinance as the provision of thrift, credit and other financial services and products of very small amounts to the poor in rural, semi-urban or urban areas for enabling them to raise their income levels and improve living standards. The Task Force emphasises that microfinance will cover not only consumption and production loans, but also loans for other credit needs such as: housing and shelter [2].

The Microfinancial Sector (Development and Regulation) Bill, (2007) defines microfinance as the provision of financial assistance and insurance services to an individual or an eligible client either directly or through a group mechanism for an amount, not exceeding rupees fifty thousand in aggregate per individual for small and tiny enterprise, agriculture, allied activities (including for consumption purposes of such individual); or an amount not exceeding rupees one lakh fifty thousand in aggregate per individual for housing or other prescribed purposes. The eligible clients which may get financial assistance under this scheme may be landless labourers and migrant labourers; artisans and micro entrepreneurs; disadvantaged cultivators of agricultural land including: oral lessees, tenants, and share croppers; and farmers owning not more than two hectares of agricultural land.

The vicious cycle of *'low income' → low savings' → low investment' → low income'* can be broken with the injection of credit in the cycle. *'Credit intended for more investment' → more income' → more savings' → more investment' → more income'* is the result that is sought through the credit intervention. The impact of microfinance on the different sectors of the economy can be well understood with the help of following diagram:

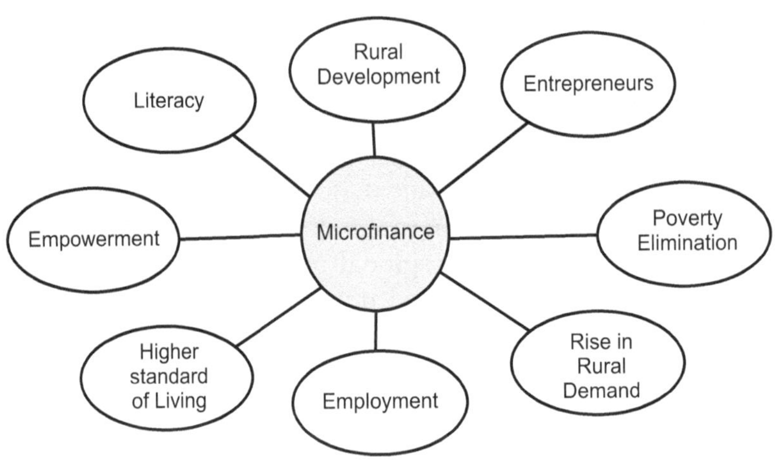

Delivery Models of Microfinance

The concept of microfinance involves informal and flexible approach to the credit needs of the poor. There is no single approach or model that fits in all the circumstances. Therefore, a number of microfinance models emerged in different countries/states according to the suitability to their local conditions. Broadly, the microfinance delivery methods can be classified into six groups as follows:

Grameen Bank Model

Grameen Bank model is one of the oldest and most successful models of microfinance. This model was developed in Bangladesh. In this model microfinance programme participants are organised into groups of five members. They make mandatory contribution to group savings and insurance fund. Each member maintains her individual saving and loan account with the bank and after contributing to the savings fund for a fixed time the group members receive individual loans from the bank. But the group is not required to give any guarantee for the loan repayment by its member. Repayment responsibility solely rests on the individual borrower and there is no form of joint liability, *i.e.,* group members are not responsible to pay on behalf of a defaulting member. Loans are provided for six months to one year duration but repayments are made weekly. Bank staff makes periodic visits to the groups, maintain individual records of group members and facilitate all the financial transactions. This creates ease in working but hindrance in the empowerment of members. The members remain dependent on field officers regarding their all group related activities. Grameen model has been replicated in more than 40 countries in Asia, Africa, and Latin America with modifications to suit local conditions and cultures. The programme of BancoSol in Bolivia and most of the solidarity groups in Latin America follow this methodology. Many MFIs in India have also replicated this model.

Joint Liability Group Model

In this model, 4 to 10 individuals are organised in a group known as a Joint Liability Group (JLG). The group members can avail bank loans against mutual guarantee and there is no condition of their own saving fund. All members sign a joint liability contract, making each one jointly liable for repayment of all loans taken by all individuals in the group. Thus, only social collateral is provided to the lending institution. The JLGs are intended primarily to be credit groups and regular savings by the JLG members are not mandatory. The group exists only because its individual members are legally bound to one another. In this model, the progress of empowerment of group members remains very limited. In India these type of groups are generally made by most of the MFIs because such groups are easy to make as there are very less restrictions regarding the utilisation of loan. NABARD is using this model for providing credit to the tenant farmers, cultivating land either as oral lessees or share croppers, and small farmers who do not have proper title of their land holding. Many other countries are also using this model. There were segments within the poor, such as: share croppers/oral lessees/tenant farmers, who were left out and whose loan requirements were much larger but who had no collaterals to fit into the traditional financing approaches of the banking system. To service such clients, Joint Liability Groups (JLGs), an upgradation of SHG model could be an effective way.

Individual Lending Model

In this method, individuals can get loans without any membership of a group. This is a straightforward credit lending model in which micro-loans are given directly to the borrowers. In this model, the financial institutions have to make frequent and close contact with individual clients to provide credit products customised to the specific needs of the individual. It is most successful for larger, urban-based, production-oriented businesses. The model is followed by many financial institutions like the Association for the Development of Micro-Enterprises (ADEMI) in Dominican Republic, Bank Rakyat Indonesia, Senegal Egypt, Self-Employment Women's Association in India, etc.

The Group Approach

The group approach delegates the entire financial process to the group rather than to the financial institutions. All financial activities like: savings, getting loans, repayment of loans and record keeping are managed at the group level. In this method, 10-20 members are organised to form a group. These group members make regular savings of fixed amount in a common fund. The amount and frequency of savings is mutually decided by the group members. After the successful working of such a group for some months the group is linked to a financial institution for getting credit. The financial institutions issue loan in the name of group and whole group is considered responsible for repayment. The amount of loan depends upon the total accumulated amount of saving of the group. Group members themselves decide about the criteria of dividing the loan among the group members. With this loan the whole group may jointly start a micro enterprise or the members may start their individual businesses. An individual may also use his loan for consumptive purpose or meeting other priority needs. The peer pressure in the group helps the timely repayment of loan. These type of group based credit delivery methods help to empower the group members because they remain involved in various group activities. They visit the bank, market and hold group meetings which help them to increase self-confidence. In India, the group based credit delivery method known as SHG-BLP is a predominant method of providing microfinance. Programme Hubungan Bank Danksm (PHBK) project in Indonesia and the Chikola groups of K-REP in Kenya are also using such group based credit delivery models.

Village Banking Model

This village banking model is an expansion of the group approach. This model was developed in Bolivia during the mid 1980s by the Foundation for International Community Assistance (FINCA), a non-profit microfinance organization. In this model, a Village Bank is developed by grouping 30 to 100 low-income individuals who seek to improve their lives through self-employment activities. The bank is financed by internal mobilisation of members' saving fund as well as loans provided by the sponsoring MFIs. The MFIs lend capital to the bank, which then lends the money to its members. Members themselves run the village bank, they choose their members, elect their own officers, establish their own by-laws, distribute loans to individuals and collect savings and payments. Loan amounts are linked to the aggregate amount saved by individual bank members. Loans are repaid weekly in small installments. Thus, village banks have a high degree of democratic control and independence. The model is used by various MFIs like Co-operative for Assistance and Relief Everywhere (CARE) in Guatemala; Save the Children in El Salvador; Burkina Faso in Bolivia, Mali, and Ghana; Freedom from Hunger and Catholic Relief Services in Thailand and Benin, Opportunity International, Consultative Group for Assisting the Poor (CGAP), etc.

Credit Unions and Co-operatives

A credit union is a democratic, not-for-profit financial co-operative. It is owned and governed by its members, who are at the same time the owners and the customers of their co-operative society. Co-operatives are often created by persons belonging to the same local or professional community or sharing a common interest. Co-operatives generally provide their members with a wide range of banking and financial services. Members participate in all the major decisions and democratically elect officers from among themselves to monitor the administration of the co-operative. Loans are granted only to the members. SANASA Development Bank of Sri Lanka is an example of rural credit co-operative which is successfully working as a microfinance service provider.

Microfinance Institutions

Microfinance institutions (MFIs) are the organizations or associations of individuals that provide financial services to the poor. In India, there is a wide range of such organizations with diverse legal forms, varying significantly in size, outreach, mission and credit delivery methodologies. Fig. 3.1 Represents the hierarchy of financial institutions for the microfinance disbursement.

Institutional Arrangement for Microfinance Disbursement in India

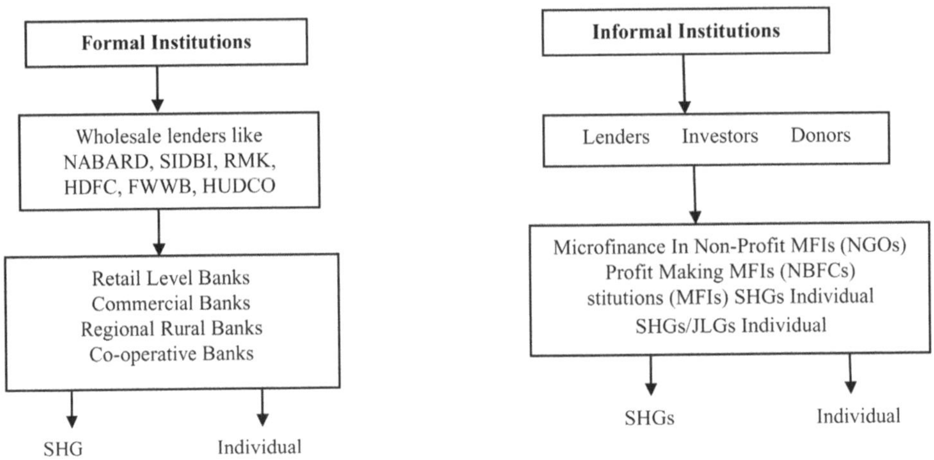

Fig. 3.1

Prospects of Microfinance

Microfinance programme has witnessed phenomenal growth in India in the past years. Studies show that this programme is helping the poor in many ways. However, the focus of most of the microfinance service providers has remained on expanding the outreach of microfinance programme with little attention on the depth, quality and viability of the financial services. Besides removing these problems there is a lot which can be done in this field to make this programme more effective. Some future prospects.

In order to expand the microfinance programme, SHGs may be linked with the post offices for disbursement of credit to rural poor by utilizing the vast network of post offices in rural areas. NABARD has launched a pilot project of this type in Tamil Nadu.

The spread of microfinance programme is unequal among various regions of India and there is limited spread in the poorer states. So, there is ample scope to spread microfinance programme in the unreached areas including the poorer states. However, taking a step in this direction NABARD has recently identified 13 states to scale up the microfinance programme in these states in order to reduce the regional disparity.

Some main features of the microfinance programme include compulsory savings, regular group meetings, record maintenance etc. These bindings lead to the exclusion of core poor from joining the microfinance programme. Therefore, in order to expand the outreach of the programme to the poorer people, there is a need to introduce more flexible system such as: the one adopted in Bangladesh, where even the beggars are provided with micro loans by the Grameen Bank.

REFERENCES

1. Task Force was a Group of Senior Government Officials and Prominent Microfinance Practitioners. It was Constituted by NABARD in 1999 to make a Conceptual Policy Framework for Sustainable Growth of Microfinance in India.
2. Microfinance Scenario in the Country, NABARD, Available at: http:// www.nabard.org/ pdf/publications/reports/mF_Scenario_in_the_Country.pdf [Accessed on 12.10.2008].
3. Mahajan, Vijay; and Nagasri, G. (1999). "Building Sustainable Microfinance Institutions in India", Paper Presented in Seminar on New Development Finance, Frankfurt, Germany, 29 September.
4. Satish, P. (2005). "Mainstreaming of Indian Microfinance", *Economic and Political Weekly*, Vol. 40, No. 17, p. 1733.
5. Schwiecker, S. (2004). The Impact and Outreach of Microfinance Institutions: The Effect of Interest Rates, Master's Degree Thesis, University of Tubingen, Germany.

Pages 26-34

POVERTY ALLEVIATION THROUGH MICROFINANCE
Edited by : Dr. B. Ramachandra Reddy
Edition : 2017
ISBN : 978-93-5056-865-1
Published by : Discovery Publishing House Pvt. Ltd., New Delhi (India)

4 The Role of Rashtriya Mahila Kosh in the Empowerment of Women

Dr. M. Kumudini

INTRODUCTION

Microfinance is gathering momentum to become a major force in developing countries like India. It is commonly understood as providing credit for self-employment and other financial and business services to very poor persons. It is defined as "provision of thrift, credit and other financial services and products of very small amounts to the poor for enabling them to raise their income levels and improve living standards". Microfinance came into prominence in India in 1980s, although early experiments date back 30 years in Bangladesh, Brazil and a few other countries. The typical microfinance clients are low-income persons who do not have access to formal financial institutions. In rural areas, they are usually small farmers and others who are engaged in small income-generating activities such as: food processing and petty trade. In urban areas, microfinance activities are more diverse and include: shopkeepers, service providers, artisans, street vendors, etc. Microfinance is, perhaps, the only economic programme that aims at broader range of goals that promote well being of poor and its philosophy is rooted in human welfare economics.

Need for the Study

Microfinance institutions (MFIs) play an important role to fill gap within the financial services industry. They provide credit and other financial services of very small amounts to poor in rural, semi-urban and urban areas for enabling them to raise their income and improve their standard of living. They vary in size and functions. Some are focusing entirely on microfinancing

Lecturer in Commerce, S.P.W. Degree and P.G. College, Tirupati.

while others work as extensions of large investment banks. In India, National Bank for Agriculture and Rural Development (NABARD), Small Industrial Development Bank of India (SIDBI), Rastriya Mahila Kosh (RMK), Commercial banks, co-operative banks, Non-Banking Finance Companies act as MFIs. The paper mainly focuses on the role of Rashtriya Mahila Kosh in the empowerment of women.

Objectives

The objectives of the present study are as follows:

- To study the role of RMK in the empowerment of women.
- To assess loan disbursement under various schemes.
- To evaluate region-wise loan disbursement.

Data Collection

The study is based on the secondary data which includes: books, magazines, annual reports, records, websites etc.

Period of Study

The study covered a period of 4 years form 2009-10 to 2012-13.

Scope and Limitations

The study made an attempt to enlighten the role of RMK in empowering women. The study covered aspects such as: scheme-wise loan disbursement; state-wise loan disbursement and region-wise loan disbursement. However, in spite of best efforts the data relating to the years 2013-14 and 2014-15 could not be collected.

Profile of RMK

RMK was established in 1993 as a national level organization and as an autonomous body under the aegis of the Ministry of Women and Child Development. Since its inception, it has been taking a number of promotional measures to popularise the concept of microfinancing, enterprise development, thrift and credit, formation and strengthening of women self-help groups (SHGs) through intermediary organizations. Some of the important objectives of RMK are: *(i)* socio-economic empowerment through multi-pronged effort; *(ii)* providing micro credit facilities; *(iii)* capacity building of Intermediary Organizations (IMO) and women beneficiaries; *(iv)* promoting, networking of SHGs for shaping and exchange of experience and information and to develop skills in response management and social mobilization and *(v)* promoting and supporting the expansion of entrepreneurship skills among women.

Administrative set up

RMK is administered by a governing board of 16 members consisting of the ex-officio chairperson who is Cabinet Minister in the Ministry of Women and Child Development, Government of India, 7 senior officials of Central and State Government, 7 specialists and representatives of Non-Government Organizations (NGOs) in the field of micro credit for women and the Executive Director of RMK who is also ex-officio member of secretary.

Sources of Funds

RMK raises its funds from the following sources.

1. Grants received from sponsors or members of the RMK.
2. Grants received from Central, State Governments, other trusts, societies and foundations, national and international bodies.
3. Donations from individuals or bodies.
4. Income from investments.
5. Income from other sources.
6. Loans raised by the RMK.
7. Membership fee.

Credit – Delivery Mechanism

Credit is disbursed to the poor women both rural and urban through intermediary organizations like: NGOs, Co-operative societies, Government autonomous organizations, State Women Development Corporations, Registered bodies and federations of women etc. The credit delivery of RMK is described in the following pages.

Year-wise Disbursement of Loans

Table 4.1: Year-wise Disbursement of Loans during 2009-10 and 2012-13

(Rs. Lakhs)

Year	Loan Disbursement	% of Change over Previous Year
2009-10	1563.00	–
2010-11	1249.00	-20.09
2011-12	1631.00	30.58
2012-13	1849.00	13.37

Source: Annual Reports of RMK.

It can be observed from Table 4.1 that there is gradual increase in the loan disbursement from Rs. 1563 lakhs to Rs. 1849 lakhs during the study period except the year 2010-2011 where there is a decline.

Scheme-wise Disbursement of Loan

RMK provides loan under various schemes. They are as follows:

Loan promotion scheme

Under this scheme, RMK provides smaller loan maximum up to 10 lakhs to promote the activity of thrift and credit among newer and smaller organizations having at least six months experience in formation of SHGs, thrift, credit and recovery management.

Main loan scheme

IMOs having minimum 3 years experience in thrift and credit activities are considered for loan under the scheme to a maximum up to 600 lakhs at a time.

Gold credit scheme

This scheme provides finance for medium and large NGOs. Maximum credit limit under this scheme is 500 lakhs.

Franchisee scheme

Smaller NGOs of the state can avail loan directly from franchisee appointed by RMK for that particular state without sending their proposal to RMK office at New Delhi. Under this scheme, credit is provided up to 500 lakhs to the franchisee who in turn extend to smaller NGOs in the state.

Refinance scheme

Under this scheme, RMK provides 100 per cent refinance assistance to Mahila Urban Co-operative Banks on finance which provide finance to poor women either directly or through SHGs within the norms of the RMK main loan scheme.

Repeat loan

This type of loan is available to the organizations on successful utilisation of first loan and the borrowing organization having repaid 50 per cent of its last loan.

Housing loan scheme

Under this scheme, RMK provides loans up to a maximum one lakh per beneficiary to SHG members for construction of low cost house and repairs.

It can be seen that of the total loan disbursement, RMK sanctioned more than 67 per cent of the loan to main loan scheme followed by gold credit card scheme, franchisee scheme and loan promotion scheme during the study period (Table 4.2). However, with regard to franchisee scheme, there was no loan disbursement during 2010-11 and 2012-13. It can be concluded that of all the schemes, main loan scheme occupied first place.

Table 4.2: Scheme-wise Disbursement of Loan during 2009-10 and 2012-13

(Rs. Lakhs)

Scheme	2009-10	2010-11	2011-12	2012-13
Main loan	1057.00(67.63)	992.00(79.42)	1201.00(73.64)	1694.00(91.62)
Loan promotion	18.00(1.15)	7.00(0.56)	10.00(0.61)	5.00(0.27)
Gold credit card	450.00(28.79)	250.00(20.02)	295.00(18.09)	150.00(8.11)
Franchisee	38.00(2.43)	–	125.00(7.66)	–

Note: Figures in parentheses indicate the percentage to total.

Source: As in Table 1.

Region-wise Disbursement of Loan

The loan disbursement of RMK can be also be analysed in terms of region-wise such as: southern, eastern, western, northern, central and northeastern. Southern region includes: states like: Andhra Pradesh, Tamil Nadu, Karnataka, Kerala and Union Territory like: Andaman Nicobar. States such as: Odisha, Bihar, West Bengal and Jharkhand form eastern region. Western region covers states of Gujarat, Maharashtra and Rajasthan. Northern region includes states like: Uttar Pradesh, Jammu and Kashmir, Himachal Pradesh, Uttaranchal, Haryana, Punjab and Union Territory like Delhi. The state of Madhya Pradesh alone is considered as Central region. Northeastern region covers states like: Assam, Manipur and Nagaland.

Table 4.3: Region-wise loan Disbursement During 2009-10 and 2012-13

(Rs. Lakhs)

Region	2009-10	2010-11	2011-12	2012-13
Southern	621.00(39.73)	517.50(41.43)	458.00(28.08)	435.00(23.53)
Eastern	479.75(30.69)	164.15(13.14)	362.50(22.23)	736.50(39.83)
Western	185.00(11.84)	210.00(16.81)	380.00(23.30)	520.00(28.13)
Northern	132.00(8.45)	212.50(17.01)	187.50(11.50)	60.00(3.24)
Central	103.00(6.58)	92.50(7.41)	243.00(14.89)	97.50(5.27)
Northeastern	42.28(2.71)	52.50(4.20)	–	–

Note: Figures in parentheses indicate the percentage to total.

Source: As in Table 1.

From Table 4.3 analysis, it can be inferred that in respect of region-wise loan disbursement, southern region stood first followed by eastern, western, northern and central region during 2009-10 and 1012-13. In case of northeastern region there was no loan disbursement during the last two years. It can be concluded that almost all regions witnessed fluctuations with regard to loan disbursement during the study period.

Loan Disbursement to NGOs

RMK has been providing funding assistance to more than 45 NGOs all over the country. The details in respect of loan disbursement to the number of NGOs during 2009-10 and 2012-13 are given in the following Table 4.4.

Table 4.4: Loan Disbursement to NGOs during 2009-10 and 2012-13

Year	Number of NGOs	% of Change over Previous Year
2009-10	69	–
2010-11	57	-17.39
2011-12	52	-8.77
2012-13	47	-9.62

Source: As in Table 1.

There is a continuous decline in the number of NGOs from 69 during 2009-10 to 47 during 2012-13. With regard to percentage of change over previous year, 2010-11 witnessed highest decrease of 17.39 per cent.

State-wise Loan Disbursement

RMK has provided loan assistance to nearly 23 states including union territories during the study period.

Table 4.5: State-wise Loan Disbursement during 2009-10 and 2012-13

(Rs. Lakhs)

State	2009-10	2010-11	2011-12	2012-13
Tamil Nadu	349.00 (22.33)	277.50 (22.21)	225.50 (13.83)	215.00 (11.63)
Odisha	350.00 (22.39)	55.40 (4.44)	145.00 (8.89)	210.00 (11.36)
Rajasthan	185.00 (11.84)	210.00 (16.81)	60.00 (3.68)	275.00 (14.87)
Andhra Pradesh	209.50 (13.40)	122.50 (9.81)	150.00 (9.20)	150.00 (8.11)
Madhya Pradesh	103.00 (6.59)	92.50 (7.41)	243.00 (14.90)	97.50 (5.27)
West Bengal	93.75 (5.99)	78.75 (6.30)	202.50 (12.41)	511.50 (27.67)
Maharashtra	–	–	270.00 (16.55)	235.00 (12.71)
Uttaranchal	–	75.00 (6.00)	50.00 (3.06)	25.00 (1.35)
Karnataka	42.50 (2.72)	72.50 (5.80)	57.50 (3.53)	70.00 (3.79)

Contd...

State	2009-10	2010-11	2011-12	2012-13
Jammu and Kashmir	45.00 (2.88)	10.00 (0.80)	5.00 (0.31)	–
Punjab	37.50 (2.40)	25.00 (2.00)	25.00 (1.53)	–
Uttar Pradesh	39.50 (2.53)	7.50 (0.60)	20.00 (1.23)	–
Himachal Pradesh	–	30.00 (2.42)	30.00 (1.84)	–
Manipur	33.28 (2.13)	–	–	–
Kerala	–	25.00 (2.00)	25.00 (1.53)	–
Bihar	30.00 (1.92)	30.00 (2.40)	–	10.00 (0.54)
Andaman Nicobar	20.00 (1.28)	20.00 (1.60)	–	–
Haryana	10.00 (0.64)	65.00 (5.20)	57.50 (3.53)	20.00 (1.08)
Assam	9.00 (0.58)	47.50 (3.80)	–	–
Jharkhand	6.00 (0.38)	–	15.00 (0.92)	5.00 (0.27)
Gujarat	–	–	50.00 (3.06)	10.00 (0.54)
Nagaland	–	5.00 (0.40)	–	–
Delhi	–	–	–	15.00 (0.81)

Note: Figures in parentheses indicate the percentage to total.
Source: As in Table 1.

It can be observed that of all the states, Tamil Nadu received highest amount of loan assistance during 2009-10 and 2012-13 (Table 4.5). However, the percentage to total decreased from 22.33 per cent to 11.63 per cent. The loan assistance to the states of Odisha, Rajasthan, Andhra Pradesh, Maharashtra, Madhya Pradesh, West Bengal, Uttaranchal, Karnataka and Haryana varied between 27.67 per cent and 1.35 per cent during the study period. The rest of the states got below 4 per cent funding assistance.

Evaluation of Loan Assistance

Before sanctioning credit to NGOs, first RMK conducts pre-sanction study to get itself satisfied about the experience, credibility and infrastructure facilities available with them. This is done through RMK officials or deputed institutional monitor. After sanction of loan, RMK evaluates loan assistance through post-sanction study to know the end use of loan to NGOS/ borrowers. The study includes verification of information furnished by the NGO, quality of fund management, verification of books of accounts, evaluation of accounting system, checking utilization of loans etc.

Conclusion

Microfinance came into prominence in India in 1980s, although early experiments date back 30 years in Bangladesh, Brazil and a few other countries. Perhaps, it is the only economic programme that aims at broader range of goals that promote well-being of poor and its philosophy is rooted in human welfare economics. Microfinance institutions play an important role to fill gap within the financial services industry. In India, National Bank for Agriculture and Rural Development (NABARD), Small Industrial Development Bank of India (SIDBI), Rastriya Mahila Kosh (RMK), Commercial banks, co-operative banks, Non-Banking Finance Companies act as Microfinance institutions. RMK was established in 1993 as a national level organization and as an autonomous body under the aegis of the Ministry of Women and Child Development. It is administered by a governing board consisting of 16 members. It raises funds from various sources. It provides credit to the poor women both rural and urban through intermediary organizations like NGOs, Co-operative societies, Government autonomous organizations, State Women Development Corporations, Registered bodies and federations of women etc. The total amount of loan disbursed during the study period increased from Rs. 1563 lakhs to Rs. 1849 lakhs. RMK provides loan under various schemes. It sanctioned more than 67 per cent of the loan to main loan scheme followed by gold credit card scheme, franchisee scheme and loan promotion scheme during 2009-10 and 2012-13. With regard to region-wise loan disbursement, southern region stood first followed by eastern, western, northern and central region during the study period.

Of all the states, Tamil Nadu received highest amount of loan assistance throughout the study period. RMK evaluates its loan assistance through post-sanction study to know the end use of loan to NGOS/borrowers.

REFERENCES

1. Indian Microfinance, The Challenges of Rapid Growth, Prabhu Ghate, Sage Publications, 2007.
2. Quarterly Compendium of News Clippings on Microfinance and Related Environment, Sa-Dhan, 2007.
3. Multiple Meaning of Money, Smitha Premchander, Sage Publications, 2009.
4. Transaction Cost: Financial Services and Low Income Segment, Sa-Dhan , Silver Jubilee, 1981-2006.
5. www.rmk.nic.in/chap1.htm Rashtriya Mahila Kosh
6. www.microfinancegateway.org Rashtriya Mahila Kosh (National Credit Fund for Women).
7. www.rmk.nic.in/annuale.pdf Annual report of RMK.

Pages 35-46

POVERTY ALLEVIATION THROUGH MICROFINANCE
Edited by: **Dr. B. Ramachandra Reddy**
Edition: **2017**
ISBN : 978-93-5056-865-1
Published by: **Discovery Publishing House Pvt. Ltd., New Delhi (India)**

5 Karnataka Farmers' Resource Centre (KFRC)'s Services to Farmers

Dr. Laxmanrao G.

Agriculture plays a pivotal role in the Indian economy. Although its contribution to gross domestic product (GDP) is now around one sixth, it provides employment to 56 per cent of the Indian workforce. Also, the forward and backward linkage effects of agriculture growth increase the incomes in the non-agriculture sector. The growth of some commercial crops has led to momentous potential for promoting exports of agricultural commodities and bringing about faster development of agro-based industries. Thus agriculture not only contributes to overall growth of the economy but also reduces poverty by providing employment and food security to the majority of the population in the country and thus it is the most inclusive growth sectors of the Indian economy. Indian agriculture is the home of small and marginal farmers (80%). Therefore, the future of sustainable agriculture growth and food security in India depends on the performance of small and marginal farmers. The role of small farms in development and poverty reduction is well recognized (Lipton, 2006). The world has witnessed historically unprecedented rates of escape from poverty over the past generation (Chen and Ravallion 2010, Ravallion 2013). Despite introduction of several anti poverty programmes to achieve inclusive growth in the post-independence period through the five-year plans, there is no evidence of higher rate of decline in poverty in India. In addition to this, income inequality has been increased significantly in the context of liberalised economic policies initiated from 1991 onwards (K Prasanna 2016). The incidence of poverty in SC and ST households is much higher than among non-scheduled

Vice Principal, Indo Asian Academy Degree and P.G. College, Bangalore.

households (Ira N Gang *et al.* 2008). The global experience of growth and poverty reduction shows that GDP growth originating in agriculture is at least twice as effective in reducing poverty as GDP growth originating outside agriculture (WDR, 2008). To support the developing countries a global policy response, closer international co-operation, and strong and coordinated partnerships between relevant public and private sector stakeholders at national and international level is desirable (Alliance for Financial Inclusion, 2010).

The structural reforms and stabilization policies introduced in India in 1991 initially focused on industry, tax reforms, foreign trade and investment, banking and capital markets. The economic reforms did not include any specific package specifically designed for agriculture. In the post reform (since 1991) period, India has done well in some indicators such as: economic growth, exports, balance of payments, resilience to external shocks, service sector growth, significant accumulation of foreign exchange, Information technology (IT) and stock market, improvements in telecommunications etc. GDP growth was around 8 to 9 per cent per annum in the period 2004-05 to 2007-08. India is now 2 trillion dollar economy. Investment and savings rates were quite high 32 to 36 per cent. However, there have been exclusion problems in the country. In other words, real development in terms of growth shared by all sections of the population has not taken place. We have problems of poverty, unemployment, inequalities in access to health and education and poor performance of agriculture sector. One of the excluded sectors during the reform period was agriculture which showed low growth and experienced more farmers' suicides. There are serious concerns on the performance of agriculture sector in the country. The post-reform growth was led by services. Commodity sector growth (agriculture, industry) has not been higher in the post reform period as compared to that of 1980s. Particular worry is agriculture sector which showed lower than 4 per cent per annum in the decade of mid-2000s to mid-2010s. There are also concerns on food security and livelihoods. It may be noted that agriculture is a 'state subject' under the Constitution of India. However, the central government plays a crucial role in shaping agricultural policies. Although Indian agriculture is in private hands, government policies have greatly influenced its pace and character.

The Government of India and state authorities alike have increasingly realised the importance of devoting attention to the economic betterment and development of rural poor and women in India. The Indian Constitution guarantees that there shall be no discrimination on the grounds of gender. In reality, however, rural women have harder lives and are often discriminated against with regard to land and property rights and in access to medical facilities and rural finance. Women undertake the more onerous tasks involved in the day-to-day running of households, including the collection of fuel-wood for cooking and the fetching of drinking water, and their nutritional status and literacy rates are lower than those of men. They also command lower wages as labour: Women's voice in key institutions concerned with decision making is also limited. Women's empowerment has long been a central feature of the Government of India and State Governments. Key instruments for supporting women's empowerment are Self-Help Groups (SHGs). Self-Help Groups (SHGs) have become the common vehicle of development process, integrating all development programmes. SHG–Bank Linkage Programme launched by NABARD way back in 1992 envisaging synthesis of formal financial system and informal sector has become a movement throughout the country. It is considered as the largest microfinance programme in terms of outreach in the world. At present, a large number of Self-Help Group Promoting Institutions (SHPIs), all the banking agencies and MFIs are pursuing this programme for the upliftment of the poor. This is also recognized as a part of priority sector lending and normal banking business by Reserve Bank of India. Thus, it is synonymous with microfinance programme of the country. This programme is also the main contributor towards the Financial Inclusion process in the country. In view of the large outreach and pre-dominant position of this microfinance programme, it is very important to give proper direction to all the stake-holders.

Agriculture is considered a high risk, low reward, and low esteem profession. Younger generation of the farm households is no longer interested in agriculture. In pursuit of secure livelihoods, urban migration is increasing. This distress is confounded due to several factors – dependence on high cost inputs, low entrepreneurial orientation, inefficient management of natural resources, lack of value addition, low capital investments, lack of holding capacity, financial illiteracy, high cost of private debts, and decadence of repayment values. Agriculture and livelihoods dependent on it are very critical for the growth and prosperity of the country. Changing trends in agriculture towards commercialization and dynamics of market economy necessitates Public and private initiatives to revive this sector. There is a need to build security of livelihoods of farmers, farm women, members of SHGs, etc., which shall benefit the economy. The National Commission for Enterprises in the Unorganized Sector (NCEUS) has recommended a special programme for marginal and small farmers. The report of NCEUS analyses the status and constraints faced by marginal and small farmers and focuses on the need for a special programme which aimed at capacity building of these farmers, both the farm and non-farm activities. The marginal and small farmers suffer from market failures in agriculture in terms of credit, input supplies and marketing of output, access to new technologies etc. NCUS recommended the four measures. These are: *(a)* special programmes for marginal and small farmers; *(b)* emphasis on accelerated land and water management; *(c)* credit for marginal and small farmers; *(d)* farmers' debt relief commission. It is under these circumstances, to overcome difficulties faced by small, marginal farmers and land less rural labour Karnataka Farmers' Resource Centre (KFRC) came into being and making concerted efforts to promote entrepreneurship especially among Farmers, Farm Women, Women SHG members and rural youth.

I contributed this theoretical paper to put light on innovative institutional model meant to serve the small and marginal farmers and rural entrepreneurs in India. Individual efforts of NABARD, RRBs and specially designed programmes of state and central government schemes are not effectively met the challenges of rural poor. Researchers at micro level and Policy makers suggested to combine the hands of all the institutions to face the challenges of rural poor.

Origin

The Government of India had advised all the SLBCs to take necessary steps to set up a Farmers Resource Centre with the pooled resources from Banks/Institutes/NABARD/State Government. Accordingly, SLBC, Karnataka formed a Sub-Committee under the Chairmanship of Sri. V.P. Baligar IAS, Principal Secretary, Commerce and Industries, Government of Karnataka, to discuss and finalize about the framework for setting up of the Karnataka Farmers Resource Centre (KFRC) a state level centre to cater to the training needs of farmers, SHGs, Bankers etc. On 03/02/2011 KFMC came into existence with Bagalkot head quarters. The KFRC is jointly sponsored by Government of Karnataka, NABARD, 10 Banks [*viz;* Syndicate Bank, Canara Bank, Corporation Bank, Vijaya Bank, SBI, SBM, SBH, Karnataka Vikas Grameena Bank, The Karnataka Bank Ltd., Krishna Grameena Bank] and B.V.V. Sangha (Basaveshwara Veerashyva Vidyavardaka Sangha.), Bagalkot to handle natural resources, production technology, backward and forward linkages and motivate Farmers, Farm Women, Women SHG members and Rural youth to take up farming as a respectable, profitable enterprise.

Objectives

General Objectives

1. Developing entrepreneurial culture in the rural community.
2. Fostering the culture of self-help in the rural community.
3. Developing a robust culture of healthy banking habits.

Specific Objectives

(i) Programmes for farming community

1. design and implement suitable training and mentoring;
2. programmes to the farm households to develop their capacities in orientation and motivation to take up agriculture as a first career option;
3. practicing sustainable agriculture and allied activities to maximize the returns on their resources including: soil, water and seed conservation and mitigate production risks associated with weather, biological and input uncertainties;
4. skills in value addition to enable a key role in the value chain of the produce either collectively or individually.

(ii) Promotion of banking habits

Design and implement suitable training and counseling programmes for promotion of healthy banking habits to mitigate financial risks by:

1. developing savings culture with the banking institutions;
2. developing skills in identifying avoidable wasteful expenses;
3. imparting a strong value system for repayment of loans and transparency in financial disclosures with the bank;
4. developing knowledge, skills and mind set to assess financial costs and risks of different financial services like: loan, remittance, insurance to take informed decision to manage financial risks;
5. orientation towards need based banking services and practices;
6. developing skills in compliance procedures about bank transactions.

(iii) Promotion of collective action

Design and implement suitable training and counseling programmes for promotion of collective action to mitigate marketing risks by:

1. facilitating formation of producers collectives and community based organizations and their managerial capacities for collective marketing in the value chains;
2. facilitating labour exchange culture;
3. promotion of Group Enterprises and Cluster Development in the value chains and their managerial capacities;
4. facilitating establishment and management of warehouses, collection points, cold storage houses, incubation centers, common processing centers, pooled resource centers for inputs, pooled transport services etc.

(iv) Dissemination services

Develop the capacities of Government departments, Banks, Bank sponsored organizations, Non-Governmental and Voluntary Organizations in carrying out activities in fulfillment of objects mentioned above by design and delivery of training, workshop or seminars.

(v) Promoting financial inclusion

Develop the capacities of eligible persons and institutions to provide services as Business Facilitators and Business Correspondents through customized training programmes.

(vi) Technology

Facilitate demystification, Adaptation and Promotion and transfer of Bio-Technology, Information Technology, Energy Technology to improve standard of living, by drudgery reduction and conservation and management of natural resources.

(vii) Research

To undertake research and publication in the areas of micro entrepreneurship, non-conventional energy, appropriate technology, rural development, public administration and any other developmental fields which has importance in the context of development of people, promotion of peace and improvement of international relationship

(viii) Publication

To bring out publications including journals and audio-visual presentations pertaining to all aspects of Developmental process including research and technological development, commercial and industrial information, market information, training and awareness.

(ix) Collaboration

To collaborate and establish effective liaison and coordination between governments, Industry, Commerce, Research and developmental, technical and educational agencies, national and international organizations, in all activities relating to furtherance of the objectives of the institute.

Organisational Set Up

The KFRC Institute is governed by a non-profit state level Trust. The Trust is registered under Indian Trust Act. The Income Tax department has issued exemption certificate to KFRC Trust under section 80G and 12A. The donations made to KFRC Trust are eligible for exemption under 80G of Income Tax Act 1961. The CMD, Syndicate Bank and Chairman, SLBC, Karnataka is the Chairman of the KFRC Trust. The Principal Secretary, Commerce and

Industries, Government of Karnataka and Principal Secretary, Agriculture Department, GOK and Chief General Manager, NABARD, Bangalore are the Vice-Chairmen of the Trust. The General Manger, Syndicate Bank and Convenor, SLBC is the Managing Trustee of the Trust. The General Managers of other sponsoring Commercial Banks and Chairman of RRBs and BVV Sangha are the Trustees of KFRC. The Board of Trustees is assisted by a Management Board. The Institute is supported by a Local Advisory Committee at local level.

Infrastructure of KFRC

(a) Land and Building

1. KFRC owns 8 acres of land in Bagalkot town. As per the commitment made in the SLBC meeting, the Government of Karnataka has been kind enough to provide the land at free of cost for construction of campus building of KFRC. The process of construction of campus building is in progress;
2. at present, the Institute is functioning in a building provided at free of rent by B.V.V. Sangha, Bagalkot - one of the Trustees of KFRC;
3. the KFRC has a capacity of conducting simultaneously 2 programmes covering 200 participants in the campus;
4. has got well equipped 2 Lecture halls provided with Multimedia projector, audio systems etc;
5. has got an Administrative Block accommodating offices of Executive Director, Directors, Faculties and office assistants;
6. has an Exhibition hall, a well equipped Library containing Books, Magazines, periodicals, Journals, Brochures, Newspapers etc;
7. residential accommodation (Dormitories/rooms) for 50 trainees;
8. a separate block containing Kitchen and Dining Hall for the Trainees.

(b) Resource Persons

The Executive Director of the Institute, a Chief Manager deputed from the SLBC convenor Bank *i.e.,* Syndicate Bank, possess rich experience in Agriculture Finance, development banking, rural development and administration. The Director, a senior Manager from Canara Bank, possess experience in Banking, rural development. They are exposed to professional training and Trainer's Training in the reputed organizations like: National Academy of RUDSETI, Bangalore; NIRD, Hyderabad; BIRD, Lucknow etc.

They are capable of handling Technical inputs for Agriculture and Allied activities, SHG-Bank linkage, besides behavioural inputs, managerial inputs, banking, launching formalities etc. Apart from this, the Institute has a panel of qualified and experienced resource persons drawn from technical, entrepreneurial, professional, social and other fields. The expert practitioners in the respective field, who provide their services out of social concern, impart skill training.

(c) Course Modules

Training modules of KFRC are developed through team experts by conducting brain storm sessions at different levels for several occasions. The practical experience, research and experiment facilitated for the development of the necessary course modules. KFRC reviews these course modules on an ongoing basis and revise and update them.

(d) Training Methodology

The main target group of KFRC is Farmers/Farm Women/SHGs etc., which is characterised by adult illiterate or less-literate population. This calls for typical adult learning environment. KFRC has adopted the unique training methodology. Through structured psychological exercises, the participants are stimulated to shed inhibitions and develop interest in learning. Besides lecture sessions, behaviour simulation games, exercises, field visits, hands on experience, interaction with role models, interface with supporting system, group discussions, role play, case study etc., are effectively used in the training. Training sessions are conducted in vernacular languages.

(e) Administration System

The Institute is guided by administrative manual for systematic conduct of the activities. Well-defined service conditions and staff policy is also adopted. Each Institute is subjected every year to internal management audit and financial audits by statutory auditors.

Performance

The KFRC was inaugurated on 03.02.2011. Since then, the KFRC has commenced the activities and providing Training programmes and other services to the Farmers; Farm Women; Women SHG members; members of Joint Liability Groups[JLGs]; Farmers Clubs; Raitha Shakthi Groups; Rural youth; Bankers; Business Correspondents/Business Facilitators; Students; Agri-input suppliers; Marketing enterprises; Agro-processing units/ entrepreneurs; Federations like KMF, KOF etc., staff of various line departments of centre and state governments, members of local elected bodies like Gram Panchayaths, Taluk Panchyaths, Zilla Panchyatha, Muncipal bodies etc.

Table 5.1: Events Organized by KFRC since Inception

S.No.	Event	2011-12	2012-13	2013-14	2014-15	2015-16	Total
1.	Awareness Programmes	2	8	12	16	17	55
2.	Core Programmes	12	28	34	35	36	145
3.	Governance	–	14	9	6	19	48
4.	Support System	–	–	19	23	26	68
	Total	14	50	74	83	98	316

The number of events are showing upward trend except Events related to governance. In the current year 2015-16, data is taken up to 31/12/2015. More events are scheduled in Jan, Feb and Mar of 2016.

Table 5.2: Participants Attended for the events Organized by KFRC since Inception

S.No.	Event	2011-12	2012-13	2013-14	2014-15	2015-16	Total
1.	Awareness Programmes	213	879	2289	2955	1685	8021
2.	Core Programmes	284	2268	3157	2101	697	8507
3.	Governance	–	149	398	460	383	1390
4.	Support System	–	–	1995	2300	2090	6385
	Total	497	3296	7839	7816	4855	24303

The number of participants are showing upward trend except participants in the Events related to core programmes. In the current year 2015-16, data is taken up to 31/12/2015. More events are scheduled in Jan, Feb and Mar of 2016 and more participants are expected to attend. Due to non availability of spacious seminar hall (infrastructural bottle neck) participants are restricted to maximum of 150 per event.

Details of Programme-wise/Activity-wise Performance

A	Awareness Programmes	No. of Programmes
1.	SHG members and students	13
2.	Bankers and Department officials	06
3.	Non-Government Organizations (NGOs)	08
4.	Farmers' Clubs/Village Meets	12
5.	Stall establishments in Krishi-Melas/Agri-Fairs	07
6.	Seminars/Exhibitions	09
	Total	55

Contd...

B	**Core Programmes**	
1.	SHG–Bank linkage Programmes	06
2.	Dairy Development	03
3.	Poultry Development	08
4.	Business Correspondents/Business Facilitators	13
5.	Sheep and Goat Development	09
6.	Rabbit Rearig	02
7.	Apiculture/Honey Bee rearing	05
8.	Agri Clinic and Agri Business	06
9.	Commodity Trading	15
10.	Food Processing	06
11.	Crop Specific – Sugar Cane crop	05
12.	Crop Specific – Banana Crop	08
13.	Crop Specific – Cotton Crop	11
14.	Crop Specific – Vegetable Crops	16
15.	Crop Specific – Fruit Crops	06
16.	Crop Specific – Major and minor Millet Crops	04
17.	Organic farming, Bio Fertilizers and Bio pesticides	07
18.	Project formulation	05
19.	Exposure visits (Taluk, District, State and National Levels)	10
	Total	145
C	**Governance Programmes**	
1.	Agriculture Department	15
2.	Horticulture Department	07
3.	Watershed Department	06
4.	Uni. of Horticultural Sciences/Colleges	08
5.	Krishi Vigyan Kendras/RUDSETIs/SIRDs	12
	Total	48

Contd...

D	Support Programmes	
1.	Non-Government Organizations	14
2.	Bankers/Financial Institutions	16
3.	Progressive farmers/Farm women/Rural Youth	17
4.	Input Out put Suppliers, Marketing Agents.	21
	Total	68
	Grand Total (A+ B+ C+D)	316

In order to take forward the activities of KFRC and to make the institute as a model one, KFRC had interactions/discussions with GMs of various Banks; Vice-Chancellors /Director of Extension/Director of Research/top officials of University of Horticulture, Bagalkot, University of Agriculture, Dharwad, University of Agricluture, Bangalore, College of Fisheries, Mangalore; College of Agriculture, Bijapur; Chief Secretary/Additional Chief Secretary, GOK; Principal Secretary, Agriculture, GOK; Principal Secretary, Commerce and Industries, GOK; Principal Secretary, RDPR, GOK; Secretary, Planning, GOK; Commissioner and Director of Agriculture, GOK; NIRD, Hyderabad; Chairman, Organic Mission, GOK; Chairman, Agricultural Mission, CGM, NABARD, RD/GM, RBI; GOK; LDMs of various districts, DDM, NABARD of various districts; Directors of various RUDSETIs/SIRDs; Programme Co-ordinators of various Krishi Vignyan Kendras; reputed NGOs and Progressive farmers of the state.

Post Training Follow-up

The KFRC has been conducting the post training follow-up to provide the required handholding support to the trainees for set up of units with or without Bank finance. It makes efforts to bring coordination among Government Departments, Banks and other agencies to help the trainees for smooth set up of units. It provides the required services like: counselling, consultancy etc., on an on-going basis.

Conclusion

Institutions relating to *(a)* land and water management; *(b)* group or cooperative approach for inputs and marketing and *(c)* value chains had not sufficient to meet the challenges of small and marginal farmers in rural areas. There is a need to review and reexamine issues relating to Poverty and it is the primary responsibility of the governments to take up innovative institutional models to reduce the poverty and achieve the inclusive growth in India.

REFERENCES

Alliance for Financial Inclusion. (2010). The AFI Survey on Financial Inclusion Policy in Developing Countries: Preliminary Findings. AFI.

Ira N Gang, Kunal Sen and Myeong-Su Yun (2008). Poverty in Rural India: Caste and Tribes Review of Income and Wealth Volume 54, Issue 1, pp. 50-70.

K. Prasanna (2016). Inclusive Growth and Poverty reduction Programmes in India, *Imperial Journal of Inter Disciplinary Research*, Vol. 2, Issue – 3.

Lipton, M. (2006). "Can Small Farmers Survive, Prosper, or be the Key Channel to cut Mass Poverty", Journal of Agricultural and Development Economics, Vol. 3, No. 1, 2006, pp. 58-85.

World Development Report (2008).

Pages 47-52

POVERTY ALLEVIATION THROUGH MICROFINANCE
Edited by : Dr. B. Ramachandra Reddy
Edition : 2017
ISBN : 978-93-5056-865-1
Published by : Discovery Publishing House Pvt. Ltd., New Delhi (India)

6 Issues and Factors Affecting the Growth of Microfinance Institutions in India

Salma Banu[1]
Dr. G. Sudarsana Reddy[2]

INTRODUCTION

In developing countries economic development is not developed but it is developing, the employment opportunities are more but the individuals do not possess the skills required for the jobs. Hence, there is unemployment and under employment in these countries. The infrastructure such as: transportation, electricity, drinking water facility, housing facility, hospital facility, telecommunication is not properly available to the mass in general. In these countries national income as well as per capita income is low, it is very difficult for the people to fulfill their needs. People need financial support to fulfill their needs and wants. Because of low income and lack of collateral security, they cannot generate the loan from formal banks. The public need financial resources to meet the necessities of life such as: food, clothing, shelter, health, education, marriage of children etc.

In India in rural areas people find it difficult to maintain the standard of living. As the agriculture is the primary occupation and income from agriculture is seasonal and not regular. So in unseasoned period it is difficult to fulfill the basic requirements.

The microfinance is a group of people who are offering the small finance to the public at a low rate of interest with feasible installments facility. It is form of a group of those poor people who are in need of microfinance,

1. Assistant Professor, Department of Commerce, University College of Arts, Tumakuru - 572 103, Karnataka.
2. Associate Professor, Department of Commerce, University College of Arts, Tumakuru - 572 103, Karnataka.

offers the loan and generate the savings from these groups and assists in fulfilling the requirements of group at large.

Microfinance – Concept

Microfinance is group which is helping the poor class to fulfill the basic needs; it is attempting to improve the social and economic conditions of people at large. Microfinance has been defined by Micro Credit Summit held in Washington D.C., in February 1997 as "programmes that provide credit for self-employment, other financial and business services to very poor persons".[1]

The definition interprets the micro credit or microfinance in a broader sense, it is providing the small loans not only to fulfill the basic needs but to generate the employment opportunities, and other diversified financial requirements. It is also helping the poor persons in commencing the business services which will fulfill the social and economic needs, increases the standard of living and in turn develops the economic condition of the country.

National Bank for Agricultural Development (NABARD) has defined microfinance as "provision of thrift, credit and other financial services and products of very small amounts to the poor in rural, semi-urban and urban provided to customers to meet the financial needs; with only qualification that transactions value is small and customers are poor".[2]

Progress of Microfinance in India

In India it is estimated that 350 million people live below poverty line, nearly 75 million households benefited through microfinance with an annual credit demand is Rs. 60,000 Crores. But, a cumulative disbursement under microfinance is only Rs. 5,000 Crores, total outstanding of microfinance India is only Rs. 1,600 Crores, only about five per cent f rural poor have access to Microfinance, and a cumulative of about 20 million. While 10 per cent lending to weaker section is required for commercial banks, the neither have the network for lending and supervision on a larger scale or confidence to offer term loan to big Microfinance institutions, and the non- poor comprise of 29 per cent of the outreach.[3]

Key Issues in Microfinance in India

The primary issues in microfinance in India are as follows:

(i) *Low Outreach:* Microfinance institutions reach is very low. It is only eight per cent as compared to 65 per cent in Bangladesh. It shows that there is lot of scope for Microfinance Institutions (MFIs) in increasing their reach and scale of operations. It has been observed that Microfinance programmes focus more attention on women.

(ii) *High Rate of Interest:* Microfinance institutions are charging very high rate of interest, which poor find it difficult to pay. It is argued that the MFIs are private entities and hence need to be financially sustainable. As they do not receive subsidy for their lending that is why, they need to recover the operational cost from borrowers.

(iii) *Negligence of Urban Poor:* It has been observed that MFIs pay more attention to rural areas and largely neglect the urban poor. Out of the more than 800 MFIs across the country only six are currently focus their attention on urban poor. However, the population of the urban poor is quite large, amounting more than 100 million. With increase of urbanisation, this number is further expected to grow rapidly in the coming years. It is suggested that MFIs should pay equal attention to urban poor because they too need financial assistance for their requirements.

(iv) *Less Client Retention:* Client retention is the big issue that creates a problem for the growth MFIs in India. There is about 28 per cent client retention in the MFIs. This occurs because people are not properly informed and educated about services and products provided by the microfinance institutions. Moreover the current client has higher default rate.[4]

(v) *Loan Default:* Loan default is another issue that created a problem in the growth and expansion of the organsation. Because around 73 per cent loan default is identified in MFIs. Lack of understanding on the part of the clients, they also cannot correctly manage the loan given to them. As a result, they are not able to payback loan.

(vi) *Low Education Level:* The level of education of the client is low. So, it creates a problem in the growth and expansion of the organsation because its percentage is around 70 per cent in MFIs. Target population of MFIs is the people of rural areas and they have no or less education level. As the percentage of people who have very less education.

(vii) *Language Barrier:* Because of low education background and variety of languages creates a difficulty in understanding the information. Around 54 per cent have language barrier identified by MFIs. For, this reason it is also difficult to the MFIs employees to make the clients to understand the policy and related details.

(viii) *Late Payments:* Late payment is an issue that creates problem in growth and expansion of the MFIs, because late payment is around 70 per cent of loans sanctioned by MFIs. This normally occurs because clients are uneducated and they do not know how to manage their debt.

(ix) *Geographic Factors:* Majority of MFIs agrees that geographic factors make it difficult to communicate with clients, which creates problem in growth and expansion of the organization. MFIs are primarily aimed to facilitate the Below Poverty Line (BPL) population of the country, but due to lack of infrastructure in those areas it becomes difficult to reach them.

(x) *Debt Management:* Clients are uneducated about debt management, majority of the clients in the MFIs are unaware of the fact that how to manage their debt. Because of lack of education and understanding on the part of client, they also cannot correctly manage the loan given to them. Hence it creates a problem in growth and expansion of MFIs.

Factors Affecting the Growth of Microfinance Institutions

The factors affecting the growth and expansion of Microfinance Institutions in India can be divided into parts: Internal Environment Factors, and External Environment Factors.

Internal Environment Factors

(i) *High Transaction Cost:* High transaction cost is the big challenge for Microfinance Institutions. The volume of the transaction is very small, whereas the fixed cost of the transaction is very high. It cannot vary with the size of loan. Higher fixed cost proportion in the total cost increases the risk in the same proportion. Moreover, if the demand for the product falls or the marginal cost increases, it becomes very difficult to adjust the cost by cutting the output. This cut will reduce the revenue out of which he has to pay principal amount as well as interest on the loan.[5]

(ii) *Lack of Access to Funding:* Another factor contributing to the lack of growth of MFIs is lack of access to funding agencies. As the MFIs are private entities, they are unable to generate resources from other formal financial institutions. They are dependent upon the funds given to the clients, which are given in the form of loan. Hence, this difficulty hinders the growth and expansion of MFIs.

(iii) *Fraud:* Majority of the MFIs agree that, the clients who have taken the loan and will not repay the principal as well as interest. Because of mismanagement among clients, which later converts into fraud affects the growth and expansion of MFIs.

External Environment Factors

(i) *Increased Competition:* Majority of MFIs agrees that increased competition affects the growth and expansion of the MFIs. The commercial banks and other financial institutions are coming forward to offer the loans in simple formalities, which affect the growth and expansion of the organization.

(ii) *Uneven Population Density:* The uneven population density is the problem, which affects the growth and expansion of the organization. The majority of the population locates in urban areas but the MFIs focuses to provide loan to the rural areas where population is low. Population density hinders the growth of MFIs.

Suggestions

The following suggestions are offered for the MFIs:

- Equal attention must be given to Urban Poor Population, which in turn leads to rapid Economic Development in the Country.
- Awareness and education about the Microfinance should be spread proper among the mass.
- Policies, terms and conditions about MFIs must be communicated proper to the clients.
- The rate of interest on the loan must be reduced.
- The fixed cost which increases the total cost should be reduced in order to attract more customers.
- The operational cost must be reduced.
- MFIs must have depth knowledge about the debt management and recovery measures.
- Proper training to the clients should be organised in an efficient way, so that they could know each and every small thing in their debt.
- The Government should assist the MFIs in providing financial assistance to the public by offering subsidies and through funding agencies.
- Formation of Regulatory Authority for Microfinance to govern the functions of MFIs for the further development as well as for safe guarding the interest of general public.

Conclusion

Microfinance institutions are the agencies, which are assisting the poor class in improving their socio-cultural and economic conditions. It is increasing standard of living of the people. It is creating the saving habit among the people, which is constituted to be the large portion of the country. It is increasing the economic development of the country. Even though MFIs are rendering social services but it is also deals with many issues, it is suggested that MFIs should give equal attention to the urban population who are also dealing with the same difficulties as the rural population. The education among the clients about the Microfinance required to be generalized to reduce the difficulties which hinder the growth and expansion of the organization. Some effort in solving the issues and creating positive environment helps improve the health of the MFIs, reach further in the rural areas, empower poor and alleviate poverty.

REFERENCES

1. Rajaram Dasgupta, "Microfinance in India, Empirical Evidence Models and Policy Imperatives", *Economical and Political Weekly,* XI, No. 2, March 2005, p. 1239.
2. Lekshmi R., Kulshreshta and Archana Gupta, "A Study of Microfinance in India-Delivery System and Impact Analysis with Special Emphasis to Women Upliftment", *Sajosps,* 3, No.1, December 2002, p. 105.
3. Tenaw. S. And K.Z. Islam, *"Rural Financial Services and Effects of Microfinance on Agricultural Productivity and on Poverty"*. University of Helsinki Department of Economics and Management (Discussion Paper Series), 2009, p. 28.
4. Ehsan, Nadia, "Issues in the Growth of Microfinance Banks: Impact of Customer, Internal and External Environment", *Interdisciplinary Journal of Contemporary Research in Business,* December 2011, p. 3-8.
5. Muhammed S.D, "Microfinance Challenges and Opportunities in Pakistan European, *Journal of Social Science,* 14(1), 2010, p. 88.

Pages 53-57

POVERTY ALLEVIATION THROUGH MICROFINANCE
Edited by: Dr. B. Ramachandra Reddy
Edition: 2017
ISBN : 978-93-5056-865-1
Published by: Discovery Publishing House Pvt. Ltd., New Delhi (India)

7 Role of Microfinance in Poverty Alleviation Through NABARD

A Study

Dr. N.K. Pradeep Kumar[1]
Prof. P. Mohan Reddy[2]

INTRODUCTION

Poverty is a social phenomenon in which a section of the society is unable to fulfill even its basic necessities of life. When a substantial segment of society is deprived of the minimum level of living and continues at bare subsistence level, that society is said to be plagued with mass poverty. In India the generally accepted definition of poverty emphasizes minimum level of living rather than a reasonable level of living. India at present has a greater share of the poor around the world. India is home to almost 1/3 of the worlds poor. At present, 29.8 per cent of the Indian population lives below the poverty line. It is expected that population in India will reach 1.5 billion by 2026 and then India will be the largest population nation in the world.

Objective of the Paper

- To identify the contribution of Microfinance in alleviating poverty through NABARD.

Research Methodology

Data used in the study is based on the secondary sources and collected through various books, journals and published annual report of the NABARD and other selected official websites have been referred and used for the purpose of the study.

1. Academic Consultant, Department of Commerce, S.V.U. College of CM and CS, S.V. University, Tirupati.
2. Professor of Commerce, S.V.U. College of CM and CS, S.V. University, Tirupati.

The Concept of Microfinance

Microfinance is the provisions of Financial Services to low income clients or solidarity lending groups including: consumers and self-employed, who rationally lack access to banking and related services. It covers a wide range of services like: credit, savings, insurance, remittance and also non-financial services like: training and counseling. Microfinance plays a major contributor to provide credit facilities. In the past few decades it has helped out remarkably in eradicating poverty. People who have taken Microfinance have been able to increase their income and thereby their standard of living.

Need for Microfinance

Many of the Indians do not have a savings bank account and they are deprived of all banking services. Poor also need financial services to fulfill their needs like consumption, building of assets and protection against risk. Microfinance institutions serve as a supplement to banks in some sense a better one too. These institutions not only offer micro credit but they also provide other financial services like: savings, insurance, remittance and non-financial services like: individual counseling, training and support to start own business. The borrower receives all these services at his or her doorstep and in most cases with a repayment schedule of borrower's confidence. But all this comes at accost and the interest rates charged by these institutions higher than commercial banks and vary widely from 10 to 30 per cent. Microfinance produces many benefits for poverty stricken, or low income households. One of the benefits is that it is very accessible. Banks today simply won't extend loans to those with little to no assets, and generally don't engage in small size loans typically associated with microfinancing. Microfinancing is based on the philosophy that even small amounts of credit can help to end the cycle of poverty. Another benefit produced from the microfinancing initiative is that it's presents opportunities, such as: extending education and jobs. As well, in relation to employment, people are more likely to open small business that will aid the creation of new jobs. Overall, the microfinancing programme is set out to improve the standard of living amongst poor communities.

Channels of Microfinance

In India microfinance operates through self-help group linkage programme and micro finance institutions.

- *Self-Help Group-Bank Linkage Programme (SBLP):* This is the bank-led microfinance channel which was initiated by NABARD in 1992. Under the Self-Help Group model, the members usually women in villages are encouraged to form groups of around 10-15. The members contribute their savings in the group periodically and from these savings small loans are provided to the members. This model has been very much successful in the past and it is becoming more popular. Efforts are being made to revive dormant SHGs and prevent the functional ones from disintegrating, through measures such as: capacity-building and hand-holding support. The self-help groups are self-sustaining and once the group becomes stable, it starts working on its own with support from NGOs and institutions like: NABARD and SIDBI.

- *Microfinance Institutions (MFIs)*: Those institutions which have microfinance as their main operation are known as microfinance institutions. These institutions lend through the concept of Joint Liability Group (JLG). A Joint liability group is an informal group consisting of 5 to 10 individual members who come together for the purpose of availing bank loans either individual or through the group mechanism against a mutual guarantee.

Microfinance Initiatives Through NABARD

The Indian microfinance is dominated by self-help groups and their linkage to banks with the launching of NABARD's pilot scheme gained concepts like: self-reliance, self-sufficiency and self-help at its core. Loans under microfinance programmes are very small (a few thousands of Rupees). Microfinance continues to target the rural and urban households, with emphazis on woman borrowers. Credit follows thrift the first stage is the formation of groups by individual themselves, followed by mobilization of petty savings and recycling this by lending to group members. The repayment period is generally very short. The amount increases based on the borrower's repayment. Group members usually create a common fund by contributing their small savings on regular basis. The average deposit and loan size of SHG account is larger than the individual accounts under the priority sector. If banks provide proper training for skill and entrepreneurship development, the SHG members would be able to diversify into income generating activities, thus improving their credit absorption capacity substantially.

Table 7.1 portrays that there were more than 74.30 lakh savings-linked SHGs, covering over 9.7 Crore poor households during the year 2013-14. The total savings of these SHGs with banks amounted to Rs. 9897.42 Crore. The number of credit-linked SHGs under the programme was 41.97 lakh.

Table7.1

Sl. No.	Particulars	Self-Help Groups*				MicrofinanceInstitutions**			
		2013		2014		2013		2014	
		Number	Amount	Number	Amount	Number	Amount	Number	Amount
1.	Loan disbursed	1219821	20585.36	1366421	24017.36	426	7839.51	545	10282.49
2.	Loans outstanding	4451434	39375.3	4197338	42927.52	2042	14425.84	2422	16517.43
3.	Savings accounts with banks	7317551	8217.25	7429500	9897.42	–	–	–	–

Note: *Figures indicate the share of Self-help groups under the Swarnajayanti Gram Swarozgar Yojana.

** Figures indicate the assistance of the SIDBI to Microfinance institutions.

Source: Compiled from the Annual Report of NABARD.

Expenditures

NABARD had spent a sum of Rs. 49.41 crore from the Financial Inclusion Fund (FIF) and the Women Self-Help Group (WSHG) Development Fund on various microfinance–related activities. These included the formation and linkage of SHGs, training and capacity-building of stakeholders, promotion of livelihoods, documentation, generation of awareness and introduction of innovations.

Support

NABARD has continued to extend support to NGOs, RRBs, District central cooperative banks (DCCBs), FCs and Individual Rural Volunteers for promoting and nurturing SHGs. A grant assistance of Rs. 88.36 crore was sanctioned to these agencies. The cumulative assistance sanctioned to various agencies for the promotion of 7.19 lakh SHGs was Rs. 339.83 crore and 4.85 lakh SHGs had been formed and grant assistance of Rs. 93.77 crore was released. The NGOs were the most dominant SHPI, forming more than 3.74 lakh SHGs.

Training

NABARD has trained and built the capacity of the stakeholders in the microfinance programme. It conducted four thousand four hundred two training programmes and trained around 1.61 lakh individuals, including stakeholders, during the year. The cumulative number of people trained was around 33.28 lakh. This has created a strong back-up team for the implementation of the programme. It organized one thousand eighty seven training programmes with thirty one thousand seventy three (31,073) participants under the WSHG Fund.

Microfinance Limitations

Microfinancing produces may benefits for poverty stricken, or low income households. Overall, the benefits outline that the microfinancing initiative is set out to improve the standard of living amongst impoverished communities. There also many challenges within microfinance initiatives which may be social or financial. Here, more articulate and better – off community members may cheat poorer or less educated neighbors. This may occur intentionally or unintentionally through loosely run organizations. As a result, many microfinance institutions require a large amount of social capital or trust in order to work effectively. Critics say that micro credit has not increased incomes, but has driven poor households into a debt trap, in some cases even leading to suicide. They add that the money from loans is often used for durable consumer goods or consumption instead of being used for productive investments, that it fails to empower women, and that is has not improve health or education. Micro credit has achieved much less that what its proponents said it would achieve, but its negative impacts have not been as drastic as some critics have argued. Micro credit is just one factor influencing the success of small businesses, whose success in influenced too much larger extent by how much an economy or a particular market grows.

Conclusion

Microfinance is effective intervention strategy for providing small credit to the rural poor in order to alleviate poverty. The Indian microfinance is dominated by self-help groups and their linkage to banks with the launching of NABARD's pilot scheme gained concepts like: self-reliance, self-sufficiency and self-help at its core. Microfinancing programmes through SHGs introduced and expanded by non-governmental organizations (NGOs) in several parts of India have the potential to minimize the problem of inadequate access of banking services to the poor. Increased availability of micro credit to the poor through microfinancing SHGs will enable rural households to take up larger productive activities, empower the poor women, decrease the dependence on exploitative local moneylenders and increase savings.

REFERENCES

1. P. Mahanta, Status of Micro-Finance in India – A Review, IJMFMR, 2012.
2. Dr. R. Neelaiah, Microfinance Growth and Impact, Manjeera Publishing House, 2015.
3. V. Krishna Naik, Poverty Eradication in India – A Brief Study, Regional Network on Poverty Eradication, 2015.
4. Annual Report of NABARD.

Pages 58-67

POVERTY ALLEVIATION THROUGH MICROFINANCE
Edited by : Dr. B. Ramachandra Reddy
Edition : 2017
ISBN : 978-93-5056-865-1
Published by : Discovery Publishing House Pvt. Ltd., New Delhi (India)

8 Performance of Microfinance and its Delivery Models in India

Dr. M. Lokanadha Reddy[1]
Dr. P. Mohan Reddy[2]

INTRODUCTION

The term 'microfinance' refers to small-ticket-size loans, savings, insurance, remittances and other financial services which meet the particular needs and characteristics of low-income individuals. Microfinance services are based on the premise that people living in poverty need a diverse range of financial services to run their businesses, build assets, smooth consumption, and manage risks, just like people from higher income groups. Microfinance gives low-income groups and those who have been excluded from formal financial services the chance to access institutional financial services rather than relying on informal providers such as: moneylenders, informal deposit collectors, etc., who provide these services at high cost and at high risk to borrowers.

Microfinance scheme provides a wide range of financial services to people who have little or nothing in the way of traditional collateral. It helps them to build up assets, survive crises and to establish small business to come out of poverty. Except extending small loans (micro credit), microfinance programme provides various other financial and non-financial services such as: savings, insurance, guidance, skill development training, capacity building and motivation to start income-generating activities to enhance the

1. **HOD and Asso. Professor, Department of MBA, Sir Vishveshwaraiah Institute of Science and Technology, Madanapalle.**
2. **Professor and BOS PG Studies, Department of Commerce, Sri Venkateswara University, Tirupathi.**

productivity of credit. This innovative programme is reaching the poor people especially women and has an impact on their socio-economic development as well as their empowerment. This programme is becoming popular and emerging as a powerful instrument for poverty alleviation in many countries of Asia, Africa, Europe and America.

Origen and Growth of Microfinance in India

Microfinance emerged as an industry almost same time all over the world. Microfinance is broadly accepted for improving income level of poor people. In 1970s and 1980s non government organizations provided micro credits to poor for opening micro enterprises. In 1970s since the effort of Mohammad Yunus founder of Grameen Bank, Microfinance has proved to be a sustainable tool for poverty alleviation. In 2006 Mohammad Yunus was awarded noble peace prize for his effort towards the economic as well as social development of poor people in Bangladesh. Microfinance industry in India can be traced back to mid of 1970s when NGO s like: PRADAN and MYRADA started promoting self-help group model as a social development tool for development of low income people.

In India, the first initiative to introduce microfinance was the establishment of Self-Employed Women's Association (SEWA) in Gujarat. SEWA was registered as a trade union of self-employed women workers of the unorganised sector in 1972. This trade union established their bank known as SEWA Bank in 1974. To establish this bank four thousand union members contributed Rs. 10 each as share capital. Since then this bank is registered as a co-operative bank and has been providing banking services to poor women and has also become a viable financial venture. The first major effort to reach these rural poor was made by NABARD in 1986-87, when it supported and funded an action research project on 'saving and Credit Management of Self-Help Groups' of Mysore Resettlement and Development Authority (MYRADA). For this purpose, a grant of Rs. one million was provided to MYRADA. The encouraging results were yielded. In 1988-89, NABARD undertook a survey of 43 NGOs spread over eleven states in India to study the functioning of the SHGs and possibilities of collaboration between the banks and SHGs in the mobilization of rural savings and improving the credit delivery to the poor. In order to meet their credit requirements, in July 1991 RBI issued a circular to the commercial banks to extend credit to the SHGs formed under the pilot project of NABARD. The programme acquired a national priority from 1999 through Government of India budget announcements. Since the time of its origin, NABARD provides policy guidance, technical and promotional support mainly for capacity building of NGOs and SHGs. These days many public and private commercial banks, regional-rural banks, co-operative banks, co-operative societies, registered and unregistered NBFCs, societies, trusts and NGOs are providing microfinance by using their branch network and through different microfinance delivery model.

Growth of Microfinance

The growth of microfinance is visible in many aspects. There are more than 2000 NGOs involved in the NABARD SHG-Bank linkage programme. Out of these, approximately 800 NGOs are involved in some form of financial intermediation. Further, there are 350 new generation co-operatives providing thrift and credit services. According to our estimate, the present total outstanding, including: Sa-Dhan members and bank linkages is approximately Rs. 700 crores (Rs. 150 crores of Sa-Dhan members and another Rs. 550 crores from the Banking system). The total client base is estimated at 6-8 million as opposed to the Government of India (GOI) intention to reach 25 million clients. The growth of community institutions has taken place with the role to take social and financial intermediation. A numbers of community banks have come into existence at village and block levels call 'Federation of Self-Help Groups'.

The inadequacies of the formal financial system to cater to the needs of the poor and the realisation of the fact that the key to success lies in the evolution and participation of community based organizations at the grassroots level led to the emergence of new generation of MFIs.

One kind of MFI is an NGO engaged in promoting Self-Help Groups (SHGs) and their federations at a cluster level and linking SHGs with Banks under the Scheme. Examples are Myrada in Karnataka, which has promoted Sanghmitra, a company of its village saving and credit sanghas, PRADAN which has established a large number of SHGs and federated them under Damodar in Bihar, Sakhi Samiti in Rajasthan.

Another kind is NGO-MFI directly lending to the poor borrowers, who are either organized into SHGs or into Grameen Bank type of groups after borrowing bulk funds from SIDBI, RMK and FWWB. Examples in this category are Rashtriya Gramin Vikas Nidhi (RGVN) which runs credit and savings programme in Assam and Orissa on the lines of Grameen Bank, Bangladesh. Also we have SHARE in AP, ASA in Tamil Nadu under this category.

There are MFIs which are specifically organized as co-operatives, such as: over 500 Mutually Aided Co-operative Thrift and Credit Socities (MACTS) in AP, promoted among others by Co-operative Development Foundation (CDF) and the SEWA Bank in Gujarat which also runs federations of SHGs in nine districts. Then we have MFIs, which are organize as Non-Banking Finance Companies (NBFC) such as: BASIX, CFTS Mirzapur, SHARE Microfin. Ltd., and Sarvodaya Nanofinance Ltd.

Performance of Microfinance in India

Microfinance sector has traversed a long journey from micro savings to micro credit and then to micro enterprises and now entered the field of micro insurance, micro pension. Financial institutions in the country continue to play a leading role in the microfinance programme for nearly two decades now. They have joined hands proactively with informal delivery channels to give microfinance sector the necessary momentum.

Loan Portfolio of Self-Help Groups and Microfinance Institution

Table 8.1 shows the Loan Portfolio of Self-Help Groups and Microfinance Institution in India from 2009-13. It may be observed that during 2009, total loan outstanding has Rs. 390 billion out of which Bank-SHGs have 272.66 billion and the remaining have MFIs. Whereas during 2013 the loan outstanding has increased to Rs. 616.75 billion.

Table 8.1: Loan Portfolio of Self-Help Groups and Microfinance Institution (Rs. Billion)

	2009	2010	2011	2012	2013
Banks-SHGs	272.66	280.38	312.21	363.41	393.75
MFI	117.34	183.44	215.56	209.13	223
Total	390	463.82	527.77	572.54	616.75

Source: NABARD Microfinance state of sector report 2013.

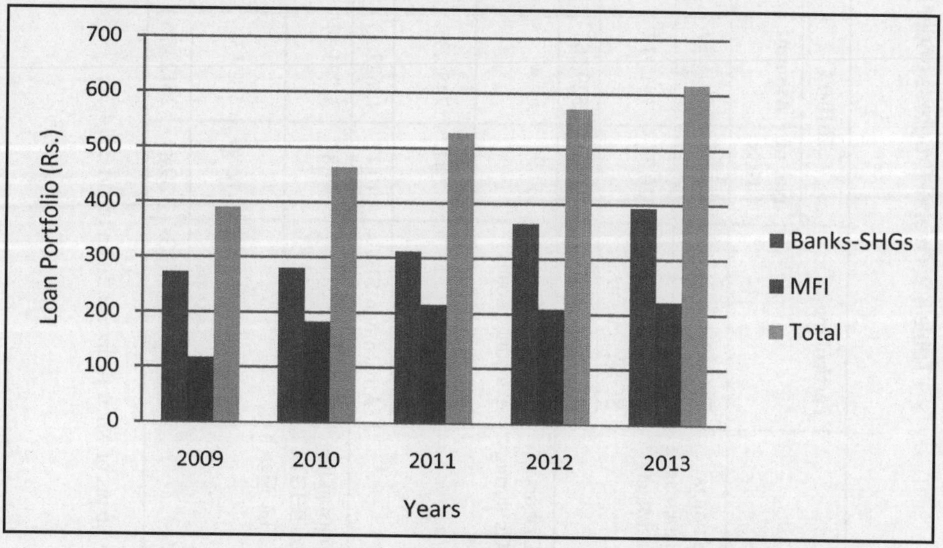

Fig. 8.1: **Chart Loan Portfolio of Self-Help Groups and Microfinance Institution (Rs. Billion)**

Table 8.2: Overall Progress under SHG-Bank Linkage Programme during last Five Years

(Numbers in lakh/Amount in Crore)

	Particulars	2010-11		2011-12		2012-13		2013-14		2014-15	
		No. of SHGs	Amount	No. of SHGs	Amount	No. of SHGs	Amount	No. of SHGs	Amount	No. of SHGs	Amount
SHG Savings with Banks as on 31st March	Total SHGs No	74.62	7016.30	79.60	6551.49	73.18	8217.25	74.30	9897.42	76.97	11059.89
	Of which SGSY groups	20.23	1817.12	21.33	1395.25	20.47	1821.65	22.62	2477.58	30.52	4424.03
	All women SHGs	60.98	5298.65	62.99	5104.33	59.38	6514.86	62.52	8012.89	66.51	9264.33
Loan Disbursed to SHGs during the year	No of SHGs extending Loans	11.96	14547.73	11.48	16534.77	12.2	20585.36	13.66	24017.36	16.26	27582.31
	Of which SGSY Groups	2.41	2480.37	2.10	2643.56	1.81	2207.47	2.26	3480.6	6.43	9487.69
	All women SHGs	10.17	12622.33	9.23	14132.02	10.37	17854.31	11.52	21037.97	14.48	24419.75
Loan outstanding Against SHGs as on 31st March	Total No SHGs Linked	47.87	31221.17	43.54	36340	44.51	39375.3	41.97	42927.52	44.68	51545.46
	Of which SGSY Groups	12.86	7829.39	12.16	8054.83	11.93	8597.09	13.07	10177.42	18.46	19752.74
	All Women SHGs	39.84	26123.75	36.49	30465.28	37.57	32840.04	34.06	36151.58	38.58	45901.95

Source: Status of Microfinance in India report 2014-15, NABARD.

It may be concluded that, the loan portfolio of SHGs and MFIs has increased gradually. Hence, both MFIs and Banks has to take initiation against to recover their loans from SHGs.

Overall Progress under SHG-Bank Linkage Programme

The SHGs-Bank Linkage programme has received wide acceptance among multiplicity of stake holders, civil society organizations, bankers and the international communities. Table 8.2 depicts the overall progress of SHGs under SHG-Bank Linkage Programme. Around 1.2 million new SHGs had credit link with banks and bank loans of Rs. 14,547 crore (including repeat loan) was disbursed to these SHGs in the financial year 2010-11. whereas during 2014-15 about 1.63 million new SHGs had credit link with banks and bank loans of Rs. 27582.31 crore (including repeat loan) was disbursed to these SHGs. During the 2010-11 about 7.46 million SHGs maintained saving account with banks. On an average, the amount of saving per SHGs was Rs. 9,405.00 as compared to the amount of credit of Rs. 65,180.00 in 2010-11. where in the year 2014-15 about 7.69 million SHGs maintained saving account with banks. On an average, the amount of saving per SHGs was Rs. 14369.09 as compared to the amount of credit of Rs. 84317.91 in 2014-15.

Table 8.3: Saving of Self-Help Groups with Banks Agency-wise Position as on 31st March 2015 **(Amount in Rs. Lakhs)**

No.of Agency	Total Savings of SHG's with Bank		Out of Total-Under NRML/SGSY and other Government Sponsored Prog		Out of Total Exclusive Women SHGs		Out of Total-Under NULM/SJSRY and other Government Sponsored Prog.	
	No. of SHGs	Saving Amount	No. of SHGs	Saving Amount	No. of SHGs	Saving Amount	No. of SHGs	Saving Amount
Commercial Banks	4135821	663067.47	3601961	571367.86	1803442	318312.5	334044	82478.58
Regional Rural Banks	2161315	234657.37	1813079	202163.96	1049122	101581.6	53884	6982.86
Co-operative Banks	1400333	208259.23	1236871	152900.79	199873	22508.89	45235	17719.52
Total	7697469	1105984.07	6651911	926432.61	3052437	442402.95	433163	107180.96

Source: Status of Microfinance in India report 2014-15, NABARD.

Delivery Models of Microfinance

The availability of credit and banking facilities to the poor and under privileged segment of the society can be reached through Microfinance. The Government and the Reserve Bank have taken several initiatives, from time to time, such as: nationalisation of banks, prescription of priority sector lending norms and concessional interest rate for the weaker section of society. It was, however, realised that further direct efforts were required to address the credit needs of poor people. In response to this requirement, the Microfinance movement started in India with the introduction of SHG bank linkage programme (SBLP) in the early 1990s. At present, there are mainly two models for delivery of Microfinance in India SBPL model and the MFI model.

The SBPL model had more borrowers and loans outstanding in comparison with other models of Microfinance. SBPL model is recognized as largest Microfinance programme in all over the world as per its coverage. Apex Institutions like: RBI, SIDBI, and NABARD have also taken a number of steps to drive movement of Microfinance programmes in India.

The developments relating to evolution of various models of the Microfinance movement are detailed in the present section. The Microfinance sector started getting recognition in India after the launch of the SBLP.

All over the world lot of basic effort had been step forwarded since 1980s which set a framework for Microfinance efforts in India. The approaches for delivery of Microfinance are varied in nature. There is no specific model which fits into all conditions rather there is an easy and elastic approach needed to meet the credit requirement of poor people. Each model has to be modified as per different situation and local requirements. Various delivery models have been adopted by Microfinance institutions and they can be categorized in to following broad categories.

SHG-Bank Linkage Model

A SHG is a small group of about 10-20 persons from a homogeneous class of rural and urban poor which promoted savings among members and used these resources for meeting their credit needs The group is democratically formed and elects its own leaders. The vital features of SHGs are it consists of members belonging to the same community or society and having common economic goal.

Their aims for formation of SHG include economic welfare of all members.

Under the SBLP, the following three different models have emerged in India:

Model I: SHGs promoted, guided and financed by banks.

Model II: SHGs promoted by NGOs/Government agencies and financed by banks.

Model III: SHGs promoted by NGOs and financed by banks using NGOs/ formal agencies as financial intermediaries.

Microfinance Institution Model

The MFI model in India is characterised by a diversity of institutional and legal forms. MFIs in India exist in a variety of forms like: trusts registered under the Indian Trust Act, 1882/Public Trust Act, 1920; societies registered under the Societies Registration Act, 1860; Co-operatives registered under the Mutually Aided Co-operative Societies Acts of the States; and non-banking financial companies (NBFC)-MFIs, which are registered under Section 25 of the Companies Act, 1956 or NBFCs registered with the Reserve Bank. These MFIs are scattered across the country and due to the multiplicity of registering authorities.

Federated Self-Help Group Model

Self-Help Groups are successful in empowering women by providing direct and indirect benefits to them. SHGs are small in size generally 10-15 members having limited in the types of financial services they can provide to its members. Federation of SHGs have more than 1000 members In Federated SHG model, there is a three tier structure the first tire is the SHG, the second tier is a cluster and the third tier is an apex body, which represents the entire SHG. At the cluster level, each SHG is represented by two of its members. The apex body usually made up of 10-15 members and they form the link between the SHGs and the NGO which is supporting to them. With the help of federations and NGO with limited resources, it has impact on a large number of poor people. Examples of Federated Self-Help Group model are PRADAN, Chaitanya and SEWA.

Bank Partnership Model

In this model, the bank is the lender and the MFI acts as an agent for handling items of work relating to credit monitoring, supervision and recovery, while the borrower is the individual. In Bank Partnership model Microfinance institutions acts as an agent of bank. Microfinance institutions are only concerned with dealing with clients for granting loan to final repayment. In this model MFI for larger funding access holds the borrower loan on its account for some time and refinance through the mean of securitization.

Grameen Bank Model

Grameen Bank model is one of the oldest and most successful models of microfinance. In 1970s Grameen Bank model was launched in village area of Bangladesh to empower the poor people through Microfinance. In this model microfinance programme participants are organised into groups of five members. They make mandatory contribution to group savings and insurance fund. Each member maintains her individual saving and loan account with the bank and after contributing to the savings fund for a fixed time the group members receive individual loans from the bank. But the group is not required to give any guarantee for the loan repayment by its member. Repayment responsibility solely rests on the individual borrower and there is no form of joint liability, *i.e.,* group members are not responsible to pay on behalf of a defaulting member. Loans are provided for six months to one year duration but repayments are made weekly. Bank staff makes periodic visits to the groups, maintain individual records of group members and facilitate all the financial transactions. This creates ease in working but hindrance in the empowerment of members.

After great success of GB Model it was created as formal Bank under special Law in 1983. The bank is owned by the poor burrowers mostly women. The Grameen bank eliminates the concept of collateral security for taking loan from bank and upturned the conventional banking practice. It is formed on mutual trust and provides credit facilities for self-employment and profit making activities to low income people. The main feature of Grameen bank model is it provides door step service to poor people. In India Grameen bank model was adopted by CASHPOR financia l and technical limited, SHARE Microfinance limited, and Activist for social alternatives (ASA).

Some of the Significant Features of Grameen Bank Model are:

- Low transaction costs.
- Loans are collateral free.
- Repayment of loans in small and short interval.
- Quick loan sanctions with little or no paper works.

Repayment of loans in small amount is one of the major reasons of high loan recovery rate of a Grameen Bank.

Banking Correspondents Model

In January 2006, the Reserve Bank permitted banks to utilise the services of NGOs, MFIs (other than NBFCs) and other civil society organizations as intermediaries in providing financial and banking services through the use of business facilitator and business correspondent (BC) models. The BC model allows banks to do 'cash in – cash out' transactions at a location much closer to the rural population, thus addressing the last mile problem. The BC model uses the MFI's ability to get close to poor clients – a necessity for savings mobilisation from the poor – while relying on the financial strength of the bank to safeguard the deposits. Pursuant to the announcement made by the Union Finance Minister in the Union Budget 2008-09, banks were permitted to engage retired bank employees, ex-servicemen and retired government employees as business correspondents (BCs) with effect from April 24, 2008, in addition to entities already permitted earlier, subject to appropriate due diligence.

Conclusion

Economic and financial services institutions long-term growth is depend on the manner that Financial Institutions approaches and taps untapped rural areas in India. Microfinance is often portrayed in literature as a tool that allows individuals excluded from the financial system to get access to sources of funding, which will help for theirs development and growth. From the above study it can be viewed that Self-help Groups are playing vital role in delivery of microfinance services which leads to increase the saving habits of poorest strata of society and contributing towards the development of poor people in India.

REFERENCES

1. Anand Vishal, (2014). Microfinance: State-of-the-art Paradigm for Women's Empowerment in Bihar, *IOSR Journal of Humanities and Social Science (IOSR-JHSS)* Volume 19, Issue 1, Ver. XI (Feb. 2014), pp. 05-08.
2. Sunitha. S, (2014). A Comprehensive Study on Microfinance Institutions in India, *Galaxy International Interdisciplinary Research Journal GIIRJ*, Vol. 2 (2), February (2014).
3. Banarjee Abhijit *et al.* (2014). The Miracle of Microfinance? Evidence from a Randomized Evaluation (http://economics.mit.edu/files/5993)
4. Mishra Sibanjan *et al.* (2013). Microfinance: A Tool for Poverty Alleviation, *American International Journal of Research in Humanities*, Arts and Social Sciences pp. 236-238.
5. Nasir Sibhatullah, (2013). Microfinance in India: Contemporary Issues and Challenges. *Middle-East Journal of Scientific Research* 15 (2): 191-199, 2013.
6. Status of Microfinance in India (2014-15) (https://www.nabard.org/english/allpublication.aspx)

Pages 68-74

POVERTY ALLEVIATION THROUGH MICROFINANCE
Edited by : Dr. B. Ramachandra Reddy
Edition : 2017
ISBN : 978-93-5056-865-1
Published by : Discovery Publishing House Pvt. Ltd., New Delhi (India)

9 Impact of Microfinance on Development of Micro and Small Enterprises

G. Damodhar[1]
Dr G. Narasimhulu[2]

Concept Microfinance

Microfinance enables the poor and excluded section of people in the society who do not have an access to formal banking to build assets, diversity livelihood options and increase income, and reduce their vulnerability to economic stress. In the past, it has been experienced that the provision for financial products and services to poor people by MFIs can cover their full costs through adequate interest spreads and by operating efficiently and effectively. Microfinance is defined as a development tool that grants or provides financial services and products such as: very small loans, saving, micro leasing, micro insurance and money transfer to assist the very or exceptionally poor in expanding or establishing their businesses (Robbinson, 1998). Microfinance is not a magic solution that will propel all of its clients out of poverty. But various impact studies have demonstrated that microfinance is really benefiting the poor households.

Evolution of Microfinance

Microfinance as an industry evolved in all the third world countries almost at the same time span. world over, it was getting widely recognized that improving income levels of low income community is essential to improve their well-being during the 1970s and 1980s the micro enterprise movement led to the emergence of Non-Governmental Organizations (NGOs) that provided small loans for the poor one of the significant events that helped it gained prominence in the 1970s was through the efforts of Mohammed

1. Research Scholar, Department of Commerce, S.V. University, Tirupati.
2. Lecturer in Commerce, SKIT, Srikalahasti.

Yunus, a microfinance pioneer and founder of the Grameen Bank of Bangladesh, In 2006, Prof. Yunus was awarded Nobel Peace prize for his efforts to create economic and social development.

Microfinance in India started in the early 1980s with small efforts at forming informal Self-Help Groups (SHGs) to provide access to much-needed savings and credit services. From this small beginning, the microfinance sector has grown significantly in the past decades. National bodies like: Small Industries Development Bank of India (SIDBI) and the National Bank for Agriculture and Rural Development (NABARD) are devoting significant time and financial resources to microfinance. The strength of the microfinance organizations (MFOS) in India is in the diversity of approaches and forms that have evolved over time.

Structure of Existing Microfinance Institutions in India

Indian Microfinance Institutions are predominantly NGOs *i.e.,* nearly 80 per cent of the Microfinance Institutions operate under the Society/Trust form which is for the not-for-profit sector with a clear development agenda. Apart from this, other important legal forms are being used by Indian Microfinance Institutions. 10 per cent of organizations operate under the company structure; 5 per cent are section 25 companies (Section 25 of the Indian Company Act, 1956); 2 per cent as cooperative; 2 per cent as Non-Banking Finance Companies (NBFCs); and 1 per cent as Local Area Banks (LAB). The Organization Structure of existing Microfinance Institutions in India is given below:

(a) Not for Profit Microfinance Institutions

1. NGO – Microfinance Institutions – 400 to 500 – Registered under Societies Registration Act, 1860 or similar provincial Acts Indian Trust Act, 1882.
2. Non-Profit Companies – 10 Registered under Section 25 of the Companies Act, 1956.

(b) Mutual Benefit Microfinance Institution

Mutually Aided Co-operative by State Government Societies (MACS) and similarly set up institutions – 200 to 250 – registered under Mutually Aided Co-operative Societies Act enacted by State Government.

(c) For Profit Microfinance Institutions

Non-Banking Financial Companies (NBFCs) – 6* - Registered under Indian Companies Act, 1956 Reserve Bank of India Act, 1934.

Note: The estimated number includes only those Microfinance Institutions, which are actually undertaking lending activity).

Source: www.nabard.org.

Micro and Small Enterprises

The major barrier to the development of Micro and Small Enterprises is access to credit. These enterprises differ in the level in which they are and the products and services offered to them by the MFIs. The micro and small enterprises need to be financed differently and the financing is determined by whether and firm is in the start-up phase or existing one and also whether it is stable, unstable, or growing. Stable survivors are those who benefit in having access to the financial services provided by MFIs to meet up with their production and consumption needs. Unstable survivors are groups that are considered not credit worthy for financial services to be provided in a sustainable way and Growth enterprises are Micro and Small Enterprises with high possibility to grow.

In identifying the market, MFIs consider whether to focus on already existing entrepreneurs or on potential entrepreneurs seeking for funds to start up a business venture. Working capital is the main hindrance in the development of already existing SMEs and to meet up, the borrow finance mostly from informal financial services which have high interest rates and services offered by the formal sector or not offered by these informal financial services.

Products and Services by Microfinance Institutions

Products and services offered by microfinance institutions in India for the development of Micro and Small Enterprises are basically classified as two *i.e.,* Financial Intermediation and Enterprise development services.

(a) Fianancial Intermediation

Providing financial assistance for small business groups in the form of business loans can be utilised for further investment in the existing business or setting up new tiny business ventures. Since the rate of interest and the repayment schedule are formulated to suit the requirements of the loan takers, there exist enormous demands for this product. MFIs extends such micro loans ranging from 5,000/- to 25,000/- for such income generating activities and few MFIs categorised their clients activities as farm based activities which includes Agriculture, Poultry, Sheep-rearing, sericulture, mushroom cultivation etc., and non-farm based activities which includes Petty-shop, Catering, Provision shop, Tailoring, Embroidery work, Beauty Shop Vegetable vendor, Fruit Vendor, Textile shop, Xerox machine, Brick making, Gold covering work, Jewelers work and others etc. The loans are taken by poor households directly as well as through groups to meet their diverse needs.

(b) Enterprise Development Services

MFIs provides cost efficient microfinance coupled with knowledge and information services that raise human capacity and organizational capability and create open access to markets resulting in more productive loans. MFIs provide skill development services, business training, marketing and technology services to their clients based on their occupation which helps them use their resources more productively.

Growth and Development of Micro and Small Enterprises

The term growth in this context can be defined as an increase in size or other objects that be quantified or a process of changes or improvements. The firm size is the results of firm growth over a period of time and it should be noted that firm growth is a process while firm size is a state (Pensore, 1995). The growth of a firm can be determined by supply of capital, labour and appropriate management and opportunities for investments that are profitable. The determining factor for a firm's growth is the availability of resources to the firm (Ghoshal, Halm and Moran, 2002.).

MFIs considering the growth of Micro and Small enterprises developed large-scale operations by offering a few highly standardized products with few advantages like: Streamlined loan administration, Simplified decision-making for field staffs, Reduced information requirements from clients, Low operational costs, Simplified repayment obligations. But this standardization also had its own disadvantages. So MFIs paid closer attention to product flexibility. Individual need-based loans are more suitable as they can be designed to cater to the specific requirements of the clients.

Reasons to Serve Microfinance Institutions in India

By definition, microfinance is the business of giving tiny loans to people who do not have access to formal banking services. Such institutions operate in the hinterland where traditional banks balk at serving. Or, so we believed. The scene has changed. MFIs have shifted their focus from rural pockets to urban India. For the first time in its 25-year history, Indian MFIs have more urban clients than rural ones. The latest data, compiled by industry self-regulatory organization Sa-Dhan, shows 67 per cent of the 37 million MFI customers live in urban India. The share of rural customers was 69 per cent in fiscal year 2012. That dropped marginally to 67 per cent in 2013. In the following two years, the share of rural customers has declined drastically. In 2014, rural customers constituted 56 per cent of the total. It dropped further to 33 per cent in the following year. This busts the myth that Indian microfinance is pre-dominantly a rural phenomenon, very different from what we see in Latin America and large parts of Africa and

Asia. The industry's outreach to urban clients was increasing every year and it has now outstripped that of rural customers. Why has this happened? Before we look for an answer, let's look at the broader picture. The industry had a customer base of 37.1 million in March 2015, up from 33 million a year ago. It included 6.5 million customers of Bandhan Financial Services Ltd, the largest MFI that turned into a bank in August. The percentage of women customers remained unchanged at 97 per cent, while the share of Scheduled Caste and Scheduled Tribe customers rose from 19 per cent to 28 per cent. The loan portfolio was close to Rs. 40,000 crores and 80 per cent of it was for income-generating activities. The average loan per borrower in the year ended 31 March rose to Rs. 13,162 from Rs. 10,079 in at the end of the previous fiscal. The quality of assets has improved. If we leave a few MFIs that had been affected by the crisis that gripped the industry following the Andhra Pradesh state law five years ago, the industry's non-performing assets were to the tune of 13 basis points as on 31 March. A basis point is one-hundredth of a percentage point. Such MFIs were referred to the so-called corporate debt restructuring cell as their equity and reserves were eroded by accumulated bad loans. About 80 per cent of 250-odd MFIs have less than 1 per cent of their loan portfolios at risk. About 12 per cent of MFIs have 1-3 per cent of their loan portfolio at risk, and 8 per cent of MFIs have more than 5 per cent of their loan portfolio at risk. The loans at risk are those that have not been serviced for 30 days.

In contrast, the quality of small loans distributed through the so-called self-help group (SHG) model is inferior. The number of SHGs to 7.71 million in 2015 from 7.43 million in the previous year even though the number of families involved in SHGs increased from 97 million to 101 million. SHGs typically a group of 20 women, save as well as offer credit to its members from money sourced from commercial banks. SHGs total savings stood at Rs. 11,307 crore in 2015 and the loan portfolio was Rs. 51,727 crore. The average loan outstanding per SHG was Rs. 1.15 lakhs and NAPs were 7.4 per cent, up from 6.8 per cent in the previous year.

One reason behind the rise in urban customers is the phenomenal growth of a few urban-focused MFIs such as: Janalakshmi Financial Services Pvt. Ltd, Ujjivan Financial Services Pvt. Ltd., and Satin Credit Card Network Ltd. These three collectively had around 5.7 million customers in March. Their growth last year had been higher than the average industry growth and most of their customers live in urban India. Till it became a bank, Bandhan had an 18 per cent market share of customers, followed by SKS Microfinance Ltd., and Shri Kshethra Dharmasthala Rural Development Project. Others among the top 10 are Janalakshmi, Equitus Microfinance Pvt. Ltd., Spandana

Spoorthy Financial Ltd., Share Microfin Ltd., Satin and Grameen Koota Financial Services Pvt Ltd., Janalakshmi, Ujjiivan and Equitus have received in-principle approval from the Reserve Bank of India to become small finance banks.

Another reason behind the growth in urban customers is the shift in the business models of many MFIs They are becoming increasingly urban-centric to cut down operational expenses and maximize operational efficiency. Under the priority sector lending norms, banks in India are required to give 40 per cent of their loans to small borrowers. As they do not have the reach, they give money to the MFIs to be on-lent to such borrowers. While fixing the loan price for small borrowers, the MFIs cannot charge more than 10 per cent over the cost of loans taken from banks. This means their profitability solely depends on operational efficiency as the cost of raising resources is almost the same for all MFIs.

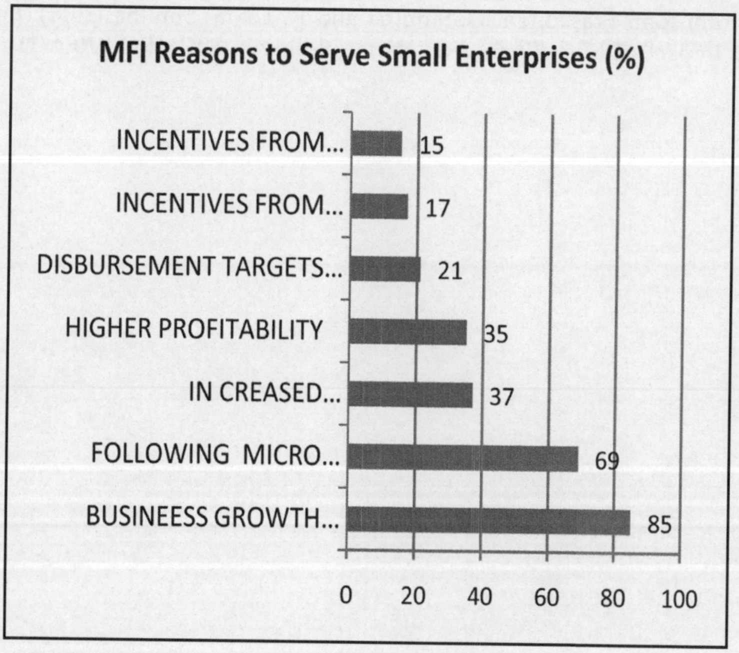

Source: CGAP MSE Industry survey 2011. Multiple answers allowed.

Conclusion

The main conclusion of this topic is that microfinance can be contribute to solve the problems of inadequate housing urban services as an integral part of poverty alleviation programmes. The challenges lies in finding the level of flexibility in the credit instruments that could make it match the multiple credit requirements of low income borrowers improving unbearably high cost of monitoring to end use lenders. A promoting solution is to provide multipurpose loans or composite credit for income generation, housing improvement and consumption support. Microfinance can indeed be sustained in long run in a profitable manner; going by the increasing number of commercial banks that have evinced interest in this area the future does seem bright.

REFERENCES

1. Robinson, M. (2003). The Microfinance Revolution: Sustainable Finance for the Poor. Washington D.C: World Bank.
2. Ranjani, K.S. (2012). Regulating Microfinance Institutions in India: A Conceptual Framework, Synergy, 10(1).
3. Chiyah Boma Ngehnevu and Forchu Zachary Nembo (2010). The Impact of Microfinance Institutions (MFIs) in the Development Small and Medium Size Business(SMEs) in Cameroon.]
4. Maruthi Ram Prasad, Dr. G. Sunitha and K. Laxmi Sunitha (2011). Emergency and Impact of Microfinance on Indian Scenario. KKIMRC IJRFA(1).

Pages 75-87

POVERTY ALLEVIATION THROUGH MICROFINANCE
Edited by : **Dr. B. Ramachandra Reddy**
Edition : **2017**
ISBN : 978-93-5056-865-1
Published by : **Discovery Publishing House Pvt. Ltd., New Delhi (India)**

10 Poverty Alleviation Programmes in India

An Overview

Dr. C. Venkateswar Rao[1]
A. Lavanya[2]
Dr. M. Venkateswarlu[3]

INTRODUCTION

Poverty is an unacceptable human condition that does not have to be inevitable. The main goal of development is to eliminate poverty and reduce social imbalances. Sustainable economic growth and appropriate social policies are keys to fighting poverty. At the same time, reducing poverty helps growth by enabling the poor to participate productively in the economy. Yet economic growth by itself does not guarantee success in eradicating poverty. Other important dimensions of poverty, such as: quality of life and participation in decision-making, need to be addressed.

This article to-know some of the Major Poverty Alleviation Programmes Launched in India. The government has relied mainly on three approaches for reduction of poverty. The first entails pursuit of higher economic growth which will improve the levels of living of all groups of people in the society including the poor, the second involves direct anti-poverty programmes and the third has stressed high priority to government expenditure on social sectors. After independence, the Government has launched several poverty alleviation programmes, the important among these are as follows:

Objectives of the Study

- To study the poverty alleviation programmes in India.
- To probe the NSAP, IAY, MGNREGS schemes progress in India.

1. Post-Doctoral Fellow.
2. Lecturer in Commerce, Viswodaya Government Degree College, Venkatagiri.
3. Professor, Department of Commerce, S.V. University.

Data Base

The study is based on secondary data. The secondary data collected from ministry of rural development, Annual reports 2004-05 to 2014-15.

1. Antyodaya plan (Annapurna).
2. National Social Assistance Programme (NSAP).
3. National Rural Employment Programme (NREP).
4. Indira Aawas Yojana.
5. Legal elimination of bonded labourers.
6. Preventing the Centralisation of wealth by modifying the law.
7. Small Farmers Development Programme (SFDP).
8. Drought Area Development Programme (DADP).
9. Twenty Point Programme.
10. Food for Work Programme.
11. Minimum Needs Programme (MNP).
12. Integrated Rural Development Programme (IRDP).
13. Rural Labour Employment Guarantee Programme (RLEGP).
14. TRYSEM Scheme.

Poverty, however, can be eradicated only when the various facilities and concessions for the upliftment of the downtrodden actually reach them. Then, there should be proper utilisation of these concessions and facilities. The focus of attention should not be on individual households but on the group of households. The assets of the individual household should be pooled together to start occupation when are technically feasible and economically viable.

The poverty alleviation programmes in India can be categorized based on whether it is targeted for rural areas or urban areas. Most of the programmes are designed to target rural poverty as the prevalence of the poverty is high in rural areas. Also targeting of the poverty is challenging in rural areas due to various geographic and infrastructure limitations. The five year plans immediately after independence tried to focus on poverty alleviation through sectoral programmes. The first five-year plan focused on agricultural production as a way of addressing poverty while second and third plans focused on massive state led investments for employment generation in public sector. While these policies did some policy-generation, they did not have enough strength to affect a sweeping effect.

1. Annapurna

This scheme was started by the government in 1999-2000 to provide food to senior citizens who cannot take care of themselves and are not under the

National Old Age Pension Scheme... (NOAPS), and who have no one to take care of them in their village. This scheme would provide 10 kg of free food grains a month for the eligible senior citizens. The number of beneficiaries covered under this scheme during the last four years is as under: (In Lakhs).

National Old Age Pension Scheme (NOAPS)

As the name suggests this scheme provides pension to old people who were above the age of 65 ('Now 60') who could not fend for themselves and did not have any means of subsistence. The pension that was given was Rs. 200 a month. This pension is given by the central government. The job of implementation of this scheme in states and union territories is given to panchayats and municipalities. The state's contribution may vary depending on the state. The amount of old age pension is Rs. 200 per month for applicants aged 60-79. For applicants aged above 80 years, the amount has been revised in Rs. 1000 a month according to the (2011-12) Budget. The scheme is administered by the Ministry of Rural Development, Government of India. It is fully funded by the Central Government, unlike some other welfare programmes where the Union government shares costs with the State Governments. Allocation of funds for NSAP by Government of India between 2009-10 and 2014-15 (in Crore Rs.). The following table shows the year wise NSAP allocations. Increase in Pension Amounts. The Government of India has urged State Governments to make matching contributions with the aim of doubling the monthly pension amounts. Monthly pension amounts in various states in India is presented in Table 10.1.

Table 10.1

State	Old age Pension (Rs.)	Widow Pension (Rs.)	Disability Pension (Rs.)
Andhra Pradesh	1000	1000	1000
Bihar	400	400	400
Delhi	1000	1500	1500
Haryana	1200	1200	1200
Himachal Pradesh	550	550	750
Jammu Kashmir	400	400	400
Kerala	600	800	800
Maharashtra	600	600	600
Odisha	300	300	300
Rajasthan	500	500	250
Sikkim	600	500	600
Tamil Nadu	400	400	400
Uttar Pradesh	300	400	300

Source: http://nsap.nic.in/nsap/NSAP-%20About%20us.pdf

National Social Assistance Programme (NSAP) beneficiaries in India are presented in Table 10.2.

Table 10.2: National Social Assistance Programme (NSAP)

Year	Allocation Rs. (in Crore)	Releases Rs. (in Crore)	Expenditure Rs. (in Crore)	No. of Beneficiaries NOAPS/ IGNOAPS	No.of Beneficiaries under NFBS	No.of Beneficiaries under Annapurna	No.of Beneficiaries under IGNWPS	No.of Beneficiaries under IGNDPS
2004-05	1189.97	1032.01	868.37	8079386	261981	820583	Introduced 2009	Introduced 2009
2005-06	1190.00	1189.71	1033.89	8002598	276737	851654		
2006-07	2489.61	2489.61	1968.28	87008837	243972	871424		
2007-08	2891.48	2889.73	3123.08	11514026	334152	1051030		
2008-09	4500.00	4500.00	3961.51	15020640	426292	1011240		
2009-10	5200.00	5155.50	4914.88	16356058	342809	1015655	3213467	699680
2010-11	5162.00	5162.00	5346.08	17059756	334924	958419	3425390	728004
2011-12	6658.00	6596.46	6188.67	21384404	330240	778682	3628467	794249
2012-13	9614.50	9112.45	5859.50	20836592	184608	639125	4879915	976713
2013-14	9541.00	NA	NA	NA	NA	NA	NA	NA
2014-15	10635.00	NA	5328.60	19097677	164814	419811	5592926	960291

Source: Ministry of Rural Development, Annual Report, 2004-05 to 14-15.

Note: Not Available.

From Table 10.2 shows that National Social Assistance Programme highest allocation was Rs. 10635.00 Cr in 2014-15 and lowest was noticed in 1189.97 Cr in 2004-05. Followed by funds release highest was 9112.45 Cr in 2012-13 and lowest funds released was noticed that 1032.01 Cr in 2004-05, NSAP expenditure was registered highest was in 6188.67 cr in 2011-12 and lowest was registered that 868.37 Cr in 2004-05. Number of beneficiaries NOAPS/IGNOAPS was highest registered 21384404 in 2011-12 and lowest was registered in 8002598 in 2005-06. Number of Beneficiaries under NFBS was highest registered 426292 in 2008-09 and lowest was noticed that 164814 in 2014-15. Number of Beneficiaries under Annapurna was highest registered was 1051030 in 2007-08 and lowest was recorded in 419811 in 2014-15. Number of Beneficiaries under IGNWPS was highest registered was 5592926 in 2014-15 and lowest was recorded in 3213467 in 2009-10. Number of Beneficiaries under IGNDPS highest registered was 976713 in 2012-13 and lowest was recorded in 699680 in 2009-10. From the table one can observed that NSAP Scheme allocation of funds, release of funds and expenditure of funds was shown an increasing trend from the study period and the remaining are showing fluctuation from the study period.

2. Rural Housing-Indira Awaas Yojana (IAY) (Initiated in 1985)

Indira Awaas Yojana is a Government of India social welfare programme to provide housing for the rural poor in India. This scheme aimed at creating housing for everyone. The differentiation is made between rural poor and urban poor for a separate set of schemes operate for the urban poor (like the Basic Services for Urban Poor). It is one of the major flagship programmes of the Rural Development Ministry to construct houses for BPL population in the villages. Under the scheme, financial assistance worth Rs. 70000/- in plain areas and Rs. 75000/- in difficult areas (high land area) is provided for construction of houses. The houses are allotted in the name of the woman or jointly between husband and wife. The construction of the houses is the sole responsibility of the beneficiary and engagement of contractors is strictly prohibited. Sanitary latrine and smokeless chullah are required to be constructed along with each IAY house for which additional financial assistance is provided from Total Sanitation Campaign and Rajiv Gandhi Grameen Vidyutikaran Yojana respectively. This scheme, operating since 1985, provides subsidies and cash-assistance to people in villages to construct their houses, themselves.

Impact of IAY

In the present form, IAY is one of the popular schemes of the Ministry of Rural Development. The popularity can be attributed to the fact that the scheme enables beneficiaries to participate and involve themselves in construction of their houses. The role of the State Government is limited to releases and to facilitating use of appropriate technology. In spite of criticism from certain quarters about IAY being a full subsidy scheme, experience reveals that houses get completed more or less on time. Not surprisingly, evaluation studies reveal high levels of occupancy and satisfaction. Providing houses to the poorest also has a positive impact on people s physical and mental health. Once the basic need of housing is fulfilled, citizens develop a sense of opportunity for livelihood, for improving living conditions and for continuing children s education. Undoubtedly, there is a direct link between a safe and secure housing and improved standards of living and reduction in vulnerability.

Table 10.3: Achievement in the 11th and 12th Five-year Plan IAY Performance (Last ten years)

(as on 31-07-2013)

Years	Total Allocation (C+S) (in crore)	Total Releases (C+S) (in crore)	Total Available Funds (in crore)	Utilization (in crore)	% Utilization	Physical Target (in lakh)
2004-05	3279.25	3842.52	*	3262.09	*	15.62
2005-06	3641.34	3650.77	4586.75	3654.09	79.67	14.41
2006-07	3874.73	3833.24	2393.01	2393.02	62.43	15.33
2007-08	5374.19	5175.10	6527.17	5464.54	83.72	21.27
2008-09	7523.85	11727.04	14460.35	8348.34	57.73	21.27
2009-10	11131.59	11316.90	15852.34	13292.46	83.85	40.52
2010-11	13181.32	13295.22	17956.54	13465.73	74.99	29.09
2011-12	12436.47	12920.36	19159.30	12926.33	67.47	27.27
2012-13	13776.21	7208.49	13531.38	9386.22	75.48	30.10
2013-14	18210.20	14420.97	16951.88	10278.67	60.63	24.80
2014-15	18464.14	11840.64	16745.17	9546.48	57.01	22.21

Source: Indira Awaas Yojana Briefing Book, 2013. Annual Reports. MRD.

From Table 10.3 shows that Achievement in the 11th and 12th Five-year plan IAY (Indira Awaas Yojana) performance highest allocation both central and state was Rs. 18464.14 Cr in 2014-15 and lowest was noticed in 3279.25 Cr in 2004-05. Followed by funds release both central and state highest was 14420.97 Cr in 2013-14 and lowest funds released was noticed that 3650.77 Cr in 2005-06. Total available funds was registered highest was in 19159.3 Cr in 2011-12 and lowest was noticed that 2393.01 Cr in 2006-07. Utilisation of funds was highest registered 13465.73 Cr in 2010-11 and lowest was observed in 2393.02 Cr in 2006-07. Per cent of Utilization was highest registered 83.85 in 2009-10 and lowest was noticed that 57.01 in 2014-15. Physical target highest registered was 40.52 in 2009-10 and lowest was recorded in 14.41 in 2005-06. From Table 10.3 one can observed that IAY Scheme allocation of funds, release of funds and expenditure of funds was shown an increasing trend from the study period and the remaining are showing fluctuation from the study period. IAY performance over last 10 years is presented in Table 10.4.

Table 10.4: IAY Performance over last 10 Years

Year	Central Allocation (Rs. Lakhs)	Central Release (Rs. Lakhs)	Utilization (Rs. Lakhs)	Target No. of. Houses Lakh	Houses Constructed/ Completed	Expenditure Rs. Cr.
2004-05	246067.00	288310.02	326208.64	15.62	15.21	3262.08
2005-06	273240.00	273822.58	365409.05	14.41	15.52	3654.09
2006-07	290753.00	290753.06	425342.45	15.33	14.98	4253.42
2007-08	403270.00	388237.01	546454.30	21.27	19.92	5464.64
2008-09	564577.00	879579.39	834834.33	21.27	21.34	8348.34
2009-10	849470.00	863573.99	1329236.40	40.52	33.86	13292.46
2010-11	1005370.00	1013945.40	1346572.75	29.08	27.15	13406.51
2011-12	949120.00	986477.80	1292632.74	27.26	24.71	12926.33
2012-13	NA	NA	NA	NA	NA	NA
2013-14	1389490.38	1297000.78	1027867.51	22.72	15.62	10278.67
2014-15	1409955.00	1040429.64	954648.31	NA	NA	9646.48

Source: Annual Reports. MRD.

From Table 10.4 shows that IAY (Indira Awaas Yojana) performance highest central allocation was Rs. 1409955 lakh in 2014-15 and lowest was noticed in 246067 lakh in 2004-05. Followed by funds release central highest was 1297001 lakh in 2013-14 and lowest funds released was noticed that 273822.6 lakh in 2005-06. Utilisation of funds was highest registered 1346573 Cr in 2010-11 and lowest was observed in 326208.6 lakh in 2004-05. Number of houses target lakh was highest registered 40.42 in 2009-10 and lowest was noticed that 14.41 in 2005-06. Houses constructed/completed highest registered was 33.86 in 2009-10 and lowest was recorded in 14.98 in 2006-

07. Expenditure highest registered was Rs. 13406.51 Cr in 2010-11 and lowest was recorded in Rs. 3262.08 Cr in 2004-05. From Table 10.4 one can observed that IAY Scheme allocation and release of funds of funds was shown an increasing trend from the study period and the remaining are showing fluctuation from the study period. Target, houses constructed (in lakhs) and Expenditure Rs. (in Crore). The year-wise allocation made by Planning Commission for the 12th Five-Year Plan is presented in Table 10.5 and 10.6.

Table 10.5: Target, Houses Constructed (in lakhs) and Expenditure Rs. in Crore

Year	Target in Lakhs	Houses Constructed (in Lakhs)	Expenditure Rs. in Crore
2009-10	40.52	33.86	13292.46
2010-11	29.09	27.15	13406.51
2011-12	27.27	24.71	12926.33
2012-13	30.10	21.86	9386.22
Total	126.98	107.58	49011.52

Table 10.6: The Year-wise Allocation made by Planning Commission for the 12th Five-Year Plan is as follows

S. No.	Year	Allocation (in crore)	Actual Budgetary Allocation (in crore)
1.	2012-13	Rs. 11075.00	Rs. 10515.00
2.	2013-14	Rs. 17127.50	Rs. 13339.10
3.	2014-15	Rs. 17127.50	Rs. 14,000.00
4.	2015-16	Rs. 17127.50	–
5.	2016-17	Rs. 17127.50	–

Source: Indira Awaas Yojana Briefing Book, 2013.

Budget 2015 allocates Rs. 14,000 crore to scheme that aims at building 6 crore houses by 2022, XII IAY in the Context of Bharat Nirman. Bharat Nirman Programme is a business plan comprising six different components addressing the rural sector and housing is one of them. Rural Housing was one of the six components of Bharat Nirman Programme. Under, Bharat Nirman, 60 lakh houses were envisaged to be constructed under the Scheme of Indira Awaas Yojana in four years from 2005-06 to 2008-09. Against this target, 71.76 lakh houses were constructed thereby exceeding the target of 'Bharat Nirman' period. The Target under Phase-II 'Bharat Nirman' is for construction of 120 lakh houses for a period of five years starting from

2009-10. During the first four years (information gathered upto 31.7.2013) of the Bharat Nirman Programme Period-Phase-II, approx. 107.58 lakh houses have been constructed. The year-wise break-up is given below: Further, for the current financial year of 2013-14, the total budgetary outlay for rural housing is Rs. 15184 crore with a physical target for construction of 24.80 lakh houses.

3. National Rural Employment Guarantee Act (NREGA)

The NREGA bill notified in 2005 and came into force in 2006 and further modified it as the Mahatma Gandhi National Rural Employment Guarantee Act (MGNREGA) in 2008. This scheme guarantees 100 days of paid work to people in the rural areas. The scheme has proved to be a major boost in Indian rural population's income. To augment wage employment opportunities by providing employment on demand and by specific guaranteed wage employment every year to households whose adult members volunteer to do unskilled manual work to thereby extend a security net to the people and simultaneously create durable assets to alleviate some aspects of poverty and address the issue of development in the rural areas.

The Ministry of Rural Development (MRD) is the nodal Ministry for the implementation of NREGA. It is responsible for ensuring timely and adequate resource support to the States and to the Central Council. It has to undertake regular review, monitoring and evaluation of processes and outcomes. It is responsible for maintaining and operating the MIS to capture and track data on critical aspects of implementation, and assess the utilization of resources through a set of performance indicators. MRD will support innovations that help in improving processes towards the achievement of the objectives of the Act. It will support the use of Information Technology (IT) to increase the efficiency and transparency of the processes as well as improve interface with the public. It will also ensure that the implementation of NREGA at all levels is sought to be made transparent and accountable to the public. Now 100 to 150 days work for all is provided.

Disbursement of MGNREGA wages through post offices Government of India enacted Mahatma Gandhi National Rural Employment Guarantee Act (MGNREGA) in September 2005. The Act seeks to provide at least 100 days of guaranteed wage employment in every financial year to every household whose adult members volunteer to do unskilled manual work. The scheme is implemented by Ministry of Rural Development and came into force in all districts in the country with effect from 1st April 2008. Scheme of disbursement of MGNREGA wages through Post Office accounts starting

Table 10.7: MGNREGS India Employment and funds utilisation different communities in India

Years	Total Job Cards Issued (in crore)	Households Provided Employment (No. in crore)	Number of MGNREGA Accounts Up to the Year (in millions)	Amount Disbursed during the Year (₹ in millions)	Available Fund	Fund Expenditure	Person days per HH (Days)				
							SCs	STs	Women	Others	Total
2006-07	3.78	2.10	NA	88233.5	12073.55	8823.35	22.95	32.98	36.40	34.56	90.5
2007-08	6.48	3.39	NA	158568.9	19305.81	15856.89	39.36	42.07	61.15	62.16	143.59
2008-09	10.01	4.51	29.21	38632.51	37397.06	27250.10	63.36	55.02	103.57	97.95	216.32
2009-10	11.25	5.25	42.50	79002.42	49579.19	37905.23	86.45	58.74	136.40	138.40	283.59
2010-11	11.98	5.49	48.97	91791.83	54172.14	39377.27	78.76	53.62	122.74	124.78	257.15
2011-12	12.50	5.06	53.84	78650.56	48832.49	38034.70	47.70	39.59	2103.81	129.06	216.34
2012-13	12.29	4.98	57.47	120141.21	39620.16	25074.69	31.42	22.14	74.74	87.10	140.66
2013-14	12.72	3.81	64.23	114033.77	42215.67	38672.40	14.45	9.59	34.91	38.53	62.57
2014-15	NA	NA	NA	NA	31467.58	26404.45	27.50	20.18	67.31	73.56	188.55
Total	81.01	34.59	296.22	769054.7	334663.7	257399.1	411.95	333.93	2741.03	786.1	1599.27
Average	18.02	7.69	84.63429	96131.84	37184.85	28599.9	45.77222	37.10333	304.5589	87.34444	177.6967
Max	12.72	5.49	64.23	158568.9	54172.14	39377.27	86.45	58.74	2103.81	138.4	283.59
Mini	3.78	2.1	29.21	38632.51	12073.55	8823.35	14.45	9.59	34.91	34.56	62.57

Source: Ministry of Rural Development. Annual Report 2014-15. Mahatma Gandhi National Rural Employment Guarantee Act, 2005. Report to the People 2nd February 2014. Department of Posts Ministry of Communications and Information Technology Government of India Annual Report 2014-15.

Note: MGNREGA accounts include both live and silent MGNREGS Accounts.

with Andhra Pradesh Postal Circle in 2005, the Scheme of disbursement of MGNREGA wages through Post Office accounts has been made operational in the entire country, with the exception of Delhi Postal Circle and Jammu and Kashmir Postal Circle. Department of Posts has taken the responsibility to disburse the wages through Post Offices by opening Post Office savings bank accounts for MGNREGA beneficiaries. The Scheme is operational through 96735 Post Offices as on 31st March, 2014. The number of accounts and amount of wages disbursed through Post Offices under MGNREGA has steadily grown over the years, are indicated in Table 10.7.

From Table 10.7 show that MGNREGS total Job Cards Issued in Cr highest was 12.72 Cr in 2013-14 and lowest was noticed in 3.78 in 2006-07. Followed by Households Provided Employment highest was 5.49 Cr in 2010-11 and lowest was noticed that 2.1 Cr In 2006-07. The number of MGNREGA Accounts Up to the Year (in millions) was highest registered 64.23 Cr in 2013-14 and lowest was observed in 29.21 Cr in 2008-09. Amount disbursed during the years in millions highest registered in 158568.9 in 2007-08 and lowest was noticed that in 38632.51 in 2008-09. Available Fund highest registered was 54172.14 in 2010-11 and lowest was recorded in 12073.55 in 2006-07. Fund Expenditure highest registered was Rs 39377.27 Cr in 2010-11 and lowest was recorded in Rs. 8823.35 Cr in 2006-07. Person₹ days per HH (Days) highest in SCs 86.45 (2009-10), STs 58.74(2009-10), women 2103.81(2011-12), Others 138.4 (2009-10) and total 283.59 (2009-10) and lowest no₹iced that SCs 14.45 (2013-14), STs 9.59 (2013-14), women 34.59 (2013-14), others 34.56 (2006-07) and total 62.57(2013-14). From Table 10.7 one can observed that MGNREGS Scheme job cards issued and house hold provide employment was shown an increasing trend from the study period and the remaining are showing fluctuation from the study period.

4. *National family Benefit Scheme (NFBS)*

In 1998, the amount of benefit under NFBS was raised to 10,000 in case of death due to natural causes as well as accidental causes. Finally with effect from 18.10.2012 amount of assistance under NFBS has been increased to 20000 and upper age limit of death of primary breadwinner has been reduced to 59 years. Hence, NFBS is presently applicable in case of death of primary breadwinner in the age group of 18-59 years. This scheme was started in August 1995 by the Government of India. This scheme is sponsored by the state government. It was transferred to the state sector scheme after 2002-03. It is under the community and rural department. This scheme provides a sum of 20000 Rs. to a person of a family who becomes the head of the family after the death of its primary breadwinner. The breadwinner is defined as a person who is above 18 who earns the most for the family and on whose earnings the family survives. It is for families below the poverty line. The number of beneficiaries covered under this scheme during the last four years is as under: (In Lakhs).

Years	2009-10	2010-11	2011-12	2012-13	2013-14	2014-15
Beneficiaries	342809	335044	336240	386005	NA	164814

5. *National Maternity Benefit Scheme (NMBS)*

This scheme provides a sum of 500 Rs. to a pregnant mother for the first two live births. The women have to be older than 19 years of age. It is given normally 12-8 weeks before the birth and in case of the death of the child the women can still avail it. Maternity Benefit Scheme Funds Allocation and Disbursement 2006-07 to 2010-11is presented in Table 10.8.

Table 10.8: Maternity Benefit Scheme Funds Allocation and Disbursement 2006-07 to 2010-11

Years	Amount Allocation (in Rs. Cr)	Amount Disbursed (in Rs. Cr)	Percent of Expenditure	No. of Beneficiaries
2006-07	100.00	100.00	100.00	241095
2007-08	300.00	296.44	98.9	679831
2008-09	350.00	349.26	99.8	579821
2009-10	360.00	358.60	99.6	599126
2010-11	360.00	326.19	90.6	544710

Source: DPH.

From Table 10.8 represent that the NMBS is implemented by states and union territories with the help of panchayats and municipalities. During 2010-11 the total allocation of funds for this scheme highest was 360 crores and the amount lowest used was Rs. 100 crore 2006-07 amount disbursed highest in 358.60 in 2009-10 and lowest was 100 Cr in 2006-07. Number of beneficiaries highest was observed in 679831 in 2007-08 and lowest noticed that 241095 in 2006-07. From Table 10.8 one can observe that Maternity Benefit Scheme Funds Allocation and Disbursement was shown increasing trend from the study period.

Conclusion

The Government of India and State Governments have been implementing above said several programmes like: (NSAP, IAY, and

MGNREGS, IRDP, JRY) for alleviation of poverty in India. While the objectives of these programmes may be commendable, they are based on a belief that spending of money is in itself a necessary and sufficient condition for poverty alleviation. This belief under plays the role of non-monetary policies and the impact they have on the lives of the people. It has been the experience of many grassroots workers that often certain government policies harm the poor much more than the benefit that accrues to them through money-oriented schemes like the IRDP.

REFERENCES

1. Vasudeva, Vikrant N. (October 1, 2010). "Legal Intervention in Poverty Alleviation: Enriching the Poor through Law" (pdf). NUJS Law Review. Retrieved January 3, 2015.
2. INDIA.GOV.IN
3. http://www.yousaytoo.com/poverty-alleviation-in-india/730838
4. Poverty Alleviation and Development Progammes by Amita Sinha ISBN 8190774840.
5. http://nsap.nic.in/nsap/NSAP-%20About%20us.pdf
6. Ministry of Rural Development, Annual Report, 2004-05 to 14-15.

Pages 88-95

POVERTY ALLEVIATION THROUGH MICROFINANCE
Edited by : **Dr. B. Ramachandra Reddy**
Edition : **2017**
ISBN : 978-93-5056-865-1
Published by : **Discovery Publishing House Pvt. Ltd., New Delhi (India)**

11

Microfinance in India

A Theoritical Frame Work

Ch. Venkataramanaiah[1]
K. Gunasekhar[2]
Dr. K. Ramakrishnaiah[3]

INTRODUCTION

Microfinance refers to all types of financial intermediation services (savings, credit funds transfer, insurance remittances etc.,) provided to low income households and enterprises in both urban and rural areas, including: employees in the public and private sectors and the self-employed (Rabinson, 2003). Effective long-term provision of these services occurs through microfinance institutions that adhere to the key principles endorsed by the consultative group to assist the poorest (CGAP). Microfinance emerged in the early 1990's to provide credit and savings services to the poor as a possible alternative to conventional bank lending. Many developing economies have developed and have been providing credit to the poor through microfinance schemes. The experience of several Asian, African as well as Latin America countries could be a typical example for this (Meyer 2002). It received further boost with involvement of several Non-governmental organizations and microfinance institutions.

The Indian state put stress on providing financial services to the poor and under privileged since independence. The commercial banks were

1. **Research Scholars, Department of Commerce, SVU College of CM and CS, S.V. University, Tirupati - 517 502.**
2. **Research Scholars, Department of Commerce, SVU College of CM and CS, S.V. University, Tirupati - 517 502.**
3. **Professor, Dean, College Development Council (CDC), Department of Commerce, SVU College of CM and CS, S.V. University, Tirupati - 517 502.**

nationalized in 1969 and were directed to lend 40 per cent of their lovable funds, at a concessional rate, to the priority sector. The priority sector included agriculture and other rural activities and the weaker strata of society in general. The aim was to provide resource to help the poor to attain self-sufficiency. They had neither resources nor employment opportunities to be financially independent let alone meet the worker consumption needs. To supplement these efforts, the credit scheme integrated rural development programme was launched in 1980. But these supply side programmes aided by computer and leakages, achieved little further, the snare of the formula financial sector in total rural credit was 56 per cent compared to the informal finance art 39.6 per cent and unspecified source at 3.8 per cent. Not only had formal credit flow been less but also uneven. The collection and paperwork based system shield away from the poor, the vacuum continued to be filled by the village money lender who charged interest rates of 2 to 3 per cent per month. Seventy per cent of land less farmers did not have a bank account and 87 per cent had no access to credit from a formal source. It was in this cheerless background that the microfinance revolution occurred worldwide. In India began in the 1980s with the formation of pockets of informal self-help groups (SHGs) engaging in micro activities financed by microfinance. But India's first microfinance institution Shri Mahila Sewa Shahkari Bank was set up as an urban Co-Operative bank by the self-employed woman's association (SEWA) soon after the group (founder Ms Ela Bhatt) was formed in 1974.

The first official effort materialized under the direction of NABARD. The Mysore resettlement and development agency sponsored project on saving and credit management of SHGs was partially financed by NABARD 1986-87.

Basically the MFIs in India of three categories:

1. Next for profile MFIs, which include the WGO.
2. Mutual benefit MFIs, which include mutually aided co-operative credit.
3. For profit MFIs which include the Non-banking financial companies.

NABARD refinances the financial institution engaged in microfinance to the extent of actual disbursement. NABARD, SIDBI are 'bulk financiers' who cleverly leverage resources obtained from a variety of sources.

Concept of Microfinance

Microfinance has evolved over the past quarter century across India into various operating forms and to a degree of success. One form of microfinance has been the development of the self-help movement (Reddy and Manak, 2005). Microfinance is a programme for the poor and by the poor to mobilize the savings and use them to meet their financial needs (Rao 2010). The task force on supportive policy and regulatory frame work for microfinance has defined microfinance as "The provision of thrift credit and other financial services to the poor in rural, semi-urban and urban areas to help raise their income levels and improve their living standards" (NABARD 1999). Microfinance is a participative model that can address the needs of the poor especially the women. The most common microfinance products are a micro credit or loan. These tiny loans are enough for hard working micro entrepreneurs particularly the rural women to start or expand their small business such as: weaving, handlooms and handicrafts embroidery and tailoring etc., and sell the products in the markets for generating their income.

Objectives of Microfinance

The following are the fundamental objectives of microfinance:

(i) To offer cost effective approach to formal institutions for expanding the outreach to the poor.

(ii) To develop collateral substitutes.

(iii) To focus on the rural and the urban poor generally and women in particular.

(iv) To pilot test other micro credit delivery mechanism as alternative channels to the formal banks.

(v) To effectively pursue the objectives of micro economic growth.

(vi) The social empowerment through:

- increased status, participation and powers of division-making of women in household;
- increased status, participation and powers of division-making of women in community and village;
- breaking cultural barriers for equal development of women;
- increased status, participation and powers of division making of women in democratic institutions.

(vii) The economic empowerment through:

- greater access to financial resources outside the household;
- reduced vulnerability of the poor women to crisis famine and the like;
- increasing access and control over resources at the household level;
- financial self-reliance of women.

(viii) Capacity building (a strategy and an end in itself) through:

- improvement in functional literacy, innumeracy;
- better communication skills;

- better leadership skills;
- self-help and mutual help;

(ix) Political empowerment through:

- participation to Panchayat Raj Institution;
- negotiating political power;
- accessing political power;
- collective identity;

(x) To increasing the consumption for poor.

Assessment of Microfinance

Assuming that a need assessment process concludes that there is excess demand for microfinance products and services, and that the situation is such that setting up a microfinance institution is adequate, what are the main steps forward?

Considering the fact that a wrong set up might do more harm than good there are several considerations to be done.

1. Market Analysis, competition and products.
2. Institutional capacity and competence.
3. Plan for reaching financial sustainability.
4. Funding.
5. Monitoring system.
6. Reporting, audit and rating.
7. Structure and ownership.

1. Market Analysis

Various tools for market analysis have been developed; for different methods and experience in the field. The main challenge is to capture the demand from potential clients and address actual and potential competition.

2. Institutional Capacity

Seen from a donor's point of view, the first step would be to consider the potential in working with already existing organizations. Do they have the capacity of providing what the market asks for in a professional way, or is setting up a new institution a better way as indicated above, most of the organizations involved in microfinance are multipurpose, and have microfinance as one of their activities, We then need to verify how they are organized, and if necessary challenge them to separate microfinance from other activities. It is of crucial importance to identify real costs and income on microfinance activities, regardless of the level of financial sustainability. Some argue that due to the nature of target groups, local economics etc., financial sustainability is merely a dream, indicating the need for subsidizing operations also in the longer run. Regardless of this argument, it is necessary to separate flow of capital due to loan activities from other transactions. In any case, if sustainability is not perceived as a possible end goal, reengineering of the institution and/or abandoning microfinance activities should be considered.

It is worthwhile underlining that what matters is the provision of accessible financial services at reasonable costs rather than who is providing it. As a donor it is easy to 'Fall in love' with some partners, but this feeling for a partner should be dealt with a very objective and professional way when it comes to microfinance. Former good partners from other projects can end up being bad partners if they get into microfinance without having the skills and the internal culture it takes to handle the challenges involved.

3. Financial Sustainability

Financial sustainability is/must be a long-term goal for a MFI. In order to address this issue, a checklist for budget for microfinance activities is useful.

- Identify operational costs.
- Projection on financial cross (Interests losses).
- Projections on income (donor funding operations).
- Define horizon for back even.
- Calculate interest rate.

Professional partners must be willing to charge interests rates that in the long run can make the institution sustainable. Micro credit services are expensive because of the costs involved of handling a large amount of small clients. A sustainable interest level is therefore likely to be above the local interest level in the formal market.

4. Funding

In the initial face, most MFI have received donor funding for setting up the organization. The long-run goal must be financial self-sufficiency, but in order to reach a large number of clients it would generally be necessary to access loans from capital providers on commercial terms. Thus the analysis of funding includes both potential donors as well as financing partners.

5. Monitoring System

In Norway, in a joint effort by the Norxegian Development Network (Bistandsorget) NORAD and the Ministry of Foreign Affairs (MFA) guideline for appraisal and monitoring of microfinance projects have been elaborated

(Clausen 2002) These build among other on the more elaborate CGAP tools, and aim at combining the need for specific information with the necessity of a tool that is not too complicated nor costly to use. The development was based on their basic criteria; we quote.

- The formers should be simple with information strictly on a 'Need to know' basis.
- The information required should be easily available by microfinance projects to limit the transaction cost for them in meeting donor appraisal and monitoring requirements.
- The performance indicators should be simple and easy to interpret but at the same time provide comprehensive overviews of overall performance of the microfinance project.

Three sets of indicators must be considered.

- Outreach indicators efficiency number of clients and poverty bracket (using average loan in per cent of GDP per capita). Savings can be added when pertinent.
- Institutional indicators focus on effectiveness; defined as productivity of staff (loans per staff) financial productivity (Administrative costs per loan) and efficiency (administrative costs over portfolio).
- Financial performance portfolio risk, that is sustainability books at operational sustainability (income versus expenditures) portfolio yield and portfolio quality (arrears).

All of the above indicators do provide important information regarding the different aspects of an MFI.

Due to the variety of contexts in which MFI operate, there are no global standards for most of the indicators compare whether a microfinance project is performing well or not. However, the micro Banking presents at regular intervals some of these indicators for a samples of MFI When it comes to outreach, a project with a strong poverty focus should have a low number for average loan in per cent of GDP per capita. Regarding financial sustainability based on many empirical studies, it is becoming a common understanding that an arrear, default rate above 5 per cent will make a long-run sustainability of the MFI very unlikely.

6. Reporting and Audit Procedures

Proper reporting is an intrinsic part of a well designed monitoring system. In addition to this external audits are necessary to establish institutional credibility.. In many cases this will be a legal requirement; it is also becoming more and more a pre condition for potentially new financing partners. Due to the nature of microfinance, the audit procedures required are different from those of a "Regular" NGFO Handbooks for these purposes are elaborated by a.o. CGAP.

Credit rating is gradually becoming a part also of the microfinance industry. A proper rating, carried out by professional rating institutions. Is likely to become a prerequisite in order for a MFI to attract professional investors in the future. A list of qualified rates by IABD and CGAP is found at www.mfrating org.mft/institutions/qualified raters, html Electronic Information Systems and internal control routines are two crucial points in professional microfinance and should therefore be included in all kinds of business planning for MFI.

7. *Structure and Ownership*

When a MFI grow, the question of structure and ownership becomes more important. As in any business or organization, the main stakeholders will determine the long rut. Strategy and the way the organization is structured and managed will be determinate for the long-run performance. Thus these are key factor in assuring the permanent provision of financial services.

Financial System Approach

The growth of microfinance in India has also to be seen in the light of financial sector reforms in India starting from 1991 and the global emphasis on commercialization of the sector. The financial sector reforms in India have focused on fostering a market based financial system by increasing competition and improving the quality of financial services. The new approach has been deeply influenced by the reorientation among international rural financial policy-makers centering on concepts such as: self-help, self-sustained growth and institutional viability. Under the new approach, institutional viability is of prime concern and instruments of directed credit and interest rate directives have been totally diluted or been done away with. As a consequence, banks are increasingly shying away from rural lending as well as rationalizing their branch network in rural areas.

Conclusion

At a time when financial inclusion is at the center stage of the regulatory landscape, the last mile connectivity provided by the MFIs has to be leveraged upon to include the hitherto financially excluded. Although the MFIs are facing tough times, there is a fair degree of opportunity to build long-term sustainable business around microfinance. Balancing the interests of the vulnerable borrows as also the micro finance institutions, effective regulations, well calibrated transition time and some breathing space to the institutions could help the microfinance sector to turn around expand and help the nation to achieve an inclusion growth. If the goods produced by the rural poor are sold at a right time with profitable price, then the poor will be able to improve their savings potential credit handling capacity and access to financial institutions, inculcate entrepreneurial skill develop an urge for investment and also risk taking attitude through SHGs. Thus micro-financing can do wonders to the rural poor living even in remote villages in improving their economic condition and protecting them from the clutches of the village money lenders. There are many stakeholders and each one has a definite role to play. In the core there is client. There is a second level called micro level where MFIs, NGOs, SHGs and Grameena work to provide financial support ti individual client. Apex institutions like: NABARD. SIDBI and other nationalized banks operate in Meso-level to provide infrastructure information and technical support to micro level players. Around all these levels there are financial environment, regulations, registrations and regulators called macro level. With passage of time new opportunities and new challenges are being felt in the field of microfinance. In recent years microfinance is in news for bad reasons there are a number of suicide cases of micro credit clients all over India for excess interest charges and high handedness of recovery agents in recovery of loans. So, government of India has thought out a legislation to check the high interest rate on micro credit and protect the poor from clutches of greedy MFIs.

REFERENCES

1. Meyer (2002). "Microfinance - Issues and Challenges" *The Journal of Economic and Political Weekly*, Vol. 9, pp. 75-79.
2. Robinson (2003). Microfinance in India, Himalaya Publishing House - New Delhi, pp. 34-36.
3. Reddy and Manak (2005). "Microfinance - The Role of Microfinancial Institutions" *Indian Journal of Marketing*, Vol. 4, pp. 23-25.
4. Rao (2010). Institutional Finance for Banking Sector in India, SEDME, Vol. 4, pp. 262-65.
5. George Bernard Shaw (2009) "Conceptual Frame Work of in India" *International Journal of Marketing*, Vol. 5, pp. 45-49.
6. R.C. Nagaraju (2015). Banking Finance, Vol. XXVIII, January 2015, ISSN No. 0971-4498, pp. 47-49.

Pages 96-101

POVERTY ALLEVIATION THROUGH MICROFINANCE
Edited by : **Dr. B. Ramachandra Reddy**
Edition : **2017**
ISBN : 978-93-5056-865-1
Published by : **Discovery Publishing House Pvt. Ltd., New Delhi (India)**

12 Microfinance in India
Risk Scenario and Remedies

Dr. P. Subramanyachary[1]
Dr. M. Reddi Ramu[1]

INTRODUCTION

Microfinance is probably the first concept based on the credit delivery systems aimed mainly at the poor. The in-built flexibility of choice for the purpose of credit without the formalities of collaterals and sanction conditions has made the concept popular among the people all over the world cutting across race, religion and political status of nations.

Microfinance refers to credit extended by:

Formal institutions to individuals. Formal institutions to informal groups, Informal groups to its individual members, and Formal institutions through voluntary association to Informal groups.

Micro credit is defined as a system of credit delivery and savings mobilizing scheme especially designed to meet the unique financial requirements of the poor. The financing schemes allow the recipients to improve the status of their living through access to additional capital without collateral. A borrower of micro credit must belong to a group to qualify for a loan. The original micro credit model requires that the group of individuals apply for a loan on behalf of one member. The group guaranteed repayment of a loan offered to one member at a time. Once a group member has paid off a loan, another member of group may qualify for a new loan or a repeat loan may be granted to a non-defaulting client. The original model has gone

1. **Associate Professors, Department of MBA, Siddharth Institute of Engineering and Technology, Narayanavanam Road, Puttur - 517 583. Chittor District, A.P.**

through many transformations. In most countries microfinance clients are typically self-employed and low income entrepreneurs in both urban and rural areas.

Need for Microfinance

Microfinance accelerates the growth of domestic deposits and mobilizes micro savings which will be given for investments for encouraging self-employment. It becomes ad good financial mechanism in the informal economy. Women participate in economic activities.

Through this sector which made them self-sufficient and empowerment. Microfinance facilitates national and international remittance flow of investments as well as development of local private sector and investment in innovations. Broadly the microfinance activities improve slum conditions, develop rural areas, interest in agricultural and allied activities and also improve health services.

Role of Microfinance Sector in Undeveloped Countries

Over the last twenty years micro credit is one of the most effective tools to fight poverty in under developed countries. It is an investment to reduce poverty in the world. In third world countries many statistics have shown them like: Dominican Republic, Srilanka, Poland. Sub-Sahara African countries, Bangladesh etc., microfinance made better life to the poor people.

When the observe examples in Brazil Casas Bahia has significant contribution in retail sector. In Mexico microfinance sector achieved success in cement sector by Cemex Company which is largest cement company Mexico. In cellular network sector, Gram Phone Company in Bangladesh brought significant change. In India ICICI brought recognized change lending issue. In Sub-Sahara in African Countries there is a prospect for the growth of micro entrepreneurship in at least 13 countries of the region where the size of the loan may allow the borrowers to assume a certain degree of risk. The micro credit operation in Sub-Sahara Africa can be a successful experience if reforms a company the growth of the micro credit programmers paying a way for the growth of micro entrepreneurship.

Poverty alleviation in the common and overriding objectives of the developing world. United Nations Millennium Declaration committing their nations to a new global partnership to reduce extreme poverty and setting out a series of tune-bound goals with target deadline of 2015. These goals have become known as the Millennium Developed Goals (MDG's). While income was considered as the major factor of the poverty, other factors such as: hunger, disease, lack of adequate shelter, gender equality, education and environmental sustainability were also included in these goals there as follows:

1. Eradicate extreme poverty and hunger.
2. Achieve universal primary education.
3. Promote gender equality and empower women.
4. Reduce child mortality.
5. Improve maternal health.
6. Combat HIV AIDS, Malaria and other diseases.
7. Ensure environmental sustainability.
8. Develop a global partnership for development.

These goals are also known as indicators of microfinance to achieve the mentioned goals micro credit has to play a key role.

Role of Micro Credit in India

In India microfinance started in the early 1980's by forming self-help groups which aimed at accessing saving and credit services. National Institute like: NABARD, SIDBI etc., is also contributions resources to microfinance. In Indian context there is an opinion on micro credit that:

(a) Microfinance is providing with the interest of the lender.

(b) It is something done predominantly with the poor.

(c) It is also considered as alternative commercial sector.

India has learnt so many experiments from the world countries especially from Bangladesh, Indonesia, Bolivia and some other African countries. Since micro credit is positioned as a development strategy for anti- poverty programmers, microfinance is considered as financing for the poor. Similarly the credit delivery systems through informal channel self-help groups. Self-help groups refer to involve people who have similar needs and are operated on informal and non-profit basics. Generally governmental or non-governmental organizations will form and guide these groups with emphasis on body thrift and credit activities. Through a consensual approach the group finalizes all the financial decisions. Once the groups show the maturity of financial behaviour, banks are encouraged to make loans of the SHG's in certain multiples of the accumulated savings on the SHG's.

Best Practices in Microfinance through SHG's

India has been trying to reduce the poverty and other problems of rural poor through SHG's by following credit practices. Effectiveness which refers degree of the delivery services for achieving the intended objectives:

- Equity which refers fair distribution of benefits and opportunities.
- Efficiency which refer favorable ratio of costs of outputs.

- Stability which refers should not confront with the structured barriers of inequity in the growth in communities and local power structures.
- Transparency which refer through systems, procedures and rewards.

Some other practices are positive interest rates of loan, community monitoring of the utilization of credit, pressure the member to repayment, overdue less than 10 per cent etc. Ratio of SHG will facilitate the banks to take taster decision on distributing the loans to the groups; Ratio is given on the basics of several aspects like: operations, punctuality of repayment and size, education, participation of members. Ratio's also increases competitiveness among SHG's in providing finance to poor and their performance. The following are the various Indian micro finance institutions that are active at present.

- The Activities for Social Alternatives (ASA) – Tamil Nadu.
- Bharat Integrated Social Welfare Agency (BISWA) – Orissa.
- Grameen Koota – Karnataka.
- Gram Vikar – Orissa.
- ICICI Bank – through out India.
- Kas Foundation – Orissa and Chattisgarh.
- SEWA Bank – Gujarat.
- Spandana – Andhra Pradesh.
- Basic – Throughout India.
- Mysore Resettlement and Development Agency (MYRADA) – Karnataka.
- Mutually Aided Cooperative Societies (MACS) – Andhra Pradesh.

For strengthening microfinance sector in India NGO's must be permitted to invest in the equity of micro finance organization in the countries like: Bolivia and African Countries.

Risk Scenario

Like all the other sectors microfinance sector is facing different types of risk as follows:

Political Risk

In the microfinance sector present greater risk in the interference of government by improving interest rates in addition to this RBI confirmed in august 2004 that "The interest rate applicable to loans given by different micro credit organization's to self-help groups/member beneficiaries would be left to their discretion". Some state is not supportive due to political pressure. In some states a weak rule of law may present riskier operations environmental for both MFI's and micro enterprises.

Economic Risk

India's new government is not expected to make any radical shifts in economic policy. However the goal is likely to increase social spending, which some analysis believe could hamper India's ability to service in foreign debt and pressure interest rates upward.

Currency Risk

India's exchange rate can be character as managed float in relation to the US dollar. RBI intervener in foreign exchange markets to keep the exchange rate stable. In addition as it is possible to purchase on one year forward contract on Indian currency in liquid markets, it is possible to hedge against currency risk during this period.

Geographic Concentration

Indian microfinance activity is located in south, with anywhere between 50 and 70 per cent alone in Andhra Pradesh. So some MFI's have begun to encourage their clients to engage in diverse livelihood activities and provide micro insurance as a way to minimize the covariant risks that they themselves face due to geographical concentration.

Unhealthy Competition

Many in industry feel the level and nature of MFI competition in Andhra Pradesh and Tamil Nadu is unhealthy and could potentially lead to unsound lending and reduced portfolio quality due to clients borrowing from more than one institutions.

Institutional Risk

When we come to institution risk, there will be lack of sound governance policies at the board level. Besides thus, there is lack of skills in managerial staff and accounting and financial reporting are not proper.

Some other risk perception are most borrowers are without desired entrepreneurial skills, costly exercise and small loans for many, unorganized scatter groups, low capital and low skill base, limited prospects, insufficient infrastructure, vicious financial cycle, low investment-low income-low profit, weak accounting practices, unsecured credit exposure etc.

Steps to Remove Risks

The success of microfinance institutions depends on the following factors and risk can be removed by providing some facilities.

1. Visionary leadership.
2. Supportive policy environment.
3. Effective Donors.

4. Physical and social environment.
5. Management with political economy.
6. Institutional process bearing.

Conclusion

Many of the countries in the world have adapted some form of micro credit model with a goal to reducing poverty. In the course of operating its activities microfinance sector is facing different types of risk. By removing risk the sector can be strengthened and make it the best tool for reducing poverty in the world. By making changes related microfinance sector as per needed in the global economy, it can be made as sustainable model to reduce poverty and other problems in the world.

REFERENCES

1. Mondal Wali (2002). "Micro Credit and Micro Entrepreneurship Collateral free Loan at Work in Bangladesh: Bangladesh Academic Press".
2. Piyush Tiwari and S.M. Fahad Concept Paper on Microfinance Institutions in India.
3. World Bank 2005 Report.
4. NABARD: Statement of Best Practices of SHG.
5. www. Microfinancegateway.org
6. www. Unesco.org
7. www. World Bank.Org
8. www. Micro credit summit. Org

Pages 102-110

POVERTY ALLEVIATION THROUGH MICROFINANCE
Edited by : **Dr. B. Ramachandra Reddy**
Edition : **2017**
ISBN : 978-93-5056-865-1
Published by : **Discovery Publishing House Pvt. Ltd., New Delhi (India)**

13

Multidimensional Role of NABARD in Rural Development

With Special Reference to Agriculture Microfinance and SHGs

Dr. J. Nalini
Dr. G. Venkatganarayana

INTRODUCTION

India is second largest country in population in the world and having 72 per cent of population in rural areas. Similarly many syndromes like: poverty, superstitions, child labour, caste system and illiteracy are prevailed in rural areas across the country. Even pre-independence the colonial rulers also implement development programmes in order to improve living standards regarding poor and down trodden sections in the traditional rural society. Since then the successive governments both central and state also continue the same in multidimensional ways. And to achieve all round development, numerous flagship programmes and policies are being implemented by the government through national and international organizations. But still the fruitful results are far away due to various reasons.

As Gandhiji said 'India lives in villages and the development of the nation cannot be achieved without the development of villages'. Development of the nation depends upon the rural development as well as quality of life of the common man. Development is often confused with economic growth. But these are two different concepts having different implication. Economic growth means increase in value of goods and services produced in an economy that is measured in terms of Gross Domestic Product (GDP). Growth is a continuous expansion in the productivity which leads to rise in the GDP. On the other hand Development is a sustained improvement in material welfare, particularly for those who are poor and afflicted by poverty, illiteracy and poor health conditions. Development is, therefore, a qualitative concept involving a qualitative improvement in the general standard of living. The term 'rural development' in general is used to denote the action and initiatives taken to improve the standard of living in rural areas. In fact Rural Development is utilisation, protection and enhancement of the natural, physical and human resources needed to make long-term improvements in rural living conditions. It involves provision of jobs and income opportunities while maintaining and protecting the environment in rural areas.

Need for the Study

Poverty is the main hurdle for economic development of any country. In the world, India is one of the over populated country and standard of living is very low. Formal sectors and informal sectors are providing number of programmes and activities for eradicate the poverty. National Bank for Agriculture and Rural Development (NABARD) is an apex institution which playing vital role in economic development of the country. It provides credit services, payment services, money transfers, and insurance services, besides that it undertake social intermediation services such as: group formation, development of self-confidence, and training in financial literacy and management capabilities among members of a group. An attempt is made on impact of NABARD in Agriculture, Microfinance SHGs and its operations towards Rural Development in India. The present paper highlights Multidimensional role of NABARD, which contribute their efforts towards efficient and effective economic growth in India.

Objectives

The present study is focus on the following objectives:

- To study the role of NABARD in rural development to eradicate poverty in India.
- To analyse the growth of agriculture, microfinance and SHGs through NABARD.

Data Collection

The present study is based on secondary data only. Secondary data has collected from the research papers, books of references, standard publications, reports by institutes organizations, magazines, periodicals, and internet etc.

Scope and Limitations

Actually NABARD role in order to develop the rural areas, it is appreciable and laudable in aspects but this paper only focus on analytical part of three sectors like: *(i)* agriculture; *(ii)* microfinance and *(iii)* SHGs.

National Bank for Agriculture and Rural Development (NABARD)

NABARD is an apex financial institution constituted to co-ordinate the activities of all the institutions involved in financing rural and agricultural development activities. India is the home of agriculture and rural industries in ancient history and remains the same feature in 21st century also. Agriculture and rural industries are the base on which the Indian economy is built. But with the fast increasing population and along with them the ever increasing needs and wants became too large for agriculture sector to support. RBI combined diverse functions and duties including rural credit. RBI could not devote sufficient attention to the complex credit problems in integrated rural development and other various fields. In order to rectify the problem, in July 1982, National Bank for Agriculture and Rural Development (NABARD) was established on the basis of the recommendations of the Sivaraman committee (1978). Since then NABARD has taken over and decentralized of RBI's functions in the phase of rural credit for the promotion of agriculture, small scale industries, cottage and village industries, handicrafts and other rural crafts. It also has the mandate to support all other allied economic activities in rural areas, promote integrated and sustainable rural development and secure prosperity of rural areas. In order to discharging its functions as a facilitator for rural prosperity NABARD is entrusted with:

- Provide refinance to lending institutions in rural areas.
- Bringing about or promoting institutional development.
- Evaluating, monitoring and inspecting the client banks.

Besides this pivotal role NABARD also:

- Act as a co-ordinator in the operations of rural credit institutions.
- Extends assistance to the government the RBI and other organizations in matters relating to rural development.
- Offers training and research facilities for banks, co-operatives and organizations in matters relating to rural development.
- Helps the state government in reaching targets of providing assistance to eligible institution in organization and rural development.
- Act as regulator for co-operative banks and RRBs.

NABARD is traversing the most dynamic and challenging phase of rural India's growth paradigm. One of the biggest challenges experienced by Indian economy is enhancing viability of agriculture. In this context, capital formation 'in' and 'for' agriculture are of critical importance for the sustainability of agricultural growth, and accordingly, NABARD flagged off capital formation in rural economy. NABARD's refinance disbursement under investment credit touched Rs. 31,427 crores during 2014-15, marking a growth of 46.3 per cent over the previous year, facilitating acceleration of capital formation in rural economy. A new product was introduced medium term refinance for 18 months to 3 years during the year 2014-15. These initiatives of NABARD have been instrumental in enabling banks to record a 47.5 per cent growth in agriculture term loan disbursement during the year, reversing a declining trend in the growth rate. Rural Infrastructure Development Fund (RIDF) is an important project financing option for the state governments for creation of rural infrastructure. Projects with loan aggregating Rs. 6,001 crores were sanctioned under Warehouse Infrastructure Fund (WIF) during the year 2014-2015. With majority of projects under RIDF, WIF and NABARD Infrastructure Development Assistance (NIDA) being under agriculture, rural connectivity, storage and power sectors, NABARD could strongly demonstrate its commitment towards enhancing public investment for agriculture. With 85 per cent of the farmers in the small and marginal holding categories, major intervention aimed at facilitating and aggregating of inputs suppliers and output marketing; besides village level value addition was the need of the hour. Accordingly the Government of India created the producers Organization Development and Upliftment Corpus (PRODUCE) Fund with a corpus of Rs. 200 crores in NABARD for the promotion of 2000 farmer producer organizations.

Realizing the importance of challenges to agriculture growth due to climatic change, NABARD as a National Implementing Entity (NIE) took up new initiatives to facilitate ecologically sustainable development. The Adaptation Fund Board (AFB) of the United Nations Framework Convention for Climate Change (UNFCCC) sanctioned proposals submitted by NABARD with a financial assistance of US $ 3.2 million during the year 2014-2015. NABARD, by according high priority to the agenda of financial inclusion, has directed its efforts in bringing in new initiatives in the form of technology adoption by co-operative banks and RRBs during the year. Cooperative banks have achieved on-boarding onto the payment system and have started issuing RuPay Kissn Cards. Further, on line with the vision of Government of India for a Digital India, NABARD launched a pilot project for digitization of Self-Help Groups (SHGs) during the year 2014-15.

Agriculture

Agriculture was the predominant sector of Indian economy at the time of independence from colonial rule in 1947. The share of agriculture in total gross domestic product at the time was above 55 per cent, and about 70 per cent of workforce was engaged in agriculture sector. Through agriculture was the predominant sector at that time but its productivity was very low and output growth during 1901 to 1946 was less than half of the population growth. Indian agriculture has witnessed wide variations in growth performance during a span of six decades after independence. In the year 1966 during Green Revolution various new discoveries were implemented like: adoption of superior technology, Hybrid variety of seeds and institutional reforms were found to manifest from 1968-69 onwards. India witnessed rapid growth in the food processing sector which resulted in increased agriculture production of the sector was realised by the business community leading to diversification from grain trading to processing, initially, it was mostly rice processing, wheat milling, the paper and pulp industry, milk processing, jute industry, sugar cane processing and oil extraction through solvent plants. Agriculture and food processing industries are both inter dependents. The strong agriculture production leads to effective food processing industry the rural changes and opportunities can be capture the value added food products space in India and abroad with a large and growing consumption base as well as export potential food processing is truly India's sunrise sector.

The Praadhan Mantri Gram Sinchai Yojana introduced by the central government aim to irrigate every formers field and improve the efficiency of water use to provide 'per drop more crop'. 'Neeranchal' was introduced by the government of India in 2014 with an aimed at imparting an additional impetus to watershed development in the country. The lab to land programme can be made effective by leveraging information technology and mobile application to needy formers. Kisan TV set up by the government, will provide formers a direct interface with agriculture experts. NABARDs Former club programme, implemented by banks and NGOs aim to organize formers to facilitate access to credit, extension services. The former clubs are provided information on weather and market prices and crop advisory services through SMS on mobile phone.

During 2014-15 banks have disbursed Rs. 8,40,643 crores credit to the agriculture sector against a target of Rs. 8,00,000 crores. Commercial Banks, Co-operative Banks and Regional Rural Banks disbursed Rs. 5,99,691 crores, Rs. 1,38,469 crore, and Rs. 1,02,483 crores respectively.

Table 13.1: Agency-wise Ground level Credit flow

Sl. No.	Agency	2010-11	%	2011-12	%	2012-13	%	2013-14	%	2014-15	%
1.	CBs	3,45,877	74	3,68,616	72	4,32,491	71	5,09,005	71	5,99,691	71
2.	RRBs	44,293	9	54,450	11	63,691	11	82,652	12	1,02,483	12
3.	Co-ops	78,121	17	87,963	17	1,11203	18	1,19,964	17	1,38,469	17
	Total	4,68,291	100	5,11,029	100	6,07375	100	7,11,621	100	8,40,643	100

CBs-Commercial Banks, RRBs-Regional Rural Banks, Co-ops-Co-Operative Banks.

Source: Annual Reports of NABARD.

The agency-wise share of credit flow to the agriculture sector that last five years is furnished shown in Table 13.1. Agricultural credit disbursement is dominated by CBs, followed by Co-operative banks and Regional Rural Banks. There has been an impressive growth in agricultural credit flow from 4.68 lakh crores to 8.41 lakh crores during the five year period.

Table 13.2: Sector-wise Ground level Credit Disbursement to Agriculture Sector

Sl.No.	Sector	2010-11	%	2011-12	%	2012-13	%	2013-14	%	2014-15	%
1.	Crop loans	3,35,550	72	3,96,158	78	4,73,500	78	5,73,001	81	6,36,099	76
2.	Term loans	1,32,741	28	1,14,871	22	1,33,875	22	1,38,620	19	2,04,544	24
	Total	4,68,291	100	5,11,029	100	6,07,375	100	7,11,621	100	8,40,643	100

Sector-wise Ground level Credit disbursement to Agriculture sector.

Source: Annual Reports of NABARD.

It is evident from Table 13.2 that the Crop loans credit disbursement had continuous growth from 72 per cent to 81 per cent during the 2010-11 to 2013-14 and the year 2014-15 it decline to 76 per cent. In case of Term loans credit disbursement reach to 24 per cent and there will be continuous decline from 28 per cent to 19 per cent during the years of 2010-11 to 2013-14 respectively.

Microfinance and SHGs

Microfinance is the supply of loans, savings, and other basic financial services to the poor. Financial services needed by the poor include working capital loans, consumer credit, savings, pensions, insurance, and money transfer services. The poor rarely access services through the formal financial sector. They mostly depend upon the informal financial sectors which include: money lenders, indigenous banks, and other individuals. Micro credit is defined as provision of thrift, credit and other financial services and products of very small amount to the poor in rural, semi-urban and urban areas for enabling them to raise their income levels and improving standards. Micro Credit Institutions are those which provide these facilities usually through Self-Help Groups.

The concept of Self-Help Groups (SHGs) occupies significant role in general and rural India in particular. About 60 per cent of women population is members in SHGs. In fact, women is the base for ideal family and governments also focusing to prepare women to be independent by empowering her in financial and social issues for which various reforms and recommendations taken at apex level. The SHGs movement originated in Bangladesh under the Leadership of Noble Laureate Mohanmed Yunus. In order to achieve the mission of reaching those families who did not access to credit by any formal financial institution and, therefore, were dependent on informal sources and money lenders. SHG means a group of 15-20 members which have become a common vehicle of development covering various development programmes. Financial intermediation is not the only objective but the purpose behind this is to combine the access to low cost financial services with a process of self-management and development. SHGs are usually formed and supported by NGOs or Government agencies. SHGs have also emerged as a powerful device and an effective medium for delivering credit to the poor in the rural economy. It helps in poverty alleviation and women empowerment. This movement has triggered off the Silent Revolution in the rural credit delivery system in India.

The Government of India has initiated various programmes and schemes in the areas of microfinance. Most important programmes are SGSY (1999) and NABARD's SBLP (1992) are using SHGs approach. Other initiatives by government like: IMY, Swa-Shakti, DWCRA, CAPART, RMK etc., these all programmes aimed at reduction of poverty and improving the living condition of rural poor with the help of economic activities. On the other hand various types of financial institutions offer microfinance programmes and schemes. There are many apex financial institutions and micro finance institutions which provide financial assistance to needy rural people. In India, micro finance progamme was initiated by NABARD's SHGs Bank Linkage Programme (SBLP) in 1992. SIDBI in second place, where refinance to the SFCs and Commercial Banks for their direct lending, RMK took third place, through providing loans to NGOs for on lending to women SHGs.

The NABARD led Pilot Project, commenced with the support of the Reserve Bank of India, in 1992 aimed to promoting and financing 500 SHGs across the country. The formal banking system has found the Micro Finance System (MFS) as an appropriate system to reach poor and also to expand their business for at low transaction costs, risk costs and with a good repayment. Apart from inculcating savings, SHG movement increased availability of micro finance to take up productive activities, income-generating activities, micro/small enterprises, empowerment of women, and decreased dependence on exploitative local money lenders. Thus in India a suitable model of the microfinance/micro credit *i.e.* SHG-bank linkage programme has been evolved based on the need and structure prevalent in the country. Subsequently, this programme was further extended to all Regional Rural Banks (RRBs) and Commercial Banks, Cooperative banks, NABARD and NGOs. While the SHG bank linkage programme experienced exponential growth over the past decade, there remain large regional disparities in the growth of the SHG movement with limited progress in certain region.

Though the SHG-Bank Linkage programme contributed to improve economic conditions, social change was not as apparent, and there are concerns to sustainability and further development of self-reliance of the institutions. The SHG-Bank Linkage Programme contain following objectives.

- To develop mutual faith and confidence between the rural poor and bankers.
- To combine sensitively, flexibility and responses of the informal credit system with the strength of administrative capabilities, technical strength and the financial resources of the formal financial institutions.
- To extent credit flow/financial services to the rural poor with less transactional costs.
- To alleviate poverty and empower the women.

The strategy behind SHGs model is to form small, cohesive and participative groups of the poor and encourage them to pool their savings regularly and use the pooled savings in order to make small interest bearing loans available to the members. Bank credit facility also available to the group to augment its resources for the purpose of lending to its members. The SHG-bank linkage programme has proved to be the major supplementary credit delivery system with a wide acceptance by banks, NGOs and various government departments.

Table 13.3: Agency-wise Microfinance – Bank Loan Disbursed to SHGs during the 2010-11 to 2014-15

Sl. No.	Name of the Agency	2010-11		2011-12		2012-13		2013-14		2014-15	
		No. of SHGs	Loans Disbursed	No. of SHGs	Loans Disbursed	No. of SHGs	Loans Disbursed	No. of SHGs	Loans Disbursed	No. of SHGs	Loans Disbursed
1.	CBs	6,69,741	9,72,455	6,00,807	9,94,204	7,35,577	13,38,500	7,67,253	16,03,749	8,55,724	17,33,413
2.	RRBs	2,29,620	1,62,556	3,04,809	5,02,605	3,12,010	5,62,653	3,33,420	6,28,813	5,22,139	7,72,522
3.	Coop	2,96,773	3,19,761	2,42,262	1,56,667	1,72,234	1,57,383	2,65,748	1,69,173	2,48,375	2,52,296
	Total	11,96,134	14,54,772	11,47,878	16,53,476	12,19,821	20,58,536	13,66,421	20,41,735	16,26,238	27,58,231

CBs-Commercial Banks, RRBs-Regional Rural Banks, Coop-Cooperative Banks.

Source: Annual Reports of NABARD.

Table 13.3 reflects that, number of SHGs are increased in CBs from 6.69741 to 8,55,724 and the loan disbursement also increased from Rs. 9,72,455 crores to Rs. 17,33,413 crores during the study period from 2010-11 to 2014-15. In case of RRBs also having continuous growth in number of SHGs as well as loan disbursed during the study period and in the year 2011-12 there was tremendous growth in number of SHGs as well as loan disbursement.

In the other hand, the Coop banks contains fluctuating trend during the study period.

Conclusion

Even after 69 years of Indian independence in which 72 per cent of people especially in rural areas depends upon agriculture and allied sectors. Similarly the successive governments also have been taking needful reforms to encourage and energies farmers but the farmers but results are not up to the mark. For instance a small farmer is not in a position to purchase seeds, chemical fertilizers and pesticides in time during season which pressurize him to approach money lenders for large interest rates and which have to be controlled as early as possible and in term implement constructive loan facilities to at least needy formers through NABARD. Regarding SHGs it is a revolutionary system in rural India. Through which tremendous awareness about many issues related to women. In fact without government involvement SHGs are enough able to solve their problems and run their families and even societies which have to be uplifted by providing loan facilities through which SHGs could start small scale and cottage industries. Similarly NABARD is playing vital role to provide micro finance to both agriculture and SHGs. Because majority representations are comes from these two sectors in Indian rural society.

REFERENCES

1. AMR - A.P. Academy of Rural Development, Rajendranar, Hyderedad - 500 030.
2. Dasai, Vasant, Rural Development in India (Past, Present and Future), Himalaya Publishing House, Mumbai, 2010.
3. Puhazhendhi, V. (2009). "Microfinance India-State of the Sector Report 2012" SAGE Publications India Pvt. Ltd., Bhandri.
4. WWW. Nabard.com
5. Annual reports of NABARD.

Pages 111-119

POVERTY ALLEVIATION THROUGH MICROFINANCE
Edited by : **Dr. B. Ramachandra Reddy**
Edition : **2017**
ISBN : 978-93-5056-865-1
Published by : **Discovery Publishing House Pvt. Ltd., New Delhi (India)**

14 Microfinance in India
A Tool for Poverty Reduction

Dr. V. Venkateswara Rao

INTRODUCTION

Microfinance in India can trace its origins back to the early 1970s when the Self-Employed Women's Association ('SEWA') of the state of Gujarat formed an urban co-operative bank, called the Shri Mahila SEWA Sahakari Bank, with the objective of providing banking services to poor women employed in the unorganised sector in Ahmadabad City, Gujarat. The microfinance sector went on to evolve in the 1980s around the concept of SHGs, informal bodies that would provide their clients with much needed savings and credit services. From humble beginnings, the sector has grown significantly over the years to become a multi-billion dollar industry, with bodies such as: the Small Industries Development Bank of India and the National Bank for Agriculture and Rural Development devoting significant financial resources to microfinance. Today, the top five private sector MFIs reach more than 20 million clients in nearly every state in India and many Indian MFIs have been recognised as global leaders in the industry.

Financial Inclusion

According to recent RBI estimates, there are over 450 million 'unbanked people' in India, most of who live in rural areas. The term 'unbanked' refers to people who have no access to formal financial services, but rather must rely on either family, or informal providers of finance, such as: the village money lender. It is undisputed that access to finance is critical for enabling individuals and communities to climb out of poverty. It is also generally

Professor in Management, Pace Institute of Technology and Sciences, Ongole.

agreed that relying on the limited resources of village money lenders exposes the poor to coercive lending practices, personal risks and high interest rates, which can be a much as 150 per cent. Therefore the Indian Government and the RBI have a policy of 'financial inclusion'. As part of this policy, the government requires Indian banks to lend to 'priority sectors', one of which is the rural poor. Until recently, banks were happy to lend money to MFIs who would then on-lend funds, primarily to poor women across rural India. The banks have welcomed this policy because historically they tended to charge MFIs average interest rates of 12-13 per cent and benefited from 100 per cent repayment rates. Thus, by lending to MFIs, banks have been able to meet their 'priority sector' lending requirements with what historically has amounted to a risk-free and very profitable arrangement.

The Goal of Financial inclusion must include the Private Sector

Microfinance in India is currently being provided by three sectors: the government, the private sector and charities. These three sectors, as large as they are, have only a small fraction of the capital and geographic scale required to meet the overwhelming need for finance amongst India's rural poor. The top 10 private sector microfinance providers in India together serve less than 5 per cent of the unbanked population of India – approximately 20 million clients. For Private sector MFIs have an essential role to play if the goal of financial inclusion is to be realised, as neither the government nor charities have the capital nor business model required to meet the insatiable demand for finance in rural India. As the public listing of SKS Microfinance underscored, private sector institutions are able to attract increasingly large amounts of private capital, in order to accelerate the growth of the industry, which is essential to expanding financial inclusion as far and as fast as practicable.

'Microfinance refers to small scale financial services for both credits and deposits - that are provided to people who farm or fish or herd; operate small or micro enterprise where goods are produced, recycled, repaired, or traded; provide services; work for wages or commissions; gain income from renting out small amounts of land, vehicles, draft animals, or machinery and tools; and to other individuals and local groups in developing countries in both rural and urban areas' - Marguerite S. Robinson. The Indian state put stress on providing financial services to the poor and under privileged since independence. The commercial banks were nationalized in 1969 and were directed to lend 40 per cent of their loan able funds, at a concessional rate, to the priority sector. The priority sector included agriculture and other rural activities and the weaker strata of society in general. The aim was to provide resources to help the poor to attain self-sufficiency. They had neither resources nor employment opportunities to be financially independent, let alone meet the minimal consumption needs.

To supplement these efforts, the credit scheme Integrated Rural Development Programme (IRDP) was launched in 1980. But these supply side programmes (ignoring the demand side of the economy) aided by corruption and leakages, achieved little. Further, 'The share of the formal financial sector in total rural credit was 56.6 per cent, compared to informal finance at 39.6 per cent and unspecified sources at 3.8 per cent. [RBI 1992]. Not only had formal credit flow been less but also uneven. The collateral and paperwork based system shied away from the poor. The vacuum continued to be filled by the village moneylender who charged interest rates of 2 to 30 per cent per month (Rural Credit and Self-Help Groups – Microfinance needs and Concepts in India - K.G. Karmakar 1999).

These distortions and imperfections in rural credit markets were sought to be addressed through Government interventions. With difference of range and degree, most developing countries from 1950s to the 1980s were home to interventions ranging from establishing state owned financial institutions, interest rate ceiling on deposits and credit, credit subsidy, directing credit to particular sectors and nationalization of private banks.

This 'supply led' approach in rural finance caused various qualitative issues such as: concerns about financial viability of institutions on account of high rate of loan delinquency, cornering of subsidy by well off people in what has been described as 'rent seeking' behaviour, continued presence of moneylenders, inability to reach the core poor and led to a reorientation in thinking around 1980s. United State's Agency for International Development's (USAID) spring review of Small Farmer Credit in 1972/73, covering 60 reports on specific farm credit programmes in developing countries followed by a World Conference on Credit for Farmers in Developing Countries in 1975 organised by FAO were the first landmark events pointing the deficiencies of directed and subsidized credit approach. These thoughts got crystallised during the 'Colloquium on Rural Finance in Low Income Countries' by USAID and World Bank in 1981 and shaped the emergence of new thinking in rural finance. Hulme and Mosley (1996) credit the counter revolution against Development Financial Institutions (DFIs) which were a prime symbol of Government intervention in rural credit markets to 'Ohio school' as the economists at Ohio State University provided the theoretical underpinnings to the critique of past approach and contributed to transfer of these ideas into operational policies of World Bank.

On account of the above developments, the resultant shift in rural finance discourse and operational paradigm is shown in Table 14.1.

Table 14.1:

Features	Old Paradigm	New Paradigm
Problem Definition	Overcome market imperfection	Lower risks and transaction cost
Role of financial Markets	Imperfect state plans Help the poor	Intermediate Resource Efficiency
View of users	Beneficiary	Clients
Subsidies Dependence	Create subsidy	Create independent institutions
Sustainability	Largely ignored	A major concern
Evaluations	Credit impact on beneficiaries	Performance of financial institutions

Source: Adopted from Meyer and Nagarajan (1996).

Emergence of micro credit in late 1970s and early 1980s in the backdrop of growing world attention on deficiencies of earlier approach in rural finance explains much of its dominant theoretical underpinnings. The initial micro credit innovations in disparate settings of Bangladesh, Bolivia and Indonesia demonstrated the success of micro lending to poor without collateral requirements. Rhyne (2001) observes that these interventions demonstrated techniques for lending to the poor with better outreach and cost recovery. Despite the contextual differences, the unifying thread of these early innovations lay in their certain common principles like: reliance on character or peer pressure rather than collateral as loan security, leveraging social capital, positive incentives for repayment and interest rates that approached or covered cost. These innovations acted as catalysts for replication across the globe and their underlying principles continue to form the bedrock of microfinance interventions till date.

The universal appeal of microfinance stemmed from its ability to reach the poor without social collateral and generation of near full recovery rates through what has been described as a Win-Win proposition. The mainstreaming of microfinance worldwide and its global acceptance in development community is based on this Win-Win proposition. This concept of provision of sustainable financial services at market rates has been termed as 'Financial System' approach or 'Commercial microfinance'. The progress report submitted by Micro credit summit campaign indicates that as of Dec. 31, 2004, 3,164 microcredit institutions have reached 92.27 million clients translating into micro credit interventions having reached 333 million poor families worldwide. The obsession with microfinance in development sector is succinctly captured by Remenyi (2000, p.30), "every bilateral donor and NGO seems to believe that it too must be involved in microfinance if it is to retain credibility as a development agency with an option for the poor".

Indian Microfinance Context

Indian public policy for rural finance from 1950s to till date mirrors the patterns observed worldwide. Increasing access to credit for the poor has always remained at the core of Indian planning in fight against poverty. The assumption behind expanding outreach of financial services, mainly credit was that the welfare costs of exclusion from the banking sector, especially for rural poor are very high. Starting late 1960s, India was home to one of largest state intervention in rural credit market and has been euphemistically referred to as:

'Social banking' phase. It saw nationalisation of existing private commercial banks, massive expansion of branch network in rural areas, mandatory directed credit to priority sectors of the economy, subsidised rates of interest and creation of a new set of rural banks at district level and an Apex bank for Agriculture and Rural Development (NABARD19) at national level. These measures resulted in impressive gains in rural outreach and volume of credit. As a result, between 1961 and 2000 the average population per bank branch fell tenfold from about 140 thousand to 14000 (Burgess and Pande, 200520) and the share of institutional agencies in ruralcredit increased from 7.3 per cent 1951 to 66 per cent in 199121.

These impressive gains were not without a cost. Government interventions through directed credit, state owned Rural Financial Institutions (RFI) and subsidised interest rates increased the tolerance for loan defaults, loan waivers and lax appraisal and monitoring of loans. The problem at the start of 1990s looked twofold, the institutional structure was neither profitable in rural lending nor serving the needs of the poorest. In short, it had created a structure, 'quantitatively impressive but qualitatively weak'. Microcredit emergence in India has to be seen in this backdrop for a better appreciation of current paradigm. Successful microfinance interventions across the world especially in Asia and in parts of India by NGOs provided further impetus. In this backdrop, NABARD's search for alternative models of reaching the rural poor brought the existence of informal groups of poor to the fore. It was realised that the poor tended to come together in a variety of informal ways for pooling their savings and dispensing small and unsecured loans at varying costs to group members on the basis of need. This concept of Self-help was discovered by social-development NGOs22 in 1980s. Realising that the only constraining factor in unleashing the potential of these groups was meagreness of their financial resources, NABARD designed the concept of linking these groups with banks to overcome the financial constraint. The programme has come a long way since 1992 passing through stages of pilot (1992-95) mainstreaming (1995-98) and expansion phase (1998 onwards) and emerged as the world's biggest microfinance programme in terms of outreach, covering 1.6 million groups as on March, 2005.23 It occupies a pre-eminent position in the sector accounting for nearly 80 per cent market share in India.

Under the programme, popularly known as SHG-Bank Linkage programmes are broadly three models of credit linkage of SHGs with banks. However, the underlying design feature in all remains the same *i.e.*, identification, formation and nurturing of groups either by NGOs/other development agencies or banks, and holding and initial period of inculcating habit of thrift followed by collateral free credit from bank in proportion to the group's savings. In accordance with the flexible approach, the decision to borrow, internal lending and rate of interest are left at the discretion of group members. Its design is built on combining the "collective wisdom of the poor, the organizational capabilities of the social intermediary and the financial strength of the Banks".

The success factors of the programme lie in it being beneficial for both banks and clients – another example of Win-Win proposition. The programme is an attractive proposition for banks due to high recovery rates and lowering of transaction costs by outsourcing costs associated with monitoring and appraisal of loans. Records show a recovery rate as high as 95 per cent for loans extended by banks to SHGs and a study sponsored by FDC, Australia, it was observed that the reduction in costs for the bankers is around 40 per cent as compared to earlier loans under Integrated Rural Development Programme (IRDP). Similar findings in respect of commercial benefit of SHG lending to banks were reported by Siebel and Dave (2002).

The programme's exclusive focus on reaching those sections of population, who were hitherto out of reach of financial system has increased the coverage of poor. Non reliance on physical collateral and total flexibility in loan purpose and amount has also resulted in increased coverage of the poor and the marginalised.

The programme has received strong public policy support from both Government of India and Reserve Bank of India. The importance attached to it by Government is exemplified by mention of yearly targets by Finance Minister in his annual budget speech as well as introduction of similar group based lending approach in government's poverty alleviation programme. The success of the programme in reaching financial services to the poor has won international admiration. World Bank policy paper hails the programme and states that it is particularly suited to India because the model capitalises on country's vast network of rural bank branches that are other-wise unable to reach the rural poor.

Road Ahead

Indian rural finance sector is at crossroads today. Following the financial sector reforms with its emphasis on profitability as the key performance bench-mark, banks are increasingly shying away from rural lending as well as rationalizing their branch network in rural areas. Burgess and Pande (ibid) have brought out this fact in their study by stating that while between 1977 and 1990 (pre reform period) more bank branches were opened in financially less developed areas, the pattern was reversed in post reform period. Thus while, access of credit to the rural poor has reduced in post reform period, the policy recommendation is to fill this gap through micro credit. The SHG-Bank linkage programme has witnessed phenomenal growth and the current strategy is to focus on 13 underdeveloped states as also graduate the existing SHGs to the next stage of micro enterprises.

At this stage, the paper argues that if SHG-Bank linkage programme has to contribute to poverty reduction, there is an imperative need for integrating impact assessment as a necessary design feature of the programme. The significance of bringing the focus back to 'people' from 'institutions' and adoption of localized people centric approach can hardly be overemphasized. In line with the tenets of commercial microfinance, it is critical that scarce public resources are used.

Judiciously and with better targeting. Adequate emphasis on impact assessment is an integral part of the triangle of factors necessary for judging microfinance intervention. Mainstreaming of impact assessment in the SHG-Bank linkage programme will call for extra efforts and resources as also create conflict with the present focus on numerical growth. Realisation of a substantial trade off between sustainable economic impact and exponential growth, calls for courageous public policy decisions. World Bank policy research working paper (ibid) also points that ensuring preoccupation with achievement of numeric targets does not override attention to group quality will be a key future concern for SHG-Bank linkage programme.

Conclusion

The Indian economy at present is at a crucial juncture, on one hand, the optimists are talking of India being among the top 5 economies of the world by 2050 and on the other is the presence of 260 million poor forming 26 per cent of the total population. The enormity of the task can be gauged from the above numbers and if India is to stand among the comity of developed nations, there is no denying the fact that poverty alleviation and reduction of income inequalities has to be the top most priority. India's achievement of the MDG of halving the population of poor by 2015 as well as achieving a broad based economic growth also hinges on a successful poverty alleviation strategy. In this backdrop, the impressive gains made by SHG-Bank linkage programme in coverage of rural population with financial services offers a ray of hope. The paper argues for mainstreaming of impact assessment and incorporation of local factors in service delivery to maximize impact of SHG-Bank linkage programme on achievement of MDGs and not letting go this opportunity.

REFERENCES

1. Seibel, H.D. and Parhusip, U (1990). Financial Innovations for Micro Enterprises – linking Formal and Informal Institutions. In Harper, M. (Ed.) (2003) Microfinance: Evolution, Achievement and Challenges, ITDG Publishing, London.
2. Yaron, J., Benjamin, M., and Piprek, G. (1997). Rural Finance. Issues, Design, and Best Practices, World Bank, Washington D.C.
3. Hulme, D., and Mosley, P. (1996). Finance Against Poverty, Routledge, London.
4. Dale Adams, Carlos Cuevas, Gordon Donald, Claudio Gonzalez-Vega and J.D. von Pischke are best known Members of 'Ohio School'.
5. Meyer, R.L., and Nagarajan, G. (1999). Rural Financial Markets in Asia: Policies. Paradigms, and Performance, Oxford University Press.
6. Usage of the term 'Microfinance' Started later after Extension of Financial Services other than credit also.
7. Grameen in Bangladesh, PRODEM in Bolivia and Bank Rakayat Indonesia (BRI).
8. Rhyne, E. (2001). Mainstreaming Microfinance, Kumarian Press, Connecticut, USA.

9. Micro Credit Summit Campaign (2005). State of the Micro Credit Summit Campaign Report 2005, Washington, DC.

10. Remenyi, J. "Is there a 'State of the Art' in Microfinance". In Remenyi, J., and Quinones, B. (Ed.) (2000). Microfinance and Poverty Alleviation Case Studies from Asia and the Pacific, Pinter, London.

Pages 120-128

POVERTY ALLEVIATION THROUGH MICROFINANCE
Edited by : Dr. B. Ramachandra Reddy
Edition : 2017
ISBN : 978-93-5056-865-1
Published by : Discovery Publishing House Pvt. Ltd., New Delhi (India)

15

Microfinance and its Delivery Models in India

Prof. N.R. Venkata Ramana Reddy
Ch. Kalpa Latha

INTRODUCTION

The microfinance sector in India has experienced a roller coaster trend in the last one and half-decade, during which various changes and amendments took place under the legal and regulatory ecosystem. The much awaited and long standing MFIDR Bill 2012 got lapsed in the parliament while the sector has experienced various regulatory changes in the last fiscal year. Recognition of SRO is one such positive move. In addition, RBI has also allowed NBFC-MFIs to work as Business Correspondents.

On a macro perspective, the Government of India has launched the Pradhan Mantri Jan Dhan Yojana (PMJDY) which is a mission on financial inclusion aiming at opening 7.5 crore bank accounts before Jan 26, 2015. RBI has restructured and created a separate department for financial inclusion to boost the measures for inclusive financial services. Bank licensing, guidelines on Small and Payment banks, technological innovations and above all, the business potential at the base of the pyramid is driving the agenda of financial inclusion in a big way, under a very fast changing landscape.

Microfinance offers board Range of financial services as loan, saving and insurance to poor people through different microfinance Institutions. Microfinance institutions also provide social intermediation services such as: training and education, organizational support, health and skills in line with their development objectives. Microfinance cannot eradicate all problems

Department of Economics, Vikrama Simhapuri University Post-Graduate Centre, Kavali, Nellore - 524 201.

caused by poverty but it can assist to put economic resources into hands of poor and low income people enabling them to make their own financial decision thereby improving their financial soundness.

Microfinance refers to loan; saving, insurance, transfer services and other financial products targeted at low levels clients. Microfinance in India is mainly provided through Self-Help Groups (SHGs), Microfinance Institutions (MFIs) and some other methodologies. The network of many financial institutions like public and private sector commercial banks, co-operative banks, regional rural banks (RRBs) and MFIs is used to provide microfinance services to the poor people.

Objectives of the Study

The paper has following objectives:

1. To examine the different models of microfinance in India.
2. To study the structure of microfinance models in India
3. To observe the status of microfinance in our country.

Research Methodology

The research study is based on the analysis of relevant reports on microfinance, previous studies, and various previous articles. This paper was prepared on the basis of the secondary data. The secondary data was collected through various published reports, journals, magazines, web sites.

Microfinance in India

Microfinance emerged as an industry almost same time all over the world. Microfinance is broadly accepted for improving income level of poor people. In 1970s and 1980s non-government organizations provided micro credits to poor for opening micro enterprises. In 1970s since the effort of Mohammad Yunus founder of Grameen Bank, Microfinance has proved to be a sustainable tool for poverty alleviation. The previous models of lending to low income people were state sponsored programmes like integrated rural development programme (IRDP) which were designed for social welfare of the state. In 1990s Grameen bank model and the Association for social Advancement model found rapid acceptance in Bangladesh as well as in India as a new breed for microfinance Institutions. Popularly known as the On-lending models they had the capacity for rapid up-scaling in terms of client reach.

They were less reliant on donation of funds. It enabled the microfinance institutions to borrow capital from large organizations and charging individual borrower a minimum amount as a service charge and retained margin for their own growth. The SHG model in the form of the SHG–Bank Linkage (SBLP) initiated in the 1992 by NABARD and the rapidly growing MFI on-lending models both dominate the microfinance industry.

Apex bodies like National Agriculture and Rural Development Bank (NABARD) and Small Industries Development Bank of India (SIDBI) are playing vital role for providing financial resources to microfinance these days. The main vigor of microfinance in India is variety of microfinance delivery models which emerged over a period of time. The country now has a wide-spread and efficient banking set-up with around 100,000 bank branches nationwide. The expansion of commercial baking has also led to a more favorable financial environment for the poor in India. It was following these forms that the 'Self-Help groups (SHGs) – Bank Linkage' model grew to become a key part of finance for India's poor.

The Government of India has initiated various programmes and schemes in the area of microfinance. The most important programmes are SGSY (1999) and NABARD's SBLP (1992) which are using SHGs approach. Other initiatives by government include IMY, Swa-Shakti, DWCRA, CAPART, SJSRY, IFAD, Swayamsiddha, RMK etc. These all programmes aimed at reduction of poverty and improving the living condition of rural poor with the help of economic activities.

Microfinance Delivery Models in India

The availability of credit and banking facilities to the poor and underprivileged segment of the society can be reached through Microfinance. The Government and the Reserve Bank have taken several initiatives, from time to time, such as: nationalisation of banks, prescription of priority sector lending norms and concessional interest rate for the weaker section of society. It was, however, realised that further direct efforts were required to address the credit needs of poor people. In response to this requirement, the Microfinance movement started in India with the introduction of SHG bank linkage programme (SBLP) in the early 1990s. At present, there are mainly two models for delivery of Microfinance in India SBPL model and the MFI model. All over the world lot of basic effort had been step forwarded since 1980s which set a framework for Microfinance efforts in India. The approaches for delivery of Microfinance are varied in nature. There is no specific model which fits into all conditions rather there is an easy and elastic approach needed to meet the credit requirement of poor people. Each model has to be modified as per different situation and local requirements. Various delivery models have been adopted by Microfinance institutions and they can be categorized in to following broad categories. Microfinance is a dynamic field and there is clearly no best way to deliver services to the poor and hence many delivery models have been developed over a period of time. Each delivery model has its share of problem and success. In India, various delivery models have been adopted by microfinance institutions and they can be categorized in to following broad categories, discussed one by one.

Self-Help Group – Bank Linkage Model

A SHG is a small group of about 10-20 persons from a homogeneous class of rural and urban poor which promoted savings among members and used these resources for meeting their credit needs The group is democratically formed and elects its own leaders. The vital features of SHGs are it consists of members belonging to the same community or society and having common economic goal.

Their aims for formation of SHG include economic welfare of all members.

Under the SBLP, the following three different models have emerged in India:

Model I: SHGs promoted, guided and financed by banks.

Model II: SHGs promoted by NGOs/Government agencies and financed by banks.

Model III: SHGs promoted by NGOs and financed by banks using NGOs/ formal agencies as financial intermediaries.

NABARD suggested three models for SHGBLP and monitored the progress model-wise till 2005-06. There were 22,38,565 SHGs having bank loan of Rs 11,398 crore till 2005-06. Model-wise composition was 73 per cent through model 'B', *i.e.* SHG promoted by SHPI and linked by banks directly, 20 per cent through model 'A' *i.e.* SHG promoted by banks through their staff, Farmers clubs and Rural volunteers and linked by the banks themselves. The third model 'C' of bulk lending to SHG promoting NGO by banks for on lending to SHGs promoted by these agencies constituted only 7 per cent of the total linkage. As of 31 March 2014, there were 74.30 lakh saving linked SHGs with a bank deposit of Rs 9897 crore and 41.97 lakh credit linked SHGs with bank loan outstanding of Rs. 42928 crore. During 2013-14, 13.66 lakh SHGs were provided credit assistance amounting Rs. 24017 crore by banks. All these are pointers to the sheer outreach of the SHG movement.

The Self-Help Group movement in India is sui generis because it is a savings-first programme with credit being its logical corollary. Touching over 9.44 crore households, it has become the largest Microfinance programme in the world.

Region-wise – Savings Linked SHGs

Region-wise number of SHGs savings linked during the last five years is furnished in Table 15.1. The below Table 15.1 shows about the region wise savings through SHGs-Bank Linkage programme from the year 2009-10 to 2013-14. The total savings in 2009-10 is 63.53 lakh these savings amount is increased to 79.60 lakh in year 2011-12. This 79.60 lakh savings are declined in the year 2013-14.

Table 15.1: Region-wise – Savings Linked SHGs

Region	No. of SHGs Savings Linked with Banks (No. Lakh)				
	2009-10	2010-11	2011-12	2012-13	2013-14
Northern	3.52	3.73	4.09	3.73	3.65
North Eastern	2.92	3.25	3.67	3.24	3.16
Eastern	13.74	15.27	16.26	14.71	14.69
Central	7.66	7.86	8.13	7.02	6.86
Western	9.46	9.61	10.62	9.06	8.97
Southern	32.23	34.89	36.83	35.41	36.96
Total	69.53	74.61	79.60	73.17	74.29

Source: National Microfinance Conclave – 2014.

In these all regions less savings are mobilized in northern region and more savings is in southern region. In 2010-11 the total savings are 74.61 lakh, in 2011-12 is 79.60 lakh, 73.17 lakh total savings is in the year 2012-13 and in 2013-14 the total savings is 74.29 lakh.

Table 15.2 explains about the region wise financed by banks during the year 2009-10 to 2013-14. In all these years and regions more finance is allocated to southern region (*i.e.* Andhra Pradesh, Karnataka, Kerala, Tamil Nadu) and less finance is allocated in northern region (*i.e.* Haryana, Himachal Pradesh, J&K, Delhi, Punjab, Rajasthan). In the year 2009-10 the total finance15.86 lakh is more than the remaining years.

Table 15.2: Region-wise Financed by Banks during the Year (No. Lakh)

Region	No. of SHGs Financed by Banks during the Year (No. Lakh)				
	2009-10	2010-11	2011-12	2012-13	2013-14
Northern	0.37	0.42	0.31	0.31	0.24
North Eastern	0.49	0.39	0.51	0.25	0.16
Eastern	2.77	2.48	2.01	1.83	2.97
Central	0.78	0.49	0.58	0.64	0.66
Western	1.49	0.92	1.01	0.70	0.88
Southern	9.96	7.26	7.05	8.46	8.75
Total	15.86	11.96	11.47	12.19	13.66

Source: National Microfinance Conclave – 2014.

Microfinance Institution Model

Microfinance institutions are organizations involved in the delivery of financial services to the population segment that is otherwise considered unbankable. They may range from benign and socially responsible NGOs to profit-oriented NBFCs. There has been an explosive growth in MFI activity in India over the past decade as a plethora of NGOs and private organizations have converged into this field, some having the genuine intention of socioeconomic advancement, while others cashing in on the, fortune at the bottom of the pyramid . There 4 were 237 MFIs operating in India in 2009 with a total client base of 2.66 crore people and a total loan amount outstanding of over Rs. 18, 000 crore.

It is evident that large NBFC-MFIs have a larger client outreach in contrast to other legal forms of MFIs. Among these, Bandhan Financial Services has the largest client outreach *i.e.*, approximately 16 per cent of the total client outreach of the sector. SKS, SKDRDP, Spandana are the other major players in this area. Over the years, the entries into the Top 10 MFIs have remained more or less unchanged, except for a few new players. Interestingly, SKDRDP and CASHPOR are the only non-NBFC MFIs with a large client outreach. Other than legal form, factors like: availability of funds, business plan, regulatory environment etc., also determine the scale of operation and client outreach.

Federated Self-Help Group Model

Self-Help Groups are successful in empowering women by providing direct and indirect benefits to them. SHGs are small in size generally

10-15 members having limited in the types of financial services they can provide to its members. Federation of SHGs have more than 1000 members In Federated SHG model, there is a three tier structure the first tire is the SHG, the second tier is a cluster and the third tier is an apex body, which represents the entire SHG. At the cluster level, each SHG is represented by two of its members. The apex body usually made up of 10-15 members and they form the link between the SHGs and the NGO which is supporting to them. With the help of federations and NGO with limited resources, it has impact on a large number of poor people. Examples of Federated Self-Help Group model are PRADAN, Chaitanya and SEWA.

- Sakhi Samiti, an SHG federation in Rajasthan, initially promoted by Professional Assistance for Development Action (PRADAN), an NGO. In 1999, the federation assumed responsibility for SHG promotion.
- A PRADAN programme in the Lohardaga district of Jharkhand, formed in 1992, that began promoting SHGs for savings and credit in 1996.
- Chitradurga Gramin Bank (CGB), a rural bank in Karnataka selected by NABARD in 1992 as one of nine regional rural banks to promote SHGs.

In Lohardarga, Jharkhand, where PRADAN works, SHG members reported that money lenders went out of business because of reduced demand for their services. Overall, 14 per cent of members of the sample SHGs supported by PRADAN still borrowed from money lenders. The average loan per member was 6,750 rupees, where SHGs had access to outside capital from federations or banks, and 1,450 rupees where there was no such support.

Grameen Bank Partnership Model

The Grameen Bank model has been a case of exceptional success in Bangladesh. It turns out that many organizations in India have adopted the Grameen Bank model with little variations and good success. Some of the notable examples are SHARE Microfinance Limited, Activists for Social Alternatives (ASA) and CASHPOR Financial and Technical Services Limited. Some of the significant features of Grameen bank model are low transaction costs, no collateral (peer pressure is sufficient), repayment of loans in small and short interval and quick loan sanctions with little or no paper works and no formalities. Repayment of loans in small chunk is one of the major reasons of high loan recovery rate of a Grameen Bank. Furthermore, loans are provided for all purposes like: housing loans, sanitation loans, supplementary loans etc. Also the interest rates are nominal making it easy for the poor people to repay their loans timely.

Co-Operative Model

A co-operative is an organization owned by the members who use its services. This model works on the principle that every community has enough human and financial resources to manage their own financial institutions. The members who own it are the members who use its services and can come from different sections of same community like: agriculture, retail, wholesale etc. By proper networking small scale local institutions scale up and become sustainable while locals maintain ownership and control over their institution. The organization which has been vastly successful in co-operative form in India is Sahavikasa or Co-operative Development Foundation (CDF). CDF's approach relies on the well known Credit Union model involving a savings first strategy. Found in 1975 by a group of individuals, Sahavikasa has now emerged as the leading co-operative in India.

Based on women's thrift group and men's thrift group, CDF has built up a network of financial cooperatives and had convinced the Andhra Pradesh government to form legislation for proper and flexible functioning of co-operatives in the state. The legislation is known as Mutually - Aided Societies Act (MACS). The act helps the CDF to register the thrift groups promoted by CDF under it. The activities of CDF involve assisting rural women and men in the areas of operation in forming and developing self sustainable co-operatives CDF also provide education and training to the co-operators from its work area.

Banking Correspondents Model

In January 2006, the Reserve Bank permitted banks to utilise the services of NGOs, MFIs (other than NBFCs) and other civil society organizations as intermediaries in providing financial and banking services through the use of business facilitator and business correspondent (BC) models. The Bank correspondent's model permits bank to do transaction at closer areas of rural population. Thus BC model addressed the problems of poor people from remote areas. The BC model uses the MFI's ability to get close to poor clients – a necessity for savings mobilisation from the poor – while relying on the financial strength of the bank to safeguard the deposits. Union finance minister in union budget 2008-09 allowed banks to appoint retired bank employee or retired government employee as business correspondents (BC).

Conclusion

Economic and financial services institutions long-term growth is depend on the manner that Financial Institutions approaches and taps untapped rural areas in India. Microfinance is often portrayed in literature as a tool that allows individuals excluded from the financial system to get access to sources of funding, which will help for theirs development and growth. From the above study it can be viewed that Self-help Groups are playing vital role in delivery of microfinance services which leads to increase the saving habits of poorest strata of society and contributing towards the development of poor people in India.

REFERENCES

1. National Microfinance Conclave – 2014.
2. The Bharat Microfinance Report 2014.
3. The New Microfinance Handbook (A Financial Market System Perspective).
4. Status of Microfinance in India 2012-13.
5. Microfinance in India: Discussion by R. Srinivasan and M.S Sriram.
6. Ghate, P. (2007). Microfinance in India: A State of the Sector Report, 2006, Microfinance India Publications, New Delhi.
7. Satish, P. (2005). "Mainstreaming of Indian Microfinance", *Economic and Political Weekly*, Vol. 40, No. 17, p. 1733.

Pages 129-133

POVERTY ALLEVIATION THROUGH MICROFINANCE
Edited by : **Dr. B. Ramachandra Reddy**
Edition : **2017**
ISBN : 978-93-5056-865-1
Published by : **Discovery Publishing House Pvt. Ltd., New Delhi (India)**

16 Microfinance Delivery Models

Dr. B.V. Anantha Ramu[1]
Dr. M. Guru Mohan Reddy[2]

INTRODUCTION

'Microfinance' emerged as the term of choice to refer to a range of financial services to the poor, that included not only credit, but also savings and other services such as: insurance and money transfers. In 1976, Professor Muhammad Yunus addressed the banking problem faced by the poor in Bangladesh, through a programme of action research. He designed an experimental credit programme to serve them. It spread rapidly to hundreds of villages. He founded the Grameen Bank in 1983. The initial success of Grameen Bank also stimulated the establishment of microfinance institutions in Bangladesh.

In India the failure of the formal credit institutions in effectively meeting the requirements of the rural poor has been the major reason for innovations in microfinance. The Self-Help Groups (SHG) – Bank Linkage Programme, launched by National Bank for Agriculture and Rural Development (NABARD) in 1992, is a landmark in the field of microfinancing in India.

Concept and Definition of Microfinance

'Microfinance can be defined as' "any activity that includes the provision of financial services such as: credit, savings, and insurance to low income individuals which fall just above the nationally defined poverty line, and

1. M.Com., Ph.D., Lecturer in Commerce, SKSC Degree College, Proddatur.
2. M.A., Ph.D., Lecturer in Economics, SKSC Degree College Proddatur.

poor individuals which fall below the poverty line, with the goal of creating social value. The creation of social value includes poverty alleviation and the broader impact of improving livelihood opportunities though the provision of capital for micro enterprises, and insurance and savings for risk mitigation and consumption smoothing".

Microfinance helps the poor people meet their needs for small credit and other financial services. The informal and flexible services offered to low-income borrowers for meeting their modest consumption and livelihood needs have not only made Microfinance movement grow at a rapid pace across the world, but, in turn, have also impacted the lives of millions of poor positively. Thus, Microfinance is the provision of a broad range of financial services such as: deposits, loans, payment services, money transfers, and insurance to the poor and low-income households and their micro enterprises. In the development paradigm, Microfinance has evolved as a need-based policy and programme to cater to the needs of neglected groups of society, especially women, poor, rural, deprived, and the like. The basic idea of Micro-finance is that if poor people are provided access to financial assistance, including: credit, they may be able to start or expand a micro enterprise that will allow them to break out of poverty. Microfinance has become one of the most effective interventions for economic empowerment of the poor. Microfinance is expected to play a significant role in poverty alleviation and development. Microfinance refers to small-scale financial services (including: savings, credit, insurance, business services and technical assistance) provided to the rural people who operate small or micro enterprises, provide services, work for wages or commissions and other individuals and groups working at local levels.

Micro credit programmes extend small amounts as credit to very poor people for self-employment projects that generate income, allowing them to care for themselves and their families. It is an important tool for the eradication of poverty and has been employed world over with spectacular results.

Micro credit activity has been evolved as an effective tool of economic development and its approach is intended to benefit the Below Poverty Line (B.P.L.) families, especially women. The provision of financial services attempts to save both the rural and the urban poor through social intermediation services such as: SHGs formation, development of self-confidence and training in financial, literary and management capability among the members of the SHGs. The success of this programme entirely depends on systematic planning and procedures.

Microfinance Delivery Models

India hosts the maximum number of Microfinance models, both in indigenous practices as well as in modern Microfinance practices. The models range from pure 'home-spun' varieties like the SHGs and co-operatives to adapted models like the Grameen methodology and methodology for-profit corporate models. The most important models of Micro finance are :

The SHG-Bank Linkage Model

The predominant model in the Indian Microfinance context continues to be the SHG-bank linkage model that accounts for nearly 20 million clients. Under this model, the self-help promoting institution (SHPI), usually a Non-Governmental Organization (NGO), helps groups of 15-20 individuals through an incubation period after which they are linked to banks. The bank lends to the groups after the incubation period, and this linkage may be single or multi-period. The SHPI typically receives no, or below cost, consideration either from the bank or the clients for group promotion. They meet this expense out of external grant sources. The cost estimates for this vary from Rs. 2,000 - Rs. 10,000 per group. Once the groups have been linked to the bank, the SHPI often supervises the loan portfolio. However, there is no specific incentive for the SHPI to play this on going role, which has associated expenses in terms of employees from time to time. Pricing to the clients under this model is not based on full costs, as the costs of promotion and those of transactions handled by the SHPI are not included. The financial needs of the SHGs are catered to by various financial institutions: the Commercial Banks, Co-operative Banks, Co-operative Credit Societies and Regional Rural Banks (RRB).

The SHGs had proved their efficacy over time but they suffer from a meagre resource base which handicapped their capacity to expand the economic activities of their members. Therefore, with time, it was seriously considered that SHGs should be linked with formal credit agencies. The factors perceived by the SHG members as responsible for their limited access to the formal credit institutions were, the lack of information about the banks schemes meant for them, cumbersome procedures, high incidental costs and difficulties in obtaining the required revenue and other documents, rigid lending policies of banks in respect of unit costs, unit sizes and group guarantees for loans and the general apathy of the local bank staff and government functionaries.

(a) *SHGs Formed and Financed by Banks:* In this model, banks themselves take up the work of forming and nurturing the groups, opening their savings accounts and providing them bank loans.

(b) *SHGs formed by Formal Agencies other than Banks (NGOs and others) but Directly Financed by Banks:* Here, NGOs and formal agencies in the field of Microfinance act only as facilitators. They facilitate in forming, organizing and nurturing of groups, and train them in thrift and credit management. Banks give loans directly to these SHGs.

(c) *SHGs Financed by Banks using NGOs and other Agencies as Financial Intermediaries:* This is the model wherein the NGO/MFIs take on the additional role of financial intermediaries. In areas where the formal banking system faces constraints, the NGOs are encouraged to approach a suitable bank for bulk loan assistance. This, in turn, is used by the NGO/MFI for on lending to the SHGs. In areas where a large number of SHGs have been financed by bank branches, intermediate agencies like federations of SHGs are coming up as links between bank branch and member SHGs. These federations are financed by banks who, in turn, fiancé their member SHGs.

The Grameen Model

Here the financial assistance *i.e.,* loans for productive purposes, is provided by the MFIs/NGOs directly to the members of small groups (affinity groups consisting of about 5-7 members) directly on the strength of group assurance. It is often coupled with an obligation to save by the group members.

The Co-operative Model

This has been initiated by Cooperative Development Forum (CDF), which has relied upon a 'Credit Union' involving the Savings First strategy. It has built up a network of women Thrift Groups (WTGs) and Men Thrift Groups (MTGs). They are registered under Mutually Aided Cooperative Society Act (MACs) and mobilize savings resources from the members and access outside/ supplementary resources from the institutional systems.

The Partnership Model

Under the partnership model, loans are contracted directly between the bank and the final borrower *i.e.,* loans are not reflected on the balance sheet of the MFI. The MFI continues to originate, monitor and recover the loans until maturity in exchange for service fees.

All the models are tried and tested and have shown excellent results in the contexts that they are operating in. Despite a few disadvantages, the perceived advantages of the SHG have far outweighed its disadvantages and have made the SHG as a popular model for Microfinance in India. So much so that even the government programmes have the SHG at the core of their strategy. Undoubtedly, the SHG model has emerged as the Indian model of Microfinance.

Conclusion

It can be concluded that Microfinance Models can be efficiently implemented in rural areas in order to achieve the balanced regional development through the development of Women Entrepreneurs as SHG members. The Government should strive to support the initiative of SHG women at the gross root level to over come the poverty and to empower the women to uplift their standard of living.

REFERENCES

1. The History of Microfinance, Administrator, Global envision, April, 14, 2006. pp. 1-10., www.globalenvision.org/library/4/1051.
2. www.nabard.org
3. www.rbi.org.in
4. www.nabard.org
5. www.rmk.org
6. www.myrada.org
7. www.sewa.org
8. www.pradan.org

Pages 134-139

POVERTY ALLEVIATION THROUGH MICROFINANCE
Edited by : **Dr. B. Ramachandra Reddy**
Edition : **2017**
ISBN : 978-93-5056-865-1
Published by : **Discovery Publishing House Pvt. Ltd., New Delhi (India)**

17

Genesis and Evolution of Microfinance System

T. Vinila

INTRODUCTION

The history of microfinancing can be traced back as long to the middle of the 1800s when the theorist Lysander Spooner was writing over the benefits from small credits to entrepreneurs and farmers as a way getting the people out of poverty. But it was at the end of World War II with the Marshall plan the concept had an big impact.

The today use of the expression microfinancing has it roots in the 1970s when organizations, such as: Grameen Bank of Bangladesh with the microfinance pioneer Mohammad Yunus, where starting and shaping the modern industry of microfinancing. Another pioneer in this sector is Akhtar Hameed Khan. At that time a new wave of microfinance initiatives introduced many new innovations into the sector. Many pioneering enterprises began experimenting with loaning to the under served people. The main reason why microfinance is dated to the 1970s is that the programmes could show that people can be relied on to repay their loans and that it's possible to provide financial services to poor people through market based enterprises without subsidy. Shorebank was the first microfinance and community development bank founded 1974 in Chicago.

An economical historian at Yale named Timothy Guinnane has been doing some research on Friedrich Wilhelm Raiffeisen's village bank movement

Assistant Professor of Commerce, Smt N.P. Savitramma Government College (W) Chittoor.

in Germany which started in 1864 an by the year 1901 the bank had reached 2 million rural farmers. Timothy Guinnane means that already then it was proved that micro credit could pass the two tests concerning peoples pay back moral and the possibility to provide the financial service to poor people.

Another organization, The caisse populaire movement grounded by Alphone and Dorimène Desjardins in Quebec, was also concerned about the poverty, and passed those two tests. Between 1900 to 1906 when they founded the first caisse, they passed a law governing them in the Quebec assembly, they risked their private assets and must have been very sure about the idea about micro credit.

Today the World Bank estimates that more than 16 million people are served by some 7000 microfinance institutions all over the world. CGAP experts means that about 500 million families benefits from these small loans making new business possible. In a gathering at a Micro credit Summit in Washington DC the goal was reaching 100 million of the world's poorest people by credits from the world leaders and major financial institutions.

Objectives of the Study

1. To review the genesis and growth of Microfinance System.
2. To determine the extent of success of microfinance for the economic development of the country.
3. To examine the services being extended by the Government and non-government organizations in promoting economic development through different scheme.
4. To assess various important segments of the programmes being implemented by the Government to provide an insight whether the programmes are being executed on the desired lines of poverty.

Objectives of Microfinance

1. Assess and promote the contribution of microfinance to the MFIs.
2. Make microfinance more visible for public awareness understanding as a very important part of the development situation.
3. The promotion should be inclusive the financial sector.
4. Make a supporting system for sustainable access to financial services.
5. Support strategic partnerships by encouraging new partnerships and innovation to build and expand the outreach and success of microfinance for all.

Financial Institutions

- *ACCION International*: An early pioneer, was founded by a law student, Joseph Blatchford, to address poverty in Latin America's cities. Begun as a student-run volunteer effort in the shantytowns of Caracas with $90,000 raised from private companies, ACCION today is one of the premier microfinance organizations in the world, with a network of lending partners that spans Latin America, the United States and Africa.
- *SEWA Bank*: In 1972 the Self-Employed Women's Association (SEWA) was registered as a trade union in Gujarat (India), with the main objective of "strengthening its members' bargaining power to improve income, employment and access to social security." In 1973, to address their lack of access to financial services, the members of SEWA decided to found 'a bank of their own'. Four thousand women contributed share capital to establish the Mahila SEWA Co-operative Bank. Since then it has been providing banking services to poor, illiterate, self-employed women and has become a viable financial venture with today around 30,000 active clients.
- *Grameen Bank*: In Bangladesh, Professor Muhammad Yunus addressed the banking problem faced by the poor through a programme of action-research. With his graduate students in Chittagong University in 1976, he designed an experimental credit programme to serve them. It spread rapidly to hundreds of villages. Through a special relationship with rural banks, he disbursed and recovered thousands of loans, but the bankers refused to take over the project at the end of the pilot phase. They feared it was too expensive and risky in spite of his success. Eventually, through the support of donors, the Grameen Bank was founded in 1983 and now serves more than 4 million borrowers. The initial success of Grameen Bank also stimulated the establishment of several other giant microfinance institutions like: BRAC, ASA, Proshika, etc.
- *NABARD*: Apart from giving the lead in piloting the SHG–Bank linkage and the refinance of loans by banks to SHGs, NABARD is engaged in fulfilling a variety of promotion and support functions as the apex bank for agriculture and rural development. These include:
    - developing a conducive policy framework;
    - training and sensitising bank officers;
    - capacity-building support to NGOs, SHGs and banks;
    - financial support to NGOs for SHG promotion;
    - provision of revolving fund assistance to MFIs;
    - evaluation studies and dissemination of SHG best practices.

A Microfinance Development Fund with a corpus of Rs. 100 crores has been established to scale up the bank linkage programme, build expertise in MF and support the evolution of regulatory and support mechanisms for MFIs. So far utilization has been low with 330 NGOs supported to the extent of Rs. 4 crores by October 2001. NABARD has also received the first tranche of a DM 3 million GTZ grant for capacity building of NABARD and its partner agencies.

- *SIDBI:* SIDBI has set up the Foundation for Micro credit. By 31 March 2000 it had sanctioned aggregate assistance of Rs. 52.76 crores to 160 MFIs. It also provides capacity building support to eligible MFIs. It has since increased the funding available for extending loans and equity to MFIs to Rs. 500 crores.
- *RMK*: A fund set up in 1993 by the Department of Women and Child Development, Government of India, RMK provides loans to NGOs for on-lending to women beneficiaries. It had disbursements of nearly 60 crores by March 2000. Its loans attract the lowest rates of interest at 8 per cent with concessions for timely repayment. Grants for SHG promotion are also provided.
- *HUDCO and HDFC*: These corporations are mainly involved in housing finance, including finance to economically weaker sections. HDFC had Rs. 80 crores of loans outstanding but its portfolio is not directed only at the rural poor.
- *RGVN*: RGVN is a non-profit society formed in April 1990. Operating in the neglected north-eastern region of the country, it is the only national donor agency working in this remote area. Sponsored by some of the biggest financial institutions like the Industries Development Bank of India (IDBI), Industrial Credit and Investment Corporation of India (ICICI) and SIDBI, it also recycles grant funds by extending 'returnable grants' to NGOs.
- *FWWB*: FWWB is a non-profit organization set up in 1982 as an affiliate of Women's World Banking. It started a revolving loan fund in 1989. It had outstanding loans of Rs. 17.41 crores to various MFIs by March 2001. It has also availed of a Cordaid loan repayable in rupees at 9 per cent interest.

Bank Linkage Scheme – The Model

The SHG-bank Linkage Programme has its origins in a GTZ-sponsored project in Indonesia. Launched in 1992 in India, early results achieved by SHGs promoted by NGOs such as: MYRADA, prompted NABARD to offer refinance to banks for collateral-free loans to groups, progressively up to four times the level of the group's savings deposits. SHGs thus 'linked' became micro banks able to access funds from the formal banking system. The linkage permitted the reduction of transaction costs of banks through the externalisation of costs of servicing individual loans and also ensuring their repayment through the peer pressure mechanism.

The programme encompasses three broad models of linkage:

Model I: Bank - SHG - Members

In this model the bank itself promotes and nurtures the self-help groups until they reach maturity. It accounted for 16 per cent of cumulative bank loan provided till the end of March 2002.

Model II: Bank - Facilitating Agency - SHG - Members

Here groups are formed and supported by NGOs or government agencies. The dominant model, it accounted for 75 per cent of cumulative loans of banks by March 2002.

Model III: Bank - NGO-MFI - SHG - Members

In this model NGOs act as both facilitators and MF intermediaries, and often federate SHGs into apex organizations to facilitate inter-group lending and larger access to funds. Cumulative bank loans through this channel were 9 per cent of total by March 2002.

Another model has been piloted recently by NABARD for facilitating the formation of SHGs for bank linkage in areas where there are no NGOs. This involves using the services of committed individual volunteers identified by bank branches.

Conclusion

Today, practitioners and donors are increasingly focusing on expanded financial services to the poor in frontier markets and on the integration of microfinance in financial systems development. The recent introduction by some donors of the financial systems approach in microfinance - which emphasizes favorable policy environment and institution-building - has improved the overall effectiveness of microfinance interventions. But numerous challenges remain, especially in rural and agricultural finance and other frontier markets. Today, the microfinance industry and the greater development community share the view that permanent poverty reduction requires addressing the multiple dimensions of poverty. For the international community, this means reaching specific Millennium Development Goals (MDGs) in education, women's empowerment, and health, among others. For microfinance, this means viewing microfinance as an essential element in any country'.

The role of Microfinance is development, specifically in relation to alleviating poverty was also examined. Key challenges facing MFIs today that are affecting their impact on poverty alleviation were seen to be an over-emphasis on financial sustainability over social objectives, and a failure of many MFIs to work with the poorest in society. Therefore, there is a greater need for MFIs to carefully design services that meet the needs of the poor and this can only be done 29 Consultative Group to Assist the Poor – a multi do nor effort of 25 western donor countries and international agencies formed by the World Bank to address the problems facing microfinance (Grameen Bank, 2000). Subsidies create incentives for the capture of funds by those who are better off and therefore betterable to gain access to the funds because of their social, economic and political status (Von Pischke, 1999). when MFIs understand their needs and the context within which the poor are working (Morduch, 2004). If MFIs are to meet their overall development objectives then they need to ensure financial sustainability and outreach of financial services designed to meet the needs of those most in need of such services. The impact of microfinance on poverty alleviation is a keenly debated issue as we have seen and it is generally accepted that it is not a silver bullet, it has not lived up in general to its expectation (Hulme and Mosley, 1996). However, when implemented and managed carefully, and when services are designed to meet the needs of clients, microfinance has had positive impacts, not just on clients, buton their families and on the wider community. There is however a need for greater assessment of these wider impacts if the true value of microfinance to development is to be understood (Zohir and Matin, 2004). One such tool for measuring wider impact is a livelihood security analysis based on a livelihoods framework which analyses how a project impacts on the livelihoods of beneficiaries.

REFERENCES

"Ministry of Social Justice and Empowerment, Government of India, New Delhi.

Raja Reddy, K. (2008). "What the SHGs Members Doing with Large Loans?". Paper presented in a national seminar on "SHGs and Role of Social Work Profession" organized by Department of Social Work, Andhra University, Visakhapatnam from 21st and 22nd February 2008.

Gert van Maanen, Microcredit: Sound Business or Development Instrument, Oikocredit, 2004.

Pages 140-145

POVERTY ALLEVIATION THROUGH MICROFINANCE
Edited by : Dr. B. Ramachandra Reddy
Edition : 2017
ISBN : 978-93-5056-865-1
Published by : Discovery Publishing House Pvt. Ltd., New Delhi (India)

18

Women Self-Help Groups in Andhra Pradesh

Role of NABARD

Dr. P. Thiripalu[1]
Dr. R. Harilal[2]
Dr. Morusu Siva Sankar[3]

Role on NABARD

National Bank for Agriculture and Rural Development (NABARD) is an apex development bank in India having headquarters based in Mumbai (Maharashtra) and other branches are all over the country. The Committee to Review Arrangements for Institutional Credit for Agriculture and Rural Development (CRAFICARD), set up by the Reserve Bank of India (RBI) under the Chairmanship of Shri B. Sivaraman, conceived and recommended the establishment of the National Bank for Agriculture and Rural Development (NABARD). It was established on 12 July 1982 by a special act by the parliament and its main focus was to uplift rural India by increasing the credit flow for elevation of agriculture and rural non farm sector and completed its 25 years on 12 July 2007. It has been accredited with "matters concerning policy, planning and operations in the field of credit for agriculture and other economic activities in rural areas in India". RBI sold its stake in NABARD to the Government of India, which now holds 99 per cent stake. NABARD is active in developing financial inclusion policy and is a member of the Alliance for Financial Inclusion.

1. Academic Consultant, Department of Anthropology, S.V. University, Tirupati - 517 502.
2. Associate Professor, S.V.V. University Tirupati - 517 502.
3. Academic Consultant Department of Commerce, S.V. University, Tirupati - 517 502.

The initiative of 1992 to make the traditional and formal banks to extend financial services to deprived sections through informal Self-Help Groups (SHGs), has now blossomed into a 'monolith' microfinance initiative. It has been recognized as a decentralized, cost effective and fastest growing microfinance initiative in the world, enabling over 103 million poor households' access to a variety of sustainable financial services from the banking system by becoming members of nearly 8 million SHGs. The linkage with banks has provided the members of the Groups the facility of not only pooling their thrift/savings and access to credit from the banking system, but also created a platform through which they could launch a number of livelihood initiatives and also facilitate the empowerment process.

The small beginning of linking only 500 SHGs to banks in 1992, had grown to over 0.5 million SHGs by March 2002 and further to 8 million SHGs by March 2012. From almost 100 per cent of the SHGs linked to Banks at the pilot stage from southern states, the share of southern States in the total number of SHGs linked shrank to 46 per cent by March 2012, while the share of eastern States (especially, West Bengal, Odissa, Bihar) shot up to over 20 per cent. The third decade of the programme promises to be one of maturing the linkage programme with livelihoods support, lot more innovations in the product range offered through SHGs and path breaking reforms in leveraging technology to improve efficiency, while extending its outreach to more geographical regions, especially the most resource poor regions of the country. It is widely believed that the SHGs of the poor will be the vehicles leading the march of India's emergence as a super economic power in the next decade.

Together the 8 million SHGs of the poor maintain a balance of over '6550 crore[1] in the Savings Bank accounts with the Banks, while they are estimated to have harnessed savings of over ₹ 22000 crore of which nearly 70 per cent (over ₹ 15000 crore) goes for internal lendings. Over 4.4 million SHGs are regularly availing credit facilities from the Banks. During 2011-12 alone, over 1.15 million Groups availed loans amounting to ₹ 16535 crore from Banks and together 4.4 million Groups have loans to the extent of '36340 crore outstanding against them with the financing banks as on 31.3.2012.

Micro Credit to Self-Help Groups in Andhra Pradesh Application Form

Sponsored by: State

Funding Pattern:

1. 50 per cent subsidy from Corporate.
2. 10 per cent Group Savings.
3. Remaining Bank Loan.

Owner: Andhra Pradesh Minorities Welfare Department, Andhra Pradesh

Description: To uplift Minority Women in urban and rural areas and to provide income generating activities for becoming self employable, the Andhra Pradesh State Minorities Finance Corporation has taken up the scheme of Micro Credit to Self-Help Groups.

Beneficiaries: women community

Benefit Type: Subsidy

Eligibility Criteria:

1. Minority women and must be a member in self-help group.
2. Self-help Groups having availed Revolving fund from District Rural Development Agency and Municipalities are also eligible after (6) months of availing of Revolving Fund.
3. Homogeneous (Minority) groups are eligible for availing Micro Credit from Andhra Pradesh State Minorities Finance Corporation.
4. Heterogeneous Groups (Mixed Groups) in which minorities and Scheduled Caste, Scheduled Tribe, Backward Class and Other Backward Classes are also eligible for Micro Credit.
5. Senior Self-Help Groups *i.e.* (2) years above groups who have not availed revolving fund from any Government Agency are also eligible for Micro Credit.
6. Self-help Groups who are having accounts in Mutually Aided Co-Operative Societies successfully operating are also eligible for Micro Credit loan subject to their operation in accordance to the Mutually Aided Co-operative Societies act.

How to Avail

The eligible Minority women of Self-help Groups should approach the Executive Director of Andhra Pradesh State Minorities Finance Corporation for financial assistance.

The Government of Andhra Pradesh has taken up the theme of women's empowerment as one of the strategies to tackle the socio-economic poverty. Self-Help movement through savings has been taken up as a mass movement by women a path chosen by them to shape their destiny for better. Development Agenda of the State in the last few years placing the people, especially women in the fore – front has enabled formation of a large number of Self-Help Groups (SHGs) throughout the State and majority of women are saving one rupee a day. The State government is consciously making an effort to assist SHGs by providing Revolving Fund/Matching grant under various programmes.

Fund/Matching Grant under Various Programmes

The state of Andhra Pradesh has been the focus of attention on the world map primarily due to its pro-active government and significant strides made by its SHGs. SHGs are playing an important role in optimization of natural and human resources through people's participation. The government of Andhra Pradesh has taken up Women's Empowerment as one of the main strategies to tackle socio-economic poverty. SHG movement through savings has been taken up as mass movement by women, a path chosen by them to shape their destiny for the better. Development agenda of the state in the last few years of placing the people especially women in the forefront has enabled the formation of large number of self-help groups throughout.

State where Women are Saving one Rupee per a day

Self-help groups (SHGs) gained prominence as informal institutions of women for poverty eradication and as an efficient delivery mechanism of the state aid, in Andhra Pradesh. In addition to DWCRA groups, NGOs, large scale poverty eradication programmes like: Velugu, APUSP and APRLP have been promoting SHGs and their federations in large numbers. The number of SHGs linked to banks for credit is increasing each year exponentially and the 'SHG-Bank linkage' demonstrated the potential to become a profitable business for banks.

SHGs have been initiated by NGOs in late 1980s in Andhra Pradesh. The women's savings and credit movement in Andhra Pradesh can be said to have really began in 1995, in Nellore district as 'Podupulakshmi' movement post anti-liquor campaign by women. This led to large-scale promotion of SHGs in every district of AP. The Podupulakshmi movement started with the slogan of 'save a rupee a day'.

Women from different social and economic levels are joining SHGs, including the poor, and some very poor. This process continues as the numbers grow. However, the barriers to entry for the poor are high – not only do they have lower incomes (by definition), but their incomes are usually more variable.

In this aspect, and in others too (accounting, decision-making, social action) it is likely that the poorer the women (or some of the women) in an SHG, the more careful and sustained promotion and guidance needs to be.

Improve transparency and record keeping: Record keeping at the group level has emerged as a very weak aspect of SHG functioning – with only marginal differences depending on who maintains the records. Complicated records and MIS seem to be part of the problem of poor book-keeping. Good book keeping is critical for the sustainability of financial operations and continued mutual trust among members. Good quality of book-keeping means completeness, accuracy, up-to-date information and transparency. There is a need for simple and user-friendly records and books of accounts, coupled with a similar MIS. This should be linked to monitoring – by SHPAs and Banks. Financial literacy and communication for SHGs also assumes importance (especially if SHG members move into running enterprises) and providing women with necessary knowledge in the initial years of SHG functioning would empower them better.

It does not seem necessary that SHGs (or their office bearers) have to maintain their accounts themselves. This can be a service to the group, as is being tried out through different forms of computerized account keeping – by Pardon (the computer monish), by Dhan kalanjiams and by MYRADA (in community resource centers). Their experience suggests that this may be a cost effective solution, in comparison with training and checking of records at group level. Other simple and user friendly ways of book keeping include the manual systems followed by IBTADA in Rajasthan, and a book-keeping system based on colour coding promoted by Ekgoan Technologies and Covenant Centre for Development.

Follow-up

SHPAs that have social objectives need to do more about them specifically and strategically: picking up problems, addressing them as they arise, using them as issues/examples for discussion with other groups – whether issues of social harmony, injustice or mobilizing for community development. SHPA support and guidance seems critical and mobilizing across groups seems most effective. Clustering of SHGs may have strong social potential, as in federations, though this builds in another level of capacity level and financing – still to be established as sustainable. There may be a question of time available for women. This did not come up as an issue in groups where such actions were taken, though we did notice that better-off women are more likely to be involved. There are also economic differences within the group, with some members better able to absorb credit than others.

REFERENCES

1. www.wekipedia journals
2. NABARD.
3. Www. Government of Andhra Pradesh

Pages 146-149

POVERTY ALLEVIATION THROUGH MICROFINANCE
Edited by : Dr. B. Ramachandra Reddy
Edition : 2017
ISBN : 978-93-5056-865-1
Published by : Discovery Publishing House Pvt. Ltd., New Delhi (India)

19

Microfinance in India
An Overview

Dr. S. Vijayulu Reddy[1]
Dr. B. Sakunthala[2]
Dr. M. Sriramulu[3]

INTRODUCTION

Microfinance sector has covered a long journey from micro savings to micro credit and then to micro enterprises and now entered the field of micro insurance, micro remittance, and evolutionary growth process has given a great boost to micro pension and micro livelihood. Financial institutions in India have been playing a leading role in the microfinance programme for nearly two decades. They have joined hands proactively with informal delivery channels to give microfinance sector the necessary momentum. Microfinance is the provision of financial services to low-income clients or solidarity lending groups including consumers and the self employed, who traditionally lack access to banking and related services. More broadly, it is a movement whose object is "a world in which as many poor and near poor households as possible have permanent access to an appropriate range of high quality financial services, including not just credit but also savings, insurance and fund transfers". Those who promote microfinance generally believe that such access will help poor people out of poverty.

1. Vice Principal and Reader in Commerce, Visvodaya Government Degree College, Venkatagiri. SPSR Nellore Dist. A.P.
2. Lecturer in Commerce, Government Degree College, Karvetinagaram, Chittoor Dt.
3. Lecturer in Commerce, Visvodaya Government Degree College, Venkatagiri.

The impact of microfinance programme especially through Self-Help Groups (SHGs) has been effective in making positive social change to all members, irrespective of the direct borrowers of the micro credit. Importantly, in the rural context, the SHGs have facilitated the poor to overcome the existing constraints grappling the formal credit institutions. Therefore, micro finance is a new method to meet the credit requirement in rural areas. It is being viewed as one of the most powerful tools for uplifting the economic conditions of the asset-less poor through group approach that ensures active participation and involvement of the beneficiaries in effective implementation of the programme.

Microfinance Approaches in India

Indian microfinance is dominated by two operational approaches *viz;* SHGs and Microfinance Institutions (MFIs) in addition to a few cooperative forms. The first approach is popularly known as SHG-Bank linkage model. This model is the dominant model, initiated by the NABARD through the SHG-Bank linkage programme in the early 1990s. Today the SHG model also links the informal groups of women to the mainstream system and it has the largest outreach to microfinancial clients in the world.

The second approach also called financing through MFIs, is the emerging model. This model emerged in the late 1990s to harness social and commercial funds available for open-lending to clients. These institutions assume the responsibility of making available much needed micro credit to the poor section of the society. Generally MFIs/NGOs take on the additional role of financial intermediaries. In areas where the formal banking system faces constraints, the NGO are encouraged to approach a suitable bank for bulk loan assistance.

Progress in Microfinance

Credit lines to SHGs are critically limited, as they are based on a certain multiple of SHG member's savings accounts within banks. While the cumulative savings of SHGs could serve as a low-cost source of funds for on-lending, their potential is limited by the lack of aggregated saving across SHGs. Commercial equity investments are not available for SHGs due to their informal status. Yet, there has been concerted effort both by the formal and informal sector institutions to reach out to the rural as well as urban poor masses with definite schemes of microfinance programme. Over the years there has been steady progress in the field of microfinance.

Although microfinance programmes have helped in widening the access of rural households to institutional credit, vast majority of the rural poor have still not been covered. Also, such lending done under the poverty alleviation schemes suffered high repayment defaults and left little sustainable impact on the economic condition of the beneficiaries.

Challenges Before Microfinance Sector in India

Despite the swelling numbers and the growth of microfinance credit portfolio, the SHG movement is suffering from so many deficiencies/lacunae like:

- Inadequate attention for the group formation process.
- Lack of homogeneity
- Irregular/virtually non-convening of group meetings.
- No concrete agenda for the meeting and arrears in writing proceedings/ meetings books.
- Near absence of capacity building and barring one or two members other are not aware of group affairs.
- Keeping savings in the bank and not rotating to get acquainted with fund management.
- Disbursements from banks are either equivalent to the deposits or slightly higher with no substantial gain by forming the groups and being in them.
- Equal distribution of loans which contravenes the basic norm of the needy gets the loan.
- Very poor bookkeeping resulting in bankers evading the groups.
- Problems related to MIS.
- Lack of transparency in Interest rates and other charges.
- Over Borrowing.
- Coercive methods of recovery.

Conclusion

Self-help micro credit schemes are often implemented as one of the most effective mechanisms to reach the poor, measures must be taken to ensure that the poor are not excluded. Participation of poor in formation, implementation and monitoring of the programmes affecting the poor is a necessity. The SHG-Bank linkage and financing through MFIs approaches is no doubt an effective instrument by which very poor people can access hassle free formal credit without any collateral security and simultaneously improve their thrift habits. But in order to make the approaches more useful means for poverty alleviation a sustainable rural development, there is a need for sincere intervention by the promotional agencies particularly the banks and block authorities in the areas of awareness building, skill development and training, etc., considering the number of clients, range of services and the increase involvement of both formal and informal sector institutions, there is tremendous scope for the sustaining of microfinance development in India.

REFERENCES

1. Microfinance Inclusion in India, *Banking Finance*, Kolkata, December 2011.
2. Micro Credit in Indonesia, *The Indian Banker*, Mumbai, May 2011.
3. Social Security for Women and Microfinance, Southern Economist, Bangalore, April 2013.

Pages 150-156

POVERTY ALLEVIATION THROUGH MICROFINANCE
Edited by : Dr. B. Ramachandra Reddy
Edition : 2017
ISBN : 978-93-5056-865-1
Published by : Discovery Publishing House Pvt. Ltd., New Delhi (India)

20 Rural Development Through Microfinance MGNREGA and Women Empowerment

D. Krupavathi[1]
Prof. P. Mohan Reddy[2]

INTRODUCTION

Rural development is an integral process of economic growth and social progress. It implies the development of rural sector which has many dimensions. The role of microfinance and women empowerment in this context is important because it provides an environment of sustainable improvement in the quality of life of rural women folk enabling them to form SHGs, and providing them equal opportunities in decision-making process and participation in community life. On the other, microfinance is a broad category of services which include micro credit and provision of financial services to the poor and low income groups who traditionally lack access to banking services. This paper discusses the concept and framework of microfinance. Microfinance and micro credit are used as synonyms. Absence of formal employment of the poor make them nonbank able as result of which banks seldom lend to low income families and women headed households. This forces them to borrow from local money lenders at a high rate of interest. Analyses of the role of microfinance in context of rural development. The access of the poor to bank services will break the vicious circle of poverty and removal of poverty is an effective instrument of rural development. Microfinance is community based. Poor people not

1. Ph.D. Research Schalor, Department of Commerce, S.V. University, Tirupati.
2. Chairman and BOS, Department of Commerce, S.V. University, Tirupati.

only need loans but also savings, insurance and money transfers. Community saving banks, SHGs is community based microfinance institutions which provide these services to the rural poor to undertake productive activities for rural development. Microfinance is one of the most effective poverty reducing strategies for rural development. It plays the vital role because subsidies from government are scarce and uncertain and microfinance can reach large number of poor and weaker sections and thereby promotes inclusive growth. It is different from charity which prevents cash flow. Once charity is given to a destitute family it does not come back again. But microfinance promotes cash flow by way of granting micro credit to the poor and weaker sections for self-employment and recovery of loans.

Objectives

MGNREGA, which is the largest work guarantee programme in the world, was enacted in 2015 with the primary objective of guaranteeing 200 days of wage employment per year to rural households. *Secondly*, it aims at addressing causes of chronic poverty through the 'works' (projects) that are undertaken and thus ensuring sustainable development. Finally, there is an emphasis on strengthening the process of decentralisation through giving a significant role to Panchayati Raj Institutions (PRIs) in planning and implementing these works.

Methodology

The main sources we used in secondary data documents provided by the Banks, with representatives of various institutions, organizations and journals.

Development of Microfinance

This is an age old practice. In ancient times money lenders were lending money to the poor and were charging high rate of interest. Modern microfinance developed in 1970s with a strong orientation towards private sector. It became popular in India after the institution of Grameen Bank by Md. Yunus in India. In recent times microfinance and micro credit are instruments of rural development. It is more. Popular in rural sector due to the financial needs of the poor. These needs of the poor include life cycle needs such as: weddings, funerals, childbirth, education, widowhood, old age, sickness, and injury etc. These needs are being met by commercial banks and non banking financial institutions, NGOs and village co-operatives in rural areas. Microfinance is no doubt a poverty alleviation and rural development strategy like: MGNREGA. Mahatma Gandhi National Rural

Employment Guarantee Act is landmark legislation for employment guarantee to the poor and weaker sections of our country. It is a special programme for livelihood support for the rural poor and vulnerable groups.

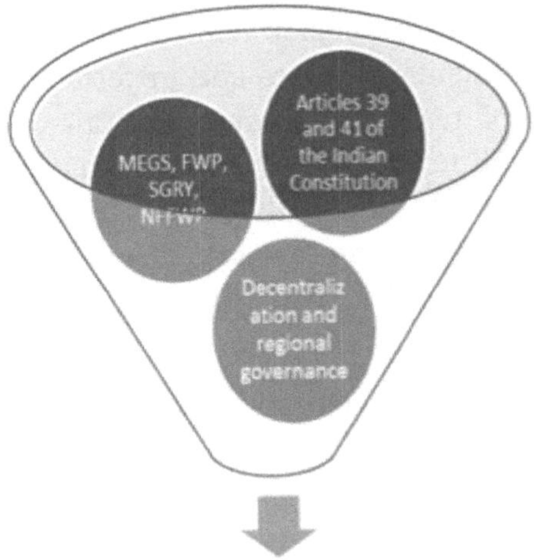

Enabling Environment
for the MGNREGA

In this paper there is a humble attempt to include MGNREGA and microfinance for the rural poor and weaker sections as two sides of rural development. MGNREGA is no doubt landmark legislation for employment guarantee to the poor for their sustenance and implementation of microfinance schemes for up lift men of weaker sections, SCs, STs and the vulnerable groups in rural sector of the district and state is the other side of rural development. MGNREGA with its right based framework was implemented first in 2014-15 in 200 districts of India is a paradigm shift from all development programmers that were traditionally supply led. It is a path breaking legislation that entitles guaranteed employment of 200 days to rural poor household as a means of sustenance. The implementation of this programme me is supported by central budget and based on demand for employment. Apart from providing livelihood to millions of households over the last five years (2010-15) the Act has played a significant role for the inclusion of marginalized and rural poor at the grass root level in its employment guarantee scheme to eradicate poverty, hunger and unemployment. MGNREGA as an endorsed employment programme and cash transfer to marginalized section of the society is a step forward for capacity building of rural poor and empowerment of women. Its provisions are par with millennium development goal of 'Eradication of Hunger and Poverty through employment generation'.

Table 20.1: Employment Generation Across the States under MGNREGA

Year	Employment Demanded by Households	Employment Provided to Households
2010-11	2,11,88,894.00	2, 10, 16,099 (99.19%)
2011-12	3,43,26,563.00	3, 39, 09,132 (98.79%)
2012-13	4,55,18,907.00	4, 51, 15,358 (99.99%)
2013-14	5,29,20,154.00	5, 25, 85,999 (99.37%)
2014-15	5,57,56,087.00	5, 49, 47,068 (98.54%)

Sources: www.nregs.nic.com in H.H. Households.

MGNREGA, Women Empowerment and Rural Development

Women empowerment is a social process that seeks to neutralize oppression of women and achieve equity in the society. It is a state without oppression of women, an environment of freedom, equity and respect for individual and a life with dignity. Realization of full identity of women folk is an important aspect of rural development. It is the expansion of assets and capabilities of women who constitute nearly half of our human resources, to participate and control the institutions that affect their life. The role of MGNREGA and microfinance in this context is important because it provides an environment of sustainable improvement in the quality of life of rural women folk for equal opportunity in decision making process and to participate in community life by forming SHGs and MFIs. In our society there is wide range of prejudices and social taboos and women have been neglected to the status of a second class citizen. The women as a class continue to be at the losing end. The role of MGNREGA and microfinance can reduce inequality and gender bias and it is a contributory factor for rural development.

The Employment Guarantee Act has contributed tremendously to women empowerment in Andhra Pradesh by providing them independent income earning opportunities to foster and expedite rural development. The act provides that out of the total employment provided. 30 per cent should be given to women workers. The priority for women in the ratio of one third of total workers. (Schedule – II (6) of the Act). The work is organized by women group. Equal wage to be paid to men and women workers (Schedule – II (34) of the Act). Crèches for the children of women workers (Schedule – II (28) of the Act). Besides these provisions of the Act, others include work within a radius of five kms. From the house, absence of supervisor and contractor and flexibility in choosing the period and month of employment. All these provisions have attracted rural women folk to the MGNREGA and women participation in work has increased significantly across the states. It is a true measure of rural development.

Table 20.2: Participation of Women under MGNREGA

Years	Total Man Days	Women	Percentage
2010-11	9050.54	3679.01	40.65
2011-12	14367.95	6109.1	42.63
2012-13	21632.86	10357.32	47.87
2013-14	28359.57	13640.51	48.16
2014-15	28359.57	13640.51	48.16

Sources: www.nregs.nic.co.in

Table 20.2 shows that participation of women in MGNREGA has increased from year to year. It is an employment generation and poverty alleviation scheme for rural development. There has been a significant dent in poverty in rural sector by increasing proper wage disbursement and increasing employment opportunities through the implementation of MGNREGA. It has increased significantly the socio-economic status of the weaker sections and particularly the rural women. The following Table 20.2 explains the employment opportunity created and poverty removed in rural household sector since the time of its implementation (2010-15) across the country.

Table 20.3: Household Employment Scenarios under MGNREGA

Year	Household Employed (in cores)
2010-11	2.10
2011-12	3.39
2012-13	4.51
2013-14	5.29
2014-15	5.49

Sources: www.nregs.nic.co.in.

Table 20.3 reveals that MGNREGA has played a positive role in increasing the employment in the country and it has contributed significantly to rural development by providing adequate employment to the rural households who are below the poverty line. Besides MGNREGA microfinance have also helped the weaker sections and rural women folk to cross the poverty line and stay put above the line. Both MGNREGA and microfinance have improved the quality of life of rural people, particularly life of rural women covering their health, education, literacy, social justice, formation of SHGs, MFIs and many others.

Conclusion

MGNREGA is the policy and programme commitment of our country to help the rural poor and weaker sections to achieve inclusive growth. Microfinance is a step forward and micro model towards eradication of poverty and rural development. Therefore, microfinance and implementation of provisions of MGNREGA are two sides of inclusive growth and rural development. The women participation in MGNREGA is increasing significantly and it is no doubt a positive aspect of women empowerment. Our society is gradually becoming women friendly. Microfinance and MGNREGA have played their vital role for the capacity building and skill up-gradation of rural women for inclusive growth both at the district and state level. Therefore MGNREGA and Microfinance is right based framework at the grass root level to generate income and employment for the rural poor and support and sustain rural development. MGNREGA is a special programme for livelihood support for the poor and vulnerable, aimed at directly increasing their income earning capabilities and at mainstreaming them in the overall inclusive growth process in order to reduce economic dualism and inequalities in socio-economic set up. MGNREGA, Microfinance and Women Empowerment seem to be a panacea in rural sector to reduce poverty and unemployment by redistributing income more equally in favour of the weaker sections and marginalized groups. Implementation of MGNREGA and Microfinance schemes have given rise to alertness among the rural poor and rural women on a continuous basis for their all round development to support a faster and sustainable growth of rural sector in our State.

REFERENCES

1. Ministry of Rural Development (2002). "Sampoorna Grameen Rozgar Yojana (SGRY) Guidelines" (PDF). "Ministry of Rural Development", Government of India. Retrieved 29 October 2013.
2. Ministry of Rural Development (2002). "Sampoorna Grameen Rozgar Yojana (SGRY) Guidelines" (PDF). "Ministry of Rural Development", Government of India. Retrieved 29 October 2013.

3. Ministry of Rural Development (2005). "Mahatma Gandhi National Rural Employment Guarantee Act (Mahatma Gandhi NREGA)" (PDF). "Ministry of Rural Development", Government of India. Retrieved 5 November 2013.

4. Ministry of Rural Development (2005). "The National Rural Employment Guarantee Act 2005 (NREGA) – Operational Guidelines" (PDF). "Ministry of Rur.

5. Saving people's livelihoodshttp://www.livemint.com/Opinion/hz2CLtVBL7q45SrIfg1BfL/Saving-peoples-livelihoods.html

6. Berg, E., Bhattacharyya, S., Durgam, R., and Ramachandra, M. (2012). Can Rural Public Works Affect Agricultural Wages? Evidence from India. CSAE Working Paper.

Pages 157-161

POVERTY ALLEVIATION THROUGH MICROFINANCE
***Edited by*: Dr. B. Ramachandra Reddy**
***Edition* : 2017**
ISBN : 978-93-5056-865-1
***Published by*: Discovery Publishing House Pvt. Ltd., New Delhi (India)**

21 The Role of Various Government Programmes in Promoting Microfinance

Dr. K. Saritha

INTRODUCTION

Micro credit has been promoted as a tool not only of women's economic empowerment, but also of social and political empowerment. An assumption of micro credit is that these programmes will significantly increase women's incomes, enable women to control that income and also enable them to negotiate improvements in their status within the household, it was also assumed that micro credit would give women access to support networks that enable them to advance their individual and collective interest at the local as well as macro level.

Microfinance

The concept of Micro credit was founded by Dr. Mohammad Yunnus and emerged in the developing world through the Grameena Bank in the country of Bangladesh in 1976. The bank was established with the practice of making small loans to the poor, pre-dominantly women to help them obtain economic self-sufficiency through micro enterprises. Micro enterprise programmes built on the unique ideas and skills of entrepreneurs would be encouraged by providing business assistance and small amounts of credit to support the development - up of a small business. Micro enterprise is proven way to earn extra income to supplement household income and it

Lecturer in Commerce, Sri Padmavathi Women's Degree and P.G. College, Tirupathi.

provides the opportunity for women to develop their talents and skills and use them to improve their financial well-being.

Self-Help Groups

Micro credit play a catalyst role in organsing women into Self-Help Groups. The empowerment of the rural through SHGs has reached a stage of irreversibility with increasing involvement of Government, Banks and NGOs. The concept made unprecedented progress in the lives of rural of the members in terms of self-confidence, involvement in decision-making processes, increased expression of their view points and participation for their own development. Saving as a habit has been the biggest asset of the programme which was other-wise incomprehensible earlier by the rural poor. Women in Self-Help Groups have been encouraged by the Government as well as Non-Government Organizations to undertake self-employment ventures with locally available raw material and other recources. Availability of micro credit helped SHG Women a lot and many women came forward and established micro enterprises.

District Poverty Initiatives Project (DPIP) which has a very good network in the district has taken the responsibility of formation of new groups and the maintance of books of accounts for all those SHGs. Since the banks are enthused by good repayment behaviour of SHGs, more and more funds are being committed by the banking sector. Many of these groups are beyond the stage of thrift and credit and given an opportunity they are eager to take up income-generating activities.

Microfinance Service Providers

- The microfinance service providers include apex institutions like: NABARD, SIDBI, Rashtriya Mahila Kosh (RMK).
- At the retail level, Commercial Banks, Regional Rural Banks and Co-operative Banks provide microfinance services.
- Today, there are about 60,000 retail credit outlets of the formal banking sector in the rural areas comprising 12,000 branches of district level co-operative banks, over 14,000 branches of the Regional Rural Banks and over 30,000 rural and semi-urban branches of commercial banks besides almost 90,000 co-operatives credit societies at the village level.
- On an average, there is at least one retail credit outlet for about 5,000 rural people.

- This physical reaching out to the far-flung areas of the country to provide savings, credit and other banking services to the rural society is an unparalleled achievement of the Indian banking system.

Government has been implementing various programmes which support specially women to take - up new ventures and start self-employment.

1. *Empowering Strategies*: Indira Mahila Yojana, Mahila Samriddhi Yojana, The Rural Women's Development and Empowerment Project, Development of Women and Children in Rural Areas.
2. *Employment and Income-generating*: Training of Rural Youth for Self-Employment, Swayamsidha, Swalamban, Support for Training and Employment Programme, Socio-economic Programme, Swarnjayanti Gram Swarozgar Yojna, Women's Vocational Training Programme, Jawahar Rozgar Yojna, Trade Related Entrepreneurship Assistance and Development, National Rural Health Mission.
3. *Welfare and Support Services*: Hostels for Working Women, Short Stay Homes, Swadhar, Creches, Day care centres for the children of working and ailing mothers.
4. *Other Enabling Measures*: Rashtriya Mahila Kosh, a national level mechanism to meet micro credit needs of poor and asset women in the informal sector. Also known as the National Credit Fund for women.

Role of Non-Government Organization (NGOs) in Rural Women Development

The major NGOs in Rural Women Development are:

1. Bihar Rural Livelihood Promotion Project (BRLP).
2. National Alliance of Young Entrepreneurs (NAYE).
3. World Assembly of Small and Medium Entrepreneurs (WASME).
4. Xavier Institute for Social Studies (XISS).
5. Self-Employment Women's Association (SEWA).
6. Association of Women Entrepreneurs of Karanataka (AWAKE).
7. Rural Development and Self-Employment Training Institute (RUDSETIs) based in Karnataka.

Various Women-Oriented Schemes of the State Governments

1. *Panchdhara Yojana*: Madhya Pradesh Government's Scheme was lunched on 1 November, 1991 for rural and tribal women which includes following five schemes.

(i) *Vatsalya Yojana* – For health care and facilities at the time of delivery of a child;

(ii) *Gramya Yojana* – For providing working capital to the rural women for small trade;

(iii) *Aayushmati Yojana* – Government subsidy is providing for medical treatment to the poorest women;

(iv) *Social Security Pension Scheme* – For orphan widows;

(v) *Kalapavraksha Scheme* – For providing employment to SC\ST women in tribal areas.

2. *Apni Beti Apna Dhan Yojana*: Haryana Government Scheme was launched on 2 October, 1994 under which an investment of Rs. 2500 is made by the Government in Indira Vikas Patra for newly born female child in SC\ST families which becomes Rs. 25000 after 18 years and given to the concerned girl.
3. *Kunwar Bainu Mamerum Scheme*: Gujarat Government Scheme was launched in 1995 in which as assistance of Rs. 5000 is provided to families having annual income of less than Rs. 7500 at the time of their daughter's marriage.
4. *Kamdhenu Yojana*: Maharashtra Government Scheme provides the financial opportunities of self-employment to the disabled, divorced women.
5. *Girl Child Protection Scheme*: Andhra Pradesh Government's Scheme aims at protecting the interest of girl child in the society.
6. The Government of India has been implementing various schemes and programmes for the welfare and empowerment of women in the areas of poverty alleviation, skill up-gradition, micro credit, development and sustainable income-generating, science and technology, education, health service, awareness generation, legal literacy and support services.

Conclusion

The main benefits of micro credit appear to be reduced vulnerability of the poor to adverse circumstances, increased consumption and empowerment of women. The major spin-off of the micro credit movement at the grassroot level has been the fact that women have used this system to come out and join the mainstream activity in the village. In many areas, particularly where there has been support from NGOs or strong SHGs, women have gained a voice and been able to use this space to come out of their traditional roles into a more 'proactive' male space. Women have been able to mobilize capital, and in the process have acquired skills that have enchanced their economic, social and political power. This positive growth has usually been where SHGs are linked with NGOs that have facilitated training and capacity-building with additional inputs and getting their talent useful to the society.

REFERENCES

1. Deepak Walokar, 'Women Entrepreneurs', Himalaya Publishing House, Nagpur.
2. Mahesh Chandra Prasad and Shandhu. P. Shah, "Management and Planning of Micro Credit for Rural Development in India" Published in the Indian Economic Association, Conference Volume 1.
3. Sandhya Rani. G., "Promoting Micro Entrepreneurship for Women's Development", *Southern Economist*, May 1 2006.
4. G. Paidi Raju, "Women Entrepreneurship In India", Problems And Prospects, 2012.
5. Internet: www.google.com.

Pages 162-172

POVERTY ALLEVIATION THROUGH MICROFINANCE
Edited by : Dr. B. Ramachandra Reddy
Edition : 2017
ISBN : 978-93-5056-865-1
Published by : Discovery Publishing House Pvt. Ltd., New Delhi (India)

22 Microfinance Institutions Delivery Models in India

Dr. Morusu Siva Sankar

Microfinance institutions (MFIs) are set to report buoyant growth over the medium term, having firmly put the Andhra Pradesh crisis behind them. Their loan assets are likely to reach Rs. 35, 000 crore by March 2015. Greater regulatory clarity, including: the recognition of the industry body MFIN as a self-regulatory organization by the Reserve Bank of India (RBI), and a stable operating environment have enhanced stake-holders' confidence in the sector. Consequently, there has been improvement in the flow of debt funding and equity capital to the sector, resulting in a 43 per cent growth in MFIs' loan assets during 2013-14 (refers to financial year, April 1 to March 31). Loans to poor people by banks have many limitations including lack of security and high operating costs. As a result, microfinance was developed as an alternative to provide loans to poor people with the goal of creating financial inclusion and equality. Muhammad Yunus, a Nobel Prize winner, introduced the concept of Microfinance in Bangladesh in the form of the 'Grameen Bank'. The National Bank for Agriculture and Rural Development (NABARD) took this idea and started the concept of microfinance in India. Under this mechanism, there exists a link between SHGs (Self-help groups), NGOs and banks. SHGs are formed and nurtured by NGOs and only after accomplishing a certain level of maturity in terms of their internal thrift and credit operations are they entitled to seek credit

Academic Consultant Department of Commerce, S.V. University, Tirupati.

from the banks. There is an involvement from the concerned NGO before and even after the SHG-Bank linkage. The SHG-Bank linkage programme, which has been in place since 1992 in India, has provided about 22.4 lakh for SHG finance by 2006. It involves commercial banks, regional rural banks (RRBs) and co-operative banks in its operations.

In developing economies and particularly in rural areas, many activities that would be classified in the developed world as financial are not monetized: that is, money is not used to carry them out. This is often the case when people need the services money can provide but do not have dispensable funds required for those services, forcing them to revert to other means of acquiring them. In their book. The Poor and Their Money, Stuart Rutherford and Sukhwinder Arora cite several types of needs:

- *Lifecycle Needs*: such as: weddings, funerals, childbirth, education, home building, widowhood and old age.
- *Personal Emergencies*: such as: sickness, injury, unemployment, theft, harassment or death.
- *Disasters*: such as: fires, floods, cyclones and man-made events like war or bulldozing of dwellings.
- *Investment Opportunities*: Expanding a business, buying land or equipment, improving housing, securing a job (which often requires paying a large bribe), etc.

People find creative and often collaborative ways to meet these needs, primarily through creating and exchanging different forms of non-cash value. Common substitutes for cash vary from country to country but typically include: livestock, grains, jewelry and precious metals. As Marguerite Robinson describes in The Microfinance Revolution, the 1980s demonstrated that "microfinance could provide large-scale outreach profitably," and in the 1990s, 'microfinance began to develop as an industry' (2001, p. 54). In the 2000s, the microfinance industry's objective is to satisfy the unmet demand on a much larger scale, and to play a role in reducing poverty. While much progress has been made in developing a viable, commercial microfinance sector in the last few decades, several issues remain that need to be addressed before the industry will be able to satisfy massive worldwide demand. The obstacles or challenges to building a sound commercial microfinance industry include:

- Inappropriate donor subsidies.
- Poor regulation and supervision of deposit-taking microfinance institutions (MFIs).
- Few MFIs that meet the needs for savings, remittances or insurance.
- Limited management capacity in MFIs.
- Institutional inefficiencies.
- Need for more dissemination and adoption of rural, agricultural microfinance methodologies.

Microfinance is the proper tool to reduce income inequality, allowing citizens from lower socio-economical classes to participate in the economy. Moreover, its involvement has shown to lead to a downward trend in income inequality.

In developing countries, financing to the rural poor through formal financial services failed to meet the credit requirements of the rural poor people. The main reason of failure was absence of any recognised employment and hence absence of collateral with the poor. The high risk and the high transaction costs of banks associated with small loans and savings deposits are other factors which make them non-bankable. The lack of loans from formal institutions leaves the poor with no other option but to borrow money from local money-lenders on huge interest rates. In different countries including India, efforts have been made by their governments to deliver formal credit to rural areas by setting up special agricultural banks/rural banks or directing commercial banks to provide loans to rural borrowers. However, these programmes have also not worked well due to various reasons. The common reasons found by many researchers are the political difficulty for governments to enforce loan repayment and the selection of relatively wealthy and influential people, rather than the poor, for bank loans (Adams *et al.* 1984; Adams and Vogel, 1986; World Bank, 1989). Women's World Banking (1995) estimated that in most developing countries, the formal financial system reaches to only top 25 per cent of the economically active population. This leaves the bottom 75 per cent without access to financial services apart from those provided by money-lenders and family. Thus, the inability of formal credit institutions to deal with the credit requirements of poor effectively has led to emergence of microfinance as an alternative credit system for the poor.

Microfinance scheme provides a wide range of financial services to people who have little or nothing in the way of traditional collateral. It helps them to build up assets, survive crises and to establish small business to come out of poverty. Except extending small loans (micro credit), microfinance programme provides various other financial and non-financial services such as: savings, insurance, guidance, skill development training, capacity building and motivation to start income-generating activities to enhance the productivity of credit. This innovative programme is reaching the poor people especially women and has an impact on their socio-economic development as well as their empowerment. This programme is becoming popular and emerging as a powerful instrument for poverty alleviation in many countries of Asia, Africa, Europe and America.

The concept of providing financial services to low income people is very old. Many informal credit groups have been operating in many countries for several years like: the *susus* in Nigeria and Ghana, *chit funds* and Rotating Savings and Credit Associations (ROSCAs) in India, *tontines* in West Africa, *pasanaku* in Bolivia, *hui* in China, *arisan* in Indonesia, *paluwagan* in Philippines etc. It is believed that initially, the informal financial institutions emerged in Nigeria dating back in the fifteenth century. Such type of institutions started establishing in Europe during the eighteenth century when in 1720 the first loan fund targeting poor people was founded in Ireland (Seibel, 2005).

In 1847, some credit co-operatives were created in Germany which served 1.4 million people by 1910. In 1880s the British controlled government of Madras in South India tried to use the German experiment to address poverty in India. This effort resulted in membership of more than nine million poor to credit co-operatives by 1946. During the same time the Dutch colonial administrators constructed a co-operative rural banking system in Indonesia which eventually became Bank Rakyat Indonesia (BRI), now one of the largest Microfinance Institutions (MFIs) of the world (Schwiecker, 2004).

In the 1970s, a paradigm shift started to take place. The failure of subsidised government or donor driven institutions to meet the demand for financial services in developing countries led to several new approaches. Bank Dagan Bali (BDB), established in Indonesia in 1970, was the earliest bank to institute commercial microfinance (Schwiecker, 2004). In 1973, ACCION International, a USA based NGO, disbursed its first loan in

Brazil at commercial interest rate to start a micro enterprise. One year later in 1974, the Self-Employed Women's Association of India (SEWA) started a bank to provide loans to poor women. In 1976, Muhammad Yunus, a professor of Economics at Chittagong University, Bangladesh initiated an experimental research project of providing credit to the rural poor. He gave a small loan of 856 Taka ($27) from his pocket to 42 poor bamboo weavers and found that small loans radically changed the lives of these people and they were able to pay back the loans with interest. The success of this idea led Yunus to establish Grameen Bank in 1983 in Bangladesh. This programme showed astonishing growth rates in Bangladesh, particularly during the 1980s and 1990s. It encouraged social innovators and organizations all over the world to begin experiments with different microfinance delivery methods to bring financial services to the poor. It is now adopted worldwide in the countries of different continents.

Many international NGOs, such as: Foundation for International Community Assistance (FINCA), Americans for Community Cooperation in Other Nations (ACCION), Freedom from Hunger, Opportunity International, Co-operative for Assistance and Relief Everywhere (CARE), Consultative Group for Assisting the Poor (CGAP), etc., are promoting microfinance programme for creating new businesses and combating poverty in a sustainable way. Over the past few decades, microfinance has been experimented in many developing countries. Bank Rakyat Indonesia (BRI) in Indonesia, Bancosol in Bolivia, Bank for Agriculture and Agricultural Co-operatives (BAAC) in Thailand, Grameen Bank, and Bangladesh Rural Advancement Committee (BRAC) of Bangladesh, NABARD in India, Amannah Ikhtiar Malaysia (AIM) of Malaysia, Agriculture Development Bank of Nepal (ADBN), K-Rep in Kenya and Mibanco in Peru have yielded encouraging results in alleviating poverty and empowering the poor through microfinance.

In India, the first initiative to introduce microfinance was the establishment of Self-Employed Women's Association (SEWA) in Gujarat. SEWA was registered as a trade union of self-employed women workers of the unorganised sector in 1972. This trade union established their bank known as SEWA Bank in 1974. To establish this bank four thousand union members contributed Rs. 10 each as share capital. Since then this bank is registered as a co-operative bank and has been providing banking services to poor women and has also become a viable financial venture.

Meaning and Function of Microfinance

The Asian Development Bank (2000) defines microfinance as the provision of broad range of services such as: savings, deposits, loans, payment services, money transfers and insurance to poor and low income households and their micro enterprises. This definition of microfinance is not restricted to the below poverty line people but it includes low income households also.

The Microfinancial Sector (Development and Regulation) Bill, (2007) defines microfinance as the provision of financial assistance and insurance services to an individual or an eligible client either directly or through a group mechanism for an amount, not exceeding rupees fifty thousand in aggregate per individual for small and tiny enterprise, agriculture, allied activities (including for consumption purposes of such individual); or an amount not exceeding rupees one lakh fifty thousand in aggregate per individual for housing or other prescribed purposes. The eligible clients which may get financial assistance under this scheme may be landless labourers and migrant labourers; artisans and micro entrepreneurs; disadvantaged cultivators of agricultural land including: oral lessees, tenants, and share croppers; and farmers owning not more than two hectares of agricultural land.

Delivery Models of Microfinance

The concept of microfinance involves informal and flexible approach to the credit needs of the poor. There is no single approach or model that fits in all the circumstances.

Therefore, a number of microfinance models emerged in different countries/states according to the suitability to their local conditions. Broadly, the microfinance delivery methods can be classified into six groups as follows:

Grameen Bank Model

Grameen Bank model is one of the oldest and most successful models of microfinance. This model was developed in Bangladesh. In this model microfinance programme participants are organized into groups of five members. They make mandatory contribution to group savings and insurance fund. Each member maintains her individual saving and loan account with the bank and after contributing to the savings fund for a fixed time the group members receive individual loans from the bank. But the group is not required to give any guarantee for the loan repayment by its member. Repayment responsibility solely rests on the individual borrower and there is no form of joint liability, *i.e.,* group members are not responsible to pay on behalf of a defaulting member. Loans are provided for six months to one year duration but repayments are made weekly. Bank staff make periodic visits to the groups, maintain individual records of group members and facilitate all the financial transactions. This creates ease in working but hindrance in the empowerment of members.

The members remain dependent on field officers regarding their all group related activities. Grameen model has been replicated in more than 40 countries in Asia, Africa, and Latin America with modifications to suit local conditions and cultures. The programme of BancoSol in Bolivia and most of the solidarity groups in Latin America follow this methodology. Many MFIs in India have also replicated this model.

Joint Liability Group Model

In this model, 4 to 10 individuals are organised in a group known as a Joint Liability Group (JLG). The group members can avail bank loans against mutual guarantee and there is no condition of their own saving fund. All members sign a joint liability contract, making each one jointly liable for repayment of all loans taken by all individuals in the group. Thus, only social collateral is provided to the lending institution. The JLGs are intended primarily to be credit groups and regular savings by the JLG members are not mandatory. The group exists only because its individual members are legally bound to one another. In this model, the progress of empowerment of group members remains very limited. In India these type of groups are generally made by most of the MFIs because such groups are easy to make as there are very less restrictions regarding the utilization of loan. NABARD is using this model for providing credit to the tenant farmers, cultivating land either as oral lessees or share croppers, and small farmers who do not have proper title of their land holding. Many other countries are also using this model. There were segments within the poor, such as: share croppers/oral lessees/tenant farmers, who were left out and whose loan requirements were much larger but who had no collaterals to fit into the traditional financing approaches of the banking system. To service such clients, Joint Liability Groups (JLGs), an up gradation of SHG model could be an effective way.

Individual Lending Model

In this method, individuals can get loans without any membership of a group. This is a straight forward credit lending model in which micro loans are given directly to the borrowers. In this model, the financial institutions have to make frequent and close contact with individual clients to provide credit products customised to the specific needs of the individual. It is most successful for larger, urban-based, production-oriented businesses. The model is followed by many financial institutions like the Association for the Development of Micro Enterprises (ADEMI) in Dominican Republic, Bank Rakyat Indonesia, Senegal Egypt, Self-Employment Women's Association in India, etc.

The Group Approach

The group approach delegates the entire financial process to the group rather than to the financial institutions. All financial activities like: savings, getting loans, repayment of loans and record keeping are managed at the group level. In this method, 10-20 members are organized to form a group. These group members make regular savings of fixed amount in a common fund. The amount and frequency of savings is mutually decided by the group members. After the successful working of such a group for some months the group is linked to a financial institution for getting credit. The financial institutions issue loan in the name of group and whole group is considered responsible for repayment. The amount of loan depends upon the total accumulated amount of saving of the group. Group members themselves decide about the criteria of dividing the loan among the group members. With this loan the whole group may jointly start a micro enterprise or the members may start their individual businesses. An individual may also use his loan for consumptive purpose or meeting other priority needs. The peer pressure in the group helps the timely repayment of loan. These type of group based credit delivery methods help to empower the group members because they remaininvolved in various group activities. They visit the bank, market and hold group meetings which help them to increase self-confidence. In India, the group based credit delivery method known as SHG-BLP is a predominant method of providing microfinance. Programme Hubungan Bank Danksm (PHBK) project in Indonesia and the Chikola groups of K-REP in Kenya are also using such group based credit delivery models.

Village Banking Model

This village banking model is an expansion of the group approach. This model was developed in Bolivia during the mid 1980s by the Foundation for International Community Assistance (FINCA), a non-profit microfinance organization. In this model, a Village Bank is developed by grouping 30 to 100 low-income individuals who seek to improve their lives through self-employment activities. The bank is financed by internal mobilisation of members' saving fund as well as loans provided by the sponsoring MFIs. The MFIs lend capital to the bank, which then lends the money to its members. Members themselves run the village bank, they choose their members, elect their own officers, establish their own by-laws, distribute loans to individuals and collect savings and payments. Loan amounts are linked to the aggregate amount saved by individual bank members. Loans are repaid weekly in small installments. Thus, village banks have a high degree of democratic control and independence. The model is used by various MFIs like Co-operative for Assistance and Relief Everywhere (CARE) in Guatemala; Save the Children in El Salvador; Burkina Faso in Bolivia, Mali, and Ghana; Freedom from Hunger and Catholic Relief Services in Thailand and Benin, Opportunity International, Consultative Group for Assisting the Poor (CGAP), etc.

Credit Unions and Co-operatives

A credit union is a democratic, not-for-profit financial co-operative. It is owned and governed by its members, who are at the same time the owners and the customers of their co-operative society. Co-operatives are often created by persons belonging to the same local or professional community or sharing a common interest. Co-operatives generally provide their members with a wide range of banking and financial services. Members participate in all the major decisions and democratically elect officers from among themselves to monitor the administration of the co-operative. Loans are granted only to the members. SANASA Development Bank of Sri Lanka is an example of rural credit co-operative which is successfully working as a microfinance service provider.

Institutional Arrangement and Disbursement of Microfinance in India

In India, there is a wide variety of institutions in public as well as private sector which provide microfinance to the poor. These institutions can be broadly divided into two types. First type is the traditional formal financial institutions, while the second type is Microfinance Institutions

(MFIs). The traditional financial institutions comprise of commercial banks, regional rural banks and co-operative banks. They provide microfinance services in addition to their general banking activities and are referred to as microfinance service providers. On the other hand MFIs are different types of financial institutions whose main financial activity is providing microfinance only. Many of these institutions are NGOs, Mutually Aided Co-operative Societies (MACS) and Non-Banking Financial Companies (NBFCs). In case of traditional financial institutions both private and public ownership are found but the MFIs are mainly in the private sector.

These financial institutions use a hierarchical network starting from the apex wholesale level to the retail level financial institutes. The retail level banks and MFIs borrow funds from apex financial institutions and use their branch network to provide microfinance at the doorstep of poor people. Some of these apex and retail level financial institutions have been discussed below:

Apex Financial Institutions

The formal microfinance service providers include a number of apex financial institutions. Some of them are like: National Bank for Agriculture and Rural Development (NABARD), Small Industries Development Bank of India (SIDBI), Rashtriya Mahila Kosh (RMK), Friends of Women World Banking (FWWB), Housing Development Finance Corporation (HDFC), Housing and Urban Development Corporation Limited (HUDCO), and Rashtriya Gramin Vikas Nidhi (RGVN). They provide bulk amount of funds to retail level banks and MFIs for on-lending to the poor. There are different terms and conditions associated with each apex financial institute. The features of some of these institutions have been highlighted. In addition to these apex financial institutions, many MFIs get funds from investors, lenders and donors also.

Retail Level Banks

At the retail level Commercial Banks, Regional Rural Banks, Co-operative Banks, and different types of MFIs provide microfinance services. In India, there are about 60,000 retail credit outlets of the formal banking sector in the rural area.

REFERENCES

1. Microfinance Self-Help Groups in India Dr. C. Venkateswarlu; Dr. Morusu Siva Sankar; Dr. B. Vijayalakshmi Asian Academic Research Journal of Social Sciences and Humanities Year 2013.
2. Anadal. N., Women and Indian Society, Rawat Publications, Jaipur and New Delhi, 2002.
3. Narasimhan, Sakuntala, Empowering Women Alternative Strategy from Rural India, Sage Publications India Pvt. Ltd., New Delhi, 1999.
4. I Puhazhendhi, V. Evaluation Study of Self-Help Groups in Tarnil Nadu, National Bank for Agriculture and Rural Development, Mumbai, 2000.
5. www.wikipedia.com

Pages 173-181

POVERTY ALLEVIATION THROUGH MICROFINANCE
Edited by : Dr. B. Ramachandra Reddy
Edition : 2017
ISBN : 978-93-5056-865-1
Published by : Discovery Publishing House Pvt. Ltd., New Delhi (India)

23 Role of Microfinance Institutions in Rural Development in India

Dr. A. Seshadri[1]
Dr. G. Manjula[2]

Poverty is the main cause of concern in improving the economic status of developing countries. A microfinance institution is an organization that offers financial services to low income populations. Almost all give loans to their members, and many offer insurance, deposit and other services. A great scale of organizations is regarded as microfinance institutes. They are those that offer credits and other financial services to the representatives of poor strata of population. Microfinance is increasingly being considered as one of the most effective tools of reducing poverty. Microfinance has a significant role in bridging the gap between the formal financial institutions and the rural poor. World to enhance credit to poor even in the absence of formal mortgage. The present paper discusses conceptual framework of a microfinance institution in India the successes and failure of various microfinance institutions around the world have been evaluated and lessons learnt have been incorporated in a model microfinance institutional mechanism for India. More than subsidies poor need assess to credit. Absence of formal employment make them non 'bankable'. This forces them to borrow from local money-lenders at exorbitant interest rates.

Microfinance and Poverty Alleviation

Most poor people manage to mobilize resources to develop their enterprises and their dwellings slowly over time. Financial services could

1. Lecturer in Economics, SGS Arts College, Tirupati. E-mail: dr.a.seshadri @gmail.com

2. Lecturer in Commerce, SGS Arts College, Tirupati.

enable the poor to leverage their initiative, accelerating the process of building incomes, assets and economic security. However, conventional finance institutions seldom lend down-market to serve the needs of low-income families and women-headed households. They are very often denied access to credit for any purpose, making the discussion of the level of interest rate and other terms of finance irrelevant. Therefore the fundamental problem is not so much of unaffordable terms of loan as the lack of access to credit itself.

The lack of access to credit for the poor is attributable to practical difficulties arising from the discrepancy between the mode of operation followed by financial institutions and the economic characteristics and financing needs of low income households. For example, commercial lending institutions require that borrowers have a stable source of income out of which principal and interest can be paid back according to the agreed terms. However, the income of many self-employed households is not stable, regardless of its size. A large number of small loans are needed to serve the poor, but lenders prefer dealing with large loans in small numbers to minimize administration costs. They also look for collateral with a clear title - which many low-income households do not have. In addition bankers tend to consider low income households a bad risk imposing exceedingly high information monitoring costs on operation.

Microfinance institutions could also serve as intermediaries between borrowers and the formal financial sector and on-lend funds backed by a public sector guarantee (Phelps 1995). Business like NGOs can offer commercial banks ways of funding micro entrepreneurs at low cost and risk, for example, through leveraged bank-NGO-client credit lines. Under this arrangement, banks make one bulk loan to NGOs and the NGOs packages it into large number of small loans at market rates and recover them (Women's World Banking 1994). There are many on-going research on this line but context specific research is needed to identify the most appropriate model. With this in mind we discuss various possible alternatives of formal-informal sector linkages in India.

In this context, following strategic, institutional and connectivity issues related to microfinance arise.

Strategic Issues

- Is there a prevailing paradigm for microfinance?
- Are there clearly visible pattern across the country?

- Is there a clearly defined foundation building blocks such as: organizing principles, gender preferences and operational imperatives?
- What are methodological issues?

Institutional Issues

- Is there a need for a new institution?
- Should it operate all India or in a state?
- Where should it be located?
- Who can lead an institution of this sort?
- What will its contextual interconnections be?
- Who will be its beneficiaries?

Connectivity Issues

- How should the Corporate Financial Sector be involved?
- What is the role of donor agencies?
- How should communities be involved?
- Are there political issues that should be explicitly considered?
- Are there government policy issues?

The Formal Sector Institutions

Traditionally, the formal sector Banking Institutions in India have been serving only the needs of the commercial sector and providing loans for middle and upper income groups. Similarly, for housing the HFIs have generally not evolved a lending product to serve the needs of the Very LIG primarily because of the perceived risks of lending to this sector. Following risks are generally perceived by the formal sector financial institutions:

- Credit risk.
- High transaction and service cost.
- Absence of land tenure for financing housing.
- Irregular flow of income due to seasonality.
- Lack of tangible proof for assessment of income.
- Unacceptable collaterals such as: crops, utensils and jewellery.

The Government has taken several initiatives to strengthen the institutional rural credit system. The rural branch network of commercial banks have been expanded and certain policy prescriptions imposed in order to ensure greater flow of credit to agriculture and other preferred sectors. The commercial banks are required to ensure that 40 per cent of total credit is provided to the priority sectors out of which 18 per cent in the form of direct finance to agriculture and 25 per cent to priority sector in favour of weaker sections besides maintaining a credit deposit ratio of 60 per cent in rural and semi-urban branches. Further the IRDP introduced in 1979 ensures supply of credit and subsidies to weaker section beneficiaries. Although these measures have helped in widening the access of rural households to institutional credit, vast majority of the rural poor have still not been covered. Also, such lending done under the poverty alleviation schemes suffered high repayment defaults and left little sustainable impact on the economic condition of the beneficiaries.

The Existing Informal Financial Sources

The informal financial sources generally include funds available from family sources or local money lenders. The local money-lenders charge exorbitant rates, generally ranging from 36 per cent to 60 per cent interest due to their monopoly in the absence of any other source of credit for non-conventional needs. Chit Funds and Bishis are other forms of credit system operated by groups of people for their mutual benefit which however have their own limitations.

Lately, few of the NGOs engaged in activities related to community mobilization for their socio-economic development have initiated savings and credit programmes for their target groups. These Community based financial systems (CBFS) can broadly be categorized into two models: Group Based Financial Intermediary and the NGO Linked Financial Intermediary.

Most of the NGOs like: Sharan in Delhi, Federation of Thrift and Credit Association (FTCA) in Hyderabad or SPARC in Bombay have adopted the first model where they initiate the groups and provide the necessary management support. Others like SEWA in Ahmedabad or Baroda Citizen's Council in Baroda pertain to the second model.

The Wholesalers will include agencies like: NABARD, Rashtriya Mahila Kosh-New Delhi and the Friends of Women's World Banking in Ahmedabad. Few of the NGOs supporting SHG Federations include MYRADA in Bangalore, SEWA in Ahmedabad, PRADAN in Tamilnadu and Bihar, ADITHI in Patna, SPARC in Mumbai, ASSEFA in Madras etc. While few of the NGOs directly retailing credit to Borrowers are SHARE in Hyderabad, ASA in Trichy, RDO Loyalam Bank in Manipur.

Strengths of Informal Sector

A synthesis that can be evolved out of the success of NGOs/CBOs engaged in microfinance is based on certain preconditions, institutional and facilitating factors.

(a) *Preconditions to Success*

Those NGOs/CBOs have been successful that have istilled financial value/discipline through savings and have demonstrated a matching value themselves before lending. A recovery system based on social intermediation and various options including non-financial mechanisms has proved to be effective. Another important feature has been the community governance. The communities in which households are direct stake holders have successfully demonstrated the success of programmes. A precondition for success is to involve community directly in the programme. Experience indicates that savings and credit are both critical for success and savings should precede credit. Chances of success more with women: Programmes designed with women are more successful.

(b) *Operating Indicators*

The operating indicators show that programmes which are designed taking into account the localized and geographical differences have been successful. Effective and responsive accounting and monitoring mechanisms have been an important and critical ingradient for the success of programmes. The operational success has been more when interest rates are at or near market rates. The experience of NGOs/CBOs indicates that low income households are willing to pay market rates. The crucial problem is not the interest rates but access to finance. Eventually in absence of such programmes households end up paying much higher rates when borrowing from informal markets. Some NGOs have experimented where members of community decide on interest rates. This is slightly different from Thailand experience where community decides on repayment terms and loan amount. A combination of the three *i.e.,* interest rates, amount and repayment period if decided by community, the programme is most likely to succeed. A programme which is able to leverage maximum funds from formal market has been successful. Experience indicates that it is possible to leverage higher funds against deposits.

The spreads should be available to meet operational costs of NGOs. Most of the directed credit programme in India like Kfw have a ceiling on the maximum interest rate and the spread available to NGOs. A flexible rate of interest scheme would indicate a wider spread for NGOs. Selected non-financial services, *viz;* business, marketing support services enhance success. Appropriate incentives for borrowing and proper graduation of credit has been essential component of success. A successful programme can not be generalized for all needs and geographical spread. The programmes which are simple and replicable in similar contexts have contributed to success.

Betterment in quality of life through better housing or better economic opportunities is a tangible indicator of success. The programmes which have been able to demonstrate on some measurable scale that the quality of life has improved have been successful. To be successful the programme productivity with outreach should match. The credit mechanism should be flexible meeting multiple credit needs. The programmes which have taken care of other needs such as: consumption, marriage etc., besides the main shelter, infrastructure or economic needs are successful.

Weaknesses of Existing Microfinance Models

One of the most successful models discussed around the world is the Grameen type. The bank has successfully served the rural poor in Bangladesh with no physical collateral relying on group responsibility to replace the collateral requirements. This model, however, has some weaknessed. It involves too much of external subsidy which is not replicable Grameen bank has not oriented itself towards mobilising peoples' resources. The repayment system of 50 weekly equal instalments is not practical because poor do not have a stable job and have to migrate to other places for jobs. If the communities are agrarian during lean seasons it becomes impossible for them to repay the loan. Pressure for high repayment drives members to money-lenders. Credit alone cannot alleviate poverty and the Grameen model is based only on credit. Microfinance is time taking process. Haste can lead to wrong selection of activities and beneficiaries.

Another model is Kerala model (Shreyas). The rules make it difficult to give adequate credit (only 40-50 per cent of amount available for lending). In Nari Nidhi/Pradan system perhaps not reaching the very poor.

Most of the existing microfinance institutions are facing problems regarding skilled labour which is not available for local level accounting. Drop out of trained staff is very high. One alternative is automation which is not looked at as yet. Most of the models do not lend for agriculture. Agriculture lending has not been experimented.

- Risk Management yield risk and price risk.
- Insurance and Commodity Future Exchange could be explored.

All the models lack in appropriate legal and financial structure. There is a need to have a sub-group to brainstorm on statutory structure/ ownership control/management/taxation aspects/financial sector prudential norms. A forum/network of microfinancier (self-regulating organization) is desired.

A New Paradigm

A new paradigm that emerges is that it is very critical to link poor to formal financial system, whatever the mechanism may be, if the goal of poverty allieviation has to be achieved. NGOs and CBOs have been involved in community development for long and the experience shows that they have been able to improve the quality of life of poor, if this is an indicator of development. The strengths and weaknesses of existing NGOs/CBOs and microfinance institutions in India indicate that despite their best of efforts they have not been able to link themselves with formal systems. It is desired that an intermediary institution is required between formal financial markets and grassroot. The intermediary should encompass the strengths of both formal financial systems and NGOs and CBOs and should be flexible to the needs of end users. There are, however, certain unresolved dilemmas regarding the nature of the intermediary institutions. There are arguments both for and against each structure. These dilemmas are very contextual and only strengthen the argument that no unique model is applicable for all situations. They have to be context specific.

Dilemmas

Community Based	Investor Owned
Community Managed	Professionally managed
Community (self) financed	Accepting outside funds for on-lending
Integrated (social and finance)	Minimalist (finance only)
Non profit/mutual benefit	For profit
Only for poor	For all under served clients
Self-regulated	Externally regulated

The four pillars of microfinance credit system are supply, demand for finance, intermediation and regulation. Whatever may the model of the intermediary institution, the end situation is accessibility of finance to poor. The following tables indicate the existing and desired situation for each component.

Demand

Existing Situation	Desired Situation
Fragmented	Professionally managed
Community Managed	Organized
Undifferentiated	Differentiated (for consumption, housing)
Addicted, corrupted by capital and subsidies	Dedicated from capital and subsides
Communities not aware of rights and responsibilities	Aware of rights and responsibilities

Supply

Existing Situation	Desired Situation
Grant based (Foreign/GOI)	Regular fund sources (borrowings/ deposits)
Directed Credit – unwilling and corrupt	Demand responsive
Not linked with mainstream	Part of mainstream (banks/FIs)
Mainly focused for credit	Add savings and insurance
Dominated	Reduce dominance of informal, unregulated suppliers

Intermediation

Existing Situation	Desired Situation
Non specialized	Specialized in financial services
Not oriented to financial analysis	Thorough in financial analysis
Non profit capital	For profit
Not linked to mainstream FIs	Link up to FIs
Not organized	Self-regulating

Regulation

Existing Situation	Desired Situation
Focused on formal service providers (informal not regulated)	Include/informal recognize *e.g.*, SHGs
Regulating the wrong things *e.g.*, interest rates	Regulate rules of game
Multiple and conflicting (FCRA, RBI, IT, ROC, MOF/FIPB, ROS/Commerce)	Coherence and coordination across regulators
Negatively oriented	Enabling environment

Conclusion

Some valuable lessons can be drawn from the experience of successful Microfinance operation. First of all, the poor repay their loans and are willing to pay for higher interest rates than commercial banks provided that access to credit is provided. The solidarity group pressure and sequential lending provide strong repayment motivation and produce extremely low default rates. *Secondly*, the poor save and hence microfinance should provide both savings and loan facilities. These two findings imply that banking on the poor can be a profitable business. However, attaining financial viability and sustainability is the major institutional challenge. Deposit mobilization is the major means for microfinance institutions to expand outreach by leveraging equity (Sacay *et al*. 1996). In order to be sustainable, microfinance lending should be grounded on market principles because large scale lending cannot be accomplished through subsidies.

Eventually it would be ideal to enhance the creditworthiness of the poor and to make them more 'bankable' to financial institutions and enable them to qualify for long-term credit from the formal sector. Microfinance institutions have a lot to contribute to this by building financial discipline and educating borrowers about repayment requirements.

REFERENCES

1. Barry, N. (1995). "The Missing Links: Financial System that Works for the Majority," Women's World Banking, New York.
2. Kim Kyung-Hwan (1995). "Access to Credit, Term of Housing Finance and Affordability of Housing," Housing Finance International, 9(4), June 22-27.
3. Otero, M. and Rhyne, E, (1994). "The New World of Micro Enterprise Finance-Building Healthy Financial Institutions for the Poor", Kumarian Press, West Harford, Connecticut.
4. UNCHS and ILO (1995). Shelter Provision and Employment Generation, Geneva.
5. Spooner, Lysander (1846). "Poverty: Its Illegal Causes and Legal Cure." Boston. Retrieved 30 January 2012.

Pages 182-193

POVERTY ALLEVIATION THROUGH MICROFINANCE
Edited by : Dr. B. Ramachandra Reddy
Edition : 2017
ISBN : 978-93-5056-865-1
Published by : Discovery Publishing House Pvt. Ltd., New Delhi (India)

24 Micro Insurance Delivery Models in India
An Overview

Dr. K. Nirmal Kumar Reddy

INTRODUCTION

The concept of insurance dates back to around 3000 BC in China where merchants and their investors shared the risks of goods lost when shipping overseas. A similar concept evolved in Babylon; the Greeks and Romans introduced the origins of health and life insurance around 600 BC when they created benevolent societies which cared for the families of deceased members. England's first fire insurance company was launched following the Great fire of London in 1666. At the same time, Mr. Edward Lloyd opened a coffee house that was a popular haunt for those in the maritime industry and became a meeting place for those wishing to insure ships and cargoes. Thus Lloyd's of London was established. At the end of the 17th century, the first mortality table was created, which marked the first step in the development of modern life insurance.

Defining Micro Insurance

The draft paper prepared by the Consultative Group to Assist the Poor (CGAP) working group on micro insurance defines micro insurance as "the protection of low income households against specific perils in exchange for premium payments proportionate to the likelihood and cost of the risk involved." The paper deliberates on the key roles to be played by all stakeholders – insurers, regulator and the Government. The working group also agrees that the cost of such cover should be affordable.

Associate Professor, Sir Vishveshwaraiah Institute of Science and Technology, Madanapalle.

Micro Insurance

The term micro insurance first appeared as a new financial service within micro finance. Micro insurance typically refers to insurance services offered to low income people in order to protect them against specific risk. It is a means of protection against specific risks in exchange for a regular payment of premium. The amount of premium payable is proportional to the likelihood and cost of the relevant risks. The term micro insurance was first published around 1999. It can be defined as a risk transfer device characterized by low premiums and low coverage limits, and designed for low income people not served by typical social insurance schemes.

Need For Micro Insurance – Risks faced by the Poor

Micro insurance is a key element in the financial services package for people at the bottom of the pyramid. The poor face more risks than the well-off, but more importantly they are more vulnerable to the same risk. Usually, the poor face two types of risks – idiosyncratic (specific to the household) and covariate (common, *e.g.*, drought, epidemic, etc.). To combat these risks, the poor do pro-active risk management – grain storage, savings, asset accumulation (specially bullocks), loans from friends and relatives, etc. However, the prevalent forms of risk management (in kind savings, self-insurance, mutual insurance) which were appropriate earlier are no longer adequate.

Poverty is not just a state of deprivation but has latent vulnerability. Micro insurance should, therefore, provide greater economic and psychological security to the poor as it reduces exposure to multiple risks and cushions the impact of a disaster. There is an overwhelming demand for social protection among the poor. Micro insurance in conjunction with micro savings and micro credit could, therefore, go a long way in keeping this segment away from the poverty trap and would truly be an integral component of financial inclusion.

Objectives of the Study

1. To study about the contribution of Life Insurance Corporation in micro insurance sector.
2. To identify major players in micro insurance sector.
3. To identify various micro insurance products.
4. To understand micro insurance delivery models.
5. To make an analysis about micro insurance products offered by LIC as a micro insurance player.

Major Players in Micro Insurance

There are 23 life insurance companies are present in India but only 14 companies are providing micro insurance products this clearly give an idea of low attraction of majority of companies towards these products. Below is the list of micro insurance products along with the name of companies:

Table 24.1

S. No.	Name of Insurer	Name of the Product	Logo
1.	Aviva Life Ins. Co. India Pvt. Ltd.	Grameen Suraksha	
2.	Bajaj Allianz Life Insurance Co. Ltd.	Bajaj Allianz Jana Vikas Yojana. Bajaj Allianz Saral Suraksha Yojana. Bajaj Allianz Alp Nivesh Yojana	
3.	Birla Sun Life Ins. Co. Ltd. B	Birla Sun Life Insurance Bima Suraksha Super. Birla Sun Life Insurance Bima Dhan Sanchay.	
4.	DLF Pramerica Life Insurance Co. Ltd.	DLF Pramerica Sarv-Suraksha.	
5.	ICICI Prudential Life Insurance Company Ltd.	ICICI Prud. Sarv Jana Suraksha	
6.	Industrial Development Bank of India (IDBI) Fortis LIC Ltd.	IDBI Fortis Group Micro insurance Plan	
7.	ING-vysya Life Insurance Company Pvt. Ltd.	ING Vysya Saral Suraksha	
8.	Life Insurance Corporation of India	LIC's Jeevan Madhur. LIC's Jeevan Mangal.	
9.	Met Life India	Met Vishwas	

Contd...

10.	Sahara India Life Insurance Co. Ltd.	Sahara Sahayog (Micro Endowment Insurance without profit plan).	
11.	SBI Life Insurance Company Ltd.	SBI Life Grameen Shakti. SBI Life Grameen Super Suraksha.	
12.	Shriram Life Insurance Co. Ltd.	Shri Sahay. Sri Sahay (AP).	
13.	Star Union Dai-ichi Life Insurance Co. Ltd.	SUD Life Paraspar Suraksha Plan	
14.	TATA AIG Life Insurance Co. Ltd.	Ayushman Yojana. Navkalyan Yojana. Sampoorn Bima Yojana. Tata AIG Sumangal Bima Yojana.	

Micro Insurance Products

Micro insurance products help low income people to cover their various risks such as: death, illness, accident, property damage, unemployment, crop failure or loss of livestock. A wide variety of micro insurance products exists to address these risks such as:

- Health insurance.
- Term life insurance.
- Death insurance.
- Crop insurance.
- Livestock/Cattle insurance.
- Insurance for theft/fire.
- Disability insurance.
- Insurance for natural disasters.

Life Micro Insurance Products

Life micro insurance products include:

- Social development plan.
- Super Suraksha.
- Janata personal accident policy.

- Janata personal accident insurance.
- Sankat Haran group insurance policy.
- Janashree Bima Yojana.
- Group personal accident policy.
- Jeevan Madhur.
- Jeevan Mangal.
- Shakthi security shield.
- Amartya siksha yojana policy.
- Krishi Shramik Samajik Suraksha Yojana.
- Accident insurance policy.

Micro Insurance Delivery Models

Methods and models for delivering 'Micro insurance products' depend on the organization, institution, and provider involved. In general, there are four main methods for offering micro insurance. Each of these models has their own advantages and disadvantages.

1. Partner agent model.
2. Provider driven model.
3. Full service model.
4. Community based model.

Partner Agent Model

A partnership is formed between the micro insurance scheme and an agent (insurance company, microfinance institution, donor, etc.), and in some cases a third-party healthcare provider. The micro insurance scheme is responsible for the delivery and marketing of products to the clients, while the agent retains all responsibility for design and development. In this model, micro insurance schemes benefit from limited risk, but are also disadvantaged in their limited control.

Full Service Model

The micro insurance scheme is in charge of everything; both the design and delivery of products to the clients, working with external healthcare providers to provide the services. This model has the advantage of offering micro insurance schemes full control, yet the disadvantage of higher risks.

Provider Driven Model

The healthcare provider is the micro insurance scheme, and similar to the full-service model, is responsible for all operations, delivery, design, and service. There is an advantage once more in the amount of control retained, yet disadvantage in the limitations on products and services.

Community-based/Mutual Model

The policy-holders or clients are in charge, managing and owning the operations, and working with external healthcare providers to offer services. This model is advantageous for its ability to design and market products more easily and effectively, yet is disadvantaged by its small size and scope of operations.

Life Insurance Corporation of India

Life Insurance Corporation of India (LIC) is an Indian state owned insurance group. It is an investment company headquartered in Mumbai. It is the largest insurance company in India. The Company was founded in 1956 when the Parliament of India passed the Life Insurance of India Act. The Act nationalized the private insurance industry in India. In order to create the state owned Life Insurance Corporation, 245 insurance companies and provident societies were merged. LIC had 5 zonal offices, 33 division offices and 212 branch offices, apart from its corporate office in the year 1956. Today LIC functions with 2048 fully computerized branch offices, 113 divisional offices, 8 zonal offices, 1381 satellite offices and the corporate office. LIC's wide area Network covers 113 divisional offices and connects all the branches through a metro area Network. LIC has tied up with some banks and service providers to offer on-line premium collection facility in overall all cities. LIC offers a variety of insurance products to its customers such as: insurance plans, pension plans, unit-linked plans, special plans and group schemes. The micro insurance portfolio has made steady progress. Many life insurers have commenced their micro insurance operations by introducing new products every year. The distribution infrastructure has also been considerably strengthened. Micro insurance business was procured largely under the group portfolio. Life Insurance Corporation of India (LIC) contributed the most both in terms of policies sold and number of micro insurance agents. With the notification of the Insurance Regulatory and Development Authority (Micro insurance) Regulations 2005, there has been a steady improvement in the design of products catering to the needs of the poor people. The flexibilities provided in the regulations allow the insurers to provide package products. With the approval of the Authority, now Insurance companies are offering approved general insurance products as micro insurance products if the sum assured for the product is within the range prescribed for micro insurance. LIC leveraged its expertise through individual endowment micro insurance products. Being experienced in selling low premium individual products, LIC did not have to take the easy credit-life way to sell micro insurance. While it provided credit-life covers through group insurance products, for individual segment, LIC launched an endowment life micro insurance product named Jeevan Madhur.

Various Micro Insurance Plans/Products Offered by LIC

1. Janashree Bima Yojana.
2. Jeevan Madhur.
3. Jeevan Mangal.
4. Jeevan Deep.
5. LIC Bhagyalakshmi.

Jeevan Madhur

Jeevan Madhur is the first micro insurance product it was launched in year 2006. It is simple savings related life insurance plan for low income persons It provides security within the reach of the poor people. The product is sold through LIC's Micro insurance Agents (MIAs). To market the product, LIC adopts a community approach. The company adopts villages with Jeevan Madhur customers as Madhur Bimagram and provides a monetary incentive to the village for social development. It is a low premium policy of endowment benefit. Minimum and maximum age level for eligibility to get the benefit of this product is 18 years and 60 years respectively.. It provides accidental coverage. Premium payable method allowed is monthly, quarterly, half yearly and yearly. Asper this policy, if a person pays two year premium fully, the insurance cover of Jeevan Madhur will exists for a period of two years consider from the date of first unpaid premium.

Additional Features

- Minimum and maximum sum assured for the product is 5000 and 30000 respectively.
- The minimum term of policy is 5 years and maximum is 15 years.
- Minimum amount of premium required is 100 per monthly and maximum is 500 per monthly.
- It provide benefit such as: in case of death 100 per cent of the sum assured and in case of maturity , considering 150 per cent of the total premium paid.
- In case of accidental death it provide additional benefit such as: 200 per cent of the sum assured to the legal heirs of the policy holder.

- Surrender value is 30 per cent of the total premium paid.
- One calendar month not less than 30 days is allowed as days of grace for yearly, half yearly and quarterly modes of payment.
- For other modes of payment, days of grace is allowed for a period of 15 days.
- Maturity benefit is varied for different terms that are it increases with the term of the policy.

Jeevan Madhur has broken the myth that stand alone life micro insurance products cannot be delivered profitably. The product has also proven that savings linked life insurance has an established demand in the micro insurance segment as well. The product has grown at an impressive rate and currently constitutes a major part of LIC's micro insurance business. With the help of this product, micro insurance constitutes 7.97 per cent of overall New Business Premium income of LIC. It is worthy to note here that following LIC, some other companies also experimented with savings.

Jeevan Mangal

It is the second micro insurance product of Life Insurance Corporation (LIC), the first being Jeevan Madhur. LIC's Jeevan mangal is a protection plan or a term assurance plan with return of premium on maturity. It facilitates the payment of premium either regularly over the term of the policy or in lumpsum. It provides double risk cover in case of accidental death. Minimum age at entry for the product is 18 years and maximum age at entry is 55 years. Maximum age at maturity is 65 years. It requires that the sum assured shall be multiples of 1000 and minimum and maximum sum assured is 10000 and 50000 respectively. As per monthly mode, the minimum installment premium is 60. It does not specify any minimum installment premium for other modes. Policy term is 5-10 years for single premium and 10-15 years for regular premium.

Additional Features

Flexible modes of premium payment have been provided that is the modes of payment may be weekly, fortnightly, monthly, quarterly, half yearly and annually:

1. Benefits

- *Death Benefit*: On death during the term of the policy the Sum Assured under the basic plan is payable, provided the policy is kept in force. Maturity Benefit: On surviving to the date of maturity, an amount equal to the total amount of premium paid during the term of the contract excluding the accident benefit premium and all extra premium, if any, is payable, provided the policy is kept in force.

2. ***Optional Rider***

- *Accidental Benefit Rider*: On death arising as a result of accident during the term of the policy, an additional amount, equal to Accident Benefit Rider Sum Assured is payable. On total and permanent disability arising due to accident (within 180 days from the date of accident), the Accident Benefit will be payable in monthly installments spread over 10 years. If the policy becomes a claim either by way of death or maturity before the expiry of the staid period of 10 years, the disability benefit installments which have not fallen due will be paid along with the claim. The disability due to accident should be total and such that the Life Assured is unable to carry out any work to earn the living. Following disabilities due to accidents are covered:
  - *(a)* irrevocable loss of the entire sight of both eyes, or
  - *(b)* amputation of both hands at or above the wrists, or
  - *(c)* amputation of both feet at or above ankles, or
  - *(d)* amputation of one hand at or above the wrist and one foot at or above the ankle. The future premiums shall be waived after the disability claim is admitted.

3. ***Exclusions***

- *Suicide:* If the Life Assured commits suicide (whether sane or insane at that time) at any time on or after the date on which the risk under the policy has commenced but before the expiry of one year from the date of commencement of risk under this policy, the sum assured under this policy shall not be payable, instead all the premiums paid under this policy shall be refunded in such cases.
- *Accident Benefit:* The Corporation shall not pay the accidental benefit in case accidental death/disability arises due to following reasons:
  - *(i)* Intentional self-injury, attempted suicide, insanity or immorality or whilst the Life Assured is under the influence of intoxicating liquor, drug or narcotic; or
  - *(ii)* Injuries resulting from riots, civil commotion, rebellion, war (whether war be declared or not), invasion, hunting, mountaineering, steeple chasing or racing of any kind; or
  - *(iii)* Result from the Life Assured committing any breach of law; or

(iv) Arises from employment of the Life Assured in the armed forces or military service of any country at war (whether war be declared or not) or from being engaged in police duty in any military, naval or police organization; or

(v) Occur after 180 days from the date of accident of the Life Assured.

Jeevan Deep

LIC's third micro insurance product Jeevan Deep is an endowment assurance product with an added feature of guaranteed additions along with provision of loyalty addition. Like other micro insurance products of LIC, it also offer customized services to low income sections of the population in order to meet their distinct needs.

Features

As per this plan, minimum sum assured is 5000 and maximum sum assured is 30000 with an optional accident benefit rider, together providing for total benefit equal to double the sum assured, on death due to accident. Flexible modes of premium payment have been provided that means the payment may be monthly, quarterly, half yearly and also annually. Single premium payment option has also been provided.

Janashree Bima Yojana

It is a group based pure term policy of insurance. Minimum and maximum age for eligibility of janashree bima yojana is 18 and 59 years respectively. It has no maturity benefit or surrender value. With this policy holders get certain additional benefit such as: educational scholarship ,accident coverage without any additional charge.. It provide benefit such as: 100 per cent of the sum assured in case of death and 250 per cent of the sum assured if death occur due to accident. It provides additional benefit as 75000 for total disability and for 37500 for partial disability.

- Minimum sum assured - 30000.
- Maximum sum assured - 30000.
- Minimum term of policy - 1 year.
- Maximum term of policy - 1 year.
- Minimum and maximum amount of premium is 200 each.
- Premium payable method is single premium.

LIC Bhagya Lakshmi

LIC Bhagyalakshmi micro insurance product is a non participating limited payment and protection oriented plan. Return of the plan is 110 per cent of total amount of premium payable on maturity. The premium paying term is 2 years less than the policy term. Minimum age at entry for the product is 18 years and maximum age at entry is 55 years. Maximum age at maturity is 65 years. Minimum and maximum sum assured is 20000 and 50000 respectively. Flexible modes of Premium payments are allowed. For all modes of payment, a grace period will be allowed for a period not less than 60 days. Minimum premium paying term is 5 years and maximum premium paying term is 13 years. The term of the policy is premium paying term plus 2 years (that is minimum 7 years and maximum 15 years).

Additional Features of LIC Bhagya Lakshmi

For yearly mode of premium, rebate allowed is 2 per cent of the Tab premium. For half yearly mode, rebate allowed is 1 per cent of the Tab prem. Commission rate is calculated as percentage of the premium net of service tax. Commission rate allowed to micro insurance agent – in first year 10 per cent and in subsequent years 7.5 per cent. Commission rate allowed to insurance and corporate agents - in first year 10 per cent and in second and third year 7.5 per cent each and in subsequent years 5 per cent each. Commission rate allowed to broker is – in first year 10 per cent, second and third year 5 per cent and also in subsequent years 5 per cent each. Sum assured on maturity is equal to 110 per cent of total amount of premium s payable during the term (excluding taxes and extra premium). Sum assured on death equal to sum assured under the policy. Paid up value or surrender value will accrue after two full year premiums are paid under policies with premium paying term less than 10 year. Paid up value or surrender value will accrue after 3 full year premiums paid under policies with premium paying term greater than 10 years Maturity paid up sum assured = sum assured on death x number of premium paid/Number of premium payable.

Conclusion

Agriculture is a volatile business. For large portions of the world population, agriculture is the main source of income. In this complex environment, farmers face a number of constraints and to reduce uncertainty and risk they depend on micro insurance products. Insurance is not an end in itself. Insurance is only a means to end. Micro insurance is only one component of a well balanced disaster risk management strategy. Various factors which demand the need for micro Insurance not only limited to agriculture but also health, death, theft or fire, disability and so on. In order to overcome the risk of all these sectors which are faced by low income people, various micro insurance players come in to the mainstream. LIC has a major role in reducing uncertainty and risks by offering various micro insurance products. It provides a practical option for low income households to protect against adverse events and it also act as a tool for governments to promote economic development and also industrial development.

REFERENCES

1. Ahuja, R. (June 2005). "Micro-Insurance in India: Trends and Strategies for Further extension" Indian Council for Research on International Economic Relations (ICRIER).
2. ILO (2004a). India: Insurance Products Provided by Insurance Companies to the Disadvantaged Groups, Strategies and Tools against Social Exclusion and Poverty (STEP), March 2004.
3. ILO (2004b). India: An Inventory of Community-based Micro Insurance Schemes, Strategies and Tools against Social Exclusion and Poverty (STEP), February 2004.
4. Deliya, M., Patel, K. and Parmar, B. (May 2012). "Awareness of Micro Insurance Product in Patan district" National Monthly Refereed Journal of Research in Commerce and Management Volume No. 1, Issue No. 5, pp. 16-35.
5. Part I: Primer on Insurance Principles and Products, November 1999.

Websites

6. www.dnb.co.in
7. www.licindia.in
8. www.MICRO INSURANCE/JeevanManga.html
9. www.MICRO INSURANCE/LICs_Bhagya_Lakshmi_.html
10. www. http://financialservices.gov.in/
11. www.policyholder.gov.in.

Pages 194-201

POVERTY ALLEVIATION THROUGH MICROFINANCE
Edited by **: Dr. B. Ramachandra Reddy**
Edition **: 2017**
ISBN : 978-93-5056-865-1
Published by **: Discovery Publishing House Pvt. Ltd., New Delhi (India)**

25

Microfinance Credit Market Structure in India

An Overview

M. Giri Kumari[*]

INTRODUCTION

Poverty is the main cause of concern in improving the economic status of developing countries. A microfinance institution is an organization that offers financial services to low income populations. Almost all give loans to their members, and many offer insurance, deposit and other services.

A great scale of organizations is regarded as microfinance institutes. They are those that offer credits and other financial services to the representatives of poor strata of population (except for extremely poor strata).

MFIs are the pivotal overseas organizations in each country that make individual micro credit loans directly to villagers, micro entrepreneurs, impoverished women and poor families. An overseas MFI is like a small bank with the same challenges and capital needs confronting any expanding small venture but with the added responsibility of serving economically-marginalized populations. Many MFIs are creditworthy and well-run with proven records of success, many are operationally self-sufficient.

The term 'transformation,' or commercialization, of a microfinance institution (MFI) refers to a change in legal status from an unregulated nonprofit or non-governmental organization (NGO) into a regulated, for-profit institution. Regulated, transformed organizations differ from non-

Academic Consultant, Department of Business Management, SPMVV, Tirupati.

profits in that they are held to performance and capital adequacy standards and are supervised by a financial authority, typically the central bank of the country where they are registered. A transformed MFI also attracts equity investors. The equity investors want to ensure that the values of their investments are maintained or enhanced and elect board members who share a common vision for the new for-profit institution. Among transformed MFIs, varying classifications of regulated institutions exist, the strictest being banks – rural banks and thrift banks – followed by non-bank financial institutions. Different countries have varied names for these regulated MFIs.

The microfinance sector consistently focuses on understanding the needs of the poor and on devising better ways of delivering services in line with their requirements, developing the most efficient and effective mechanisms to deliver finance to the poor. Continuous efforts towards automation of operations is steady improving in efficiency. The automated systems have also helped accelerate the growth rate of the microfinance sector.

Significance of the Credit Market

There is a broad consensus, among both academics and policy-makers, that a developed financial system spurs economic growth through a number of channels: *(i)* acquisition of information on firms; *(ii)* intensity with which creditors exert corporate control; *(iii)* provision of risk-reducing arrangements; *(iv)* pooling of capital and *(v)* ease of making transactions. There are two mechanisms for mobilising savings and channeling them into investments, *viz;* bank-based and market-based.

Credit institutions have the distinct advantage in information gathering and processing to monitor the efficiency and productivity of projects. In recent years the existence of banks, which are the major players in the credit market, is attributed more to their information gathering capacity arising out of the existence of asymmetric information and moral hazard problems, than to the classic explanation relating to their ability to mobilise savings and channeling them into investment. Savers usually have incomplete information on the affairs of companies, which makes it more difficult for companies to obtain direct financing from the market. Intermediation by banks mitigates such agency problems. The cost of acquiring information on a company by the providers of financial resources is high, the process of financing companies can be done more efficiently if the prospective investors are able to delegate the collection of such information to a specialised organization (Diamond, 1984). The financial intermediation is justified on the grounds of information gathering and company-monitoring functions performed by banks. By reducing the costs of acquiring and processing information, financial institutions encourage mobilisation of savings and improve resource allocation. Banks can also versify risk among a number of companies.

Firms in developing countries generally tend to rely more on debt finance, including bank credit. The emphasis on credit rather than equity arises due to various reasons. The cost of equity in developing economies is often much higher than the cost of debt due to the existence of higher perceived risk premia than in developed countries. The existence of artificially repressed interest rates contributes further to the problem. The other reasons for the heavy reliance on debt in developing countries include the fragility of their equity markets, lack of suitable accounting practices and the absence of adequate corporate governance practices. The high dependence on bank credit and lack of substitutes for external finance, firms in developing economies are generally highly sensitive to changes in the cost and flow of credit.

Credit markets in developing countries plays an important role, apart from industry, agriculture is also an important segment of the economy. There are also a large number of small and medium enterprises in the industrial and service sectors, which are not able to access the capital market and have to depend on the credit market for their funding requirements. The importance of banks and other lending institutions in developing countries can hardly be over emphasised.

Commercial banks, given their preeminent position in the regulated financial sector, dominate the credit market. The quantity of loans created by the banking system is generally a function of both the willingness and ability of banks to lend. In an economy with ceilings on lending rates, banks face a higher credit demand than they can effectively supply, necessitating reliance on a credit rationing mechanism. In a non-repressed financial system, the borrowers are, in principle, differentiated along the lines of risk characteristics and riskier borrowers are charged higher interest rates to account for default probabilities. The riskier projects bring higher returns, banks, out of sustainability consideration, need to optimise the risk of their portfolio.

Another important factor influencing the supply of credit is the amount of reserves available from the central bank to the banking system. A large pre-emption of central bank money by the Government may constrain reserve supply to the banking system, affecting their capacity for credit creation. Credit expansion could also be an endogenous process, *i.e.*, it is the demand for credit that may drive the banking system's ability to create credit in the economy.

Development of the credit market plays an important role in the monetary transmission mechanism. The traditional interest rate channel, represented by the 'money view', mainly focuses on the liability side as banks create money through chequable deposits. The asset side is not emphasised as firms' financial structure is believed to be neutral to borrowings through loans from banks or through issuance of securities. This is based on the assumption that different financial assets such as: bonds and bank loans are perfect substitutes. In terms of 'credit view', bonds and bank loans are not seen as perfect substitudes primarily because of information asymmetries. Firms facing informational problems find it more expensive to borrow through bonds than availing loans from banks. Developed financial intermediation system facilitates growth, policy makers tend to liberalise the system to facilitate financial development. The literature suggests that authorities should take adequate caution in adopting a liberalised policy frameworks intended to develop the financial sector.

Institutional Structure of the Credit Market in India

The credit market structure in India has evolved over the years. A wide range of financial institutions exist in the country to provide credit to various sectors of the economy. These include commercial banks, regional rural banks (RRBs), co-operatives [comprising urban co-operative banks (UCBs), State co-operative banks (STCBs), district central co-operative banks (DCCBs), primary agricultural credit societies (PACS), state co-operative and agricultural rural development banks (SCARDBs) and primary co-operative and agricultural rural development banks (PCARDBs)], financial institutions (FI) (term-lending institutions, both at the Centre and State level, and refinance institutions) and non-banking financial companies (NBFCs).

Scheduled commercial banks constitute the predominant segment of the credit market in India. The co-operative banking system, with two broad segments of urban and rural co-operatives, forms an integral part of the Indian financial system. Urban cooperative banks, also referred to as primary co-operative banks, play an important role in meeting the growing credit needs of urban and semi-urban areas of the country. The UCBs, which grew rapidly in the early 1990s, showed certain weaknesses arising out of lack of sound corporate governance, unethical lending, comparatively high levels of non-performing loans and their inability to operate in a liberalised environment.

The rural co-operative credit institutions have played an important role in providing institutional credit to the agricultural and rural sectors. These credit institutions, based on the nature of their lending operations, have typically been pided into two distinct segments, commonly known as the short-term co-operative credit structure (STCCS) and the long-term co-operative credit structure (LTCCS). The STCCS, comprising PACS at the village level, DCCBs at the intermediate level, and the STCBs at the apex level, provide crop and other working capital loans to farmers and rural artisans primarily for short-term purposes. The LTCCS, comprising SCARDBs at the State level and PCARDBs at the district or block level, provide typically medium and long-term loans for making investments in agriculture, rural industries and housing.

Financial institutions owed their origin to the objective of state driven planned economic development. The capital markets were relatively under developed and judged to be incapable of meeting adequately the long-term requirements of the economy. A wide range of FIs, mostly Government owned, came into existence to cater to the medium to long-term financing requirements of different sectors of the economy. FIs played a key role in extending development finance in India and for this purpose they were given access to concessional finance in the form of Government guaranteed bonds and Long-term Operations (LTO) Fund of the Reserve Bank.

NBFCs encompass a heterogeneous group of intermediaries and provide a whole range of financial services. It can be broadly classified into three categories, *viz;* asset finance companies (such as: equipment leasing and hire purchase), loan companies and investment companies.

The Credit Channel of Monetary Policy

The impact of monetary policy on the real economy operates through various channels. Under the conventional approach, referred to as the 'money view', monetary policy influences the economy *via* the interest rate.

There are two channels through which credit conditions are expected to affect monetary transmission. *First,* the 'bank lending' channel, that operates through modulation of bank reserves, is affected by monetary policy. Contractionary/expansionary policy limits or enhances the ability of banks to lend and thereby reduces/increases investment and output. The second, the 'balance sheet' channel works through net worth of the borrowers.

Policy Developments in the Credit Market in India

The credit market, with commercial banks as its predominant segment, has been the major source for meeting the finance requirements in the economy, both for the private sector and the Central and State Government enterprises. The issue of allocation of bank resources among various sectors was addressed through mechanisms such as: SLR, credit authorisation scheme (CAS), fixation of maximum permissible bank finance (MPBF) and selective credit controls. This regulated environment set in complacency in the manner in which credit institutions operated and responded to the customer needs. The interest rate played a very limited role as the equilibrating mechanism between demand and supply of resources.

1. Priority sector comprises agriculture (both direct and indirect), small scale industries, small roads and water transport operators, small business, retail trade, professional and self-employed persons, state sponsored organizations for Scheduled Castes/Scheduled Tribes, education, housing (both direct and indirect), consumption loans, micro-credit, loans to software, and food and agro-processing sector.
2. Under Section 18 of the Banking Regulation Act, 1949, all scheduled banks are required to maintain SLR, *i.e.*, a certain proportion of their demand and time liabilities (DTL) as on the last Friday of the second preceeding fortnight as liquid assets (cash, gold valued at a price not exceeding the current market price or unencumbered approved securities valued at a price as specified by the Reserve Bank from time to time).

Credit Information Bureaus

Credit bureaus (or credit reference agencies) are useful as they help lenders to assess credit worthiness of individual borrowers and their ability to pay back a loan. As credit bureaus collect and collate personal financial data on individuals from financial institutions, a form of price discrimination can be modelled taking into account credit rating and past behaviour of borrowers. The information is generally aggregated and made available on request to contributing companies for the purposes of credit assessment and credit scoring.

The CIBIL provides a vital service, which allows its members to make informed, objective and faster credit decisions. CIBIL's aim is to fulfill the need of credit granting institutions for comprehensive credit information by collecting, collating and disseminating credit information pertaining to both commercial and consumer borrowers, to a closed user group of members.

Annex IV.1: Manu of Policy Options in Responding to Rapid Credit Growth

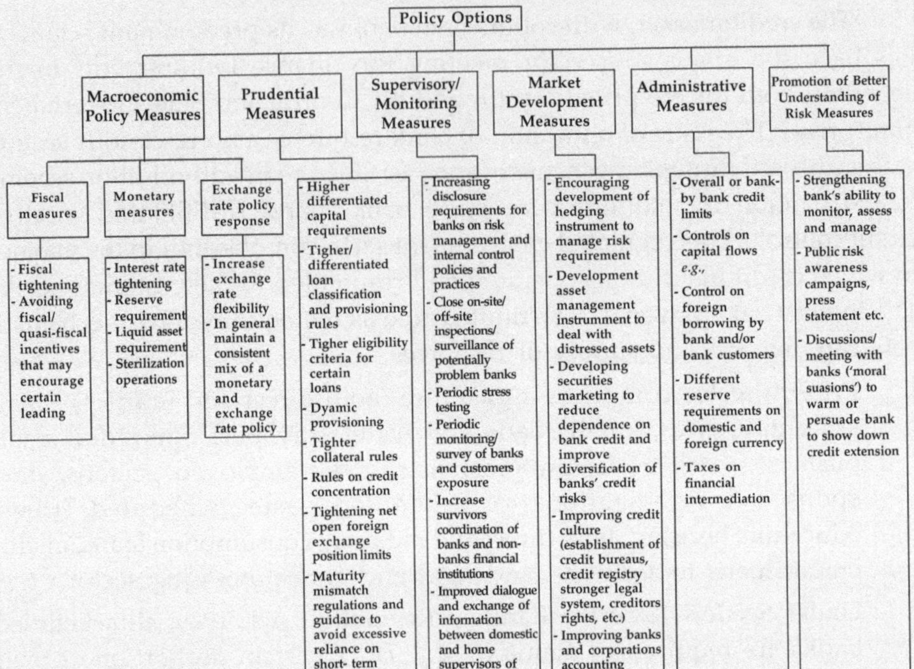

Source: Hilbers, et al. 2005

Banks, financial institutions, non-banking financial companies, housing finance companies and credit card companies use CIBIL's services.

Conclusion

The credit market is the most significant segment of the financial market structure in India. The credit market in India has witnessed significant transformation in the last 15 years in terms of type of borrowers/type of instruments and price of credit. With the conversion of two DFIs into banks and reduction in the business operations of NBFCs, the predominance of banking institutions in the credit market has increased. Enhanced freedom for business operations and increased presence of private and foreign banks and non-bank credit institutions, the credit market has become highly competitive as new banks are making every effort to increase their share in the credit market. The credit market has also persified in terms of borrowing entities and the purposes for which credit is extended.

A proper functioning of the credit market depends on adequate competition. In a competitive environment, the more efficient institutions capture the market share at the expense of less efficient ones, which improves the overall efficiency of the system. This benefits both the credit institutions and their clients. While gains to credit institutions occur in the form of higher profits, to consumers they occur in the form of lower cost of the services. The process of consolidation and restructuring that is underway in the credit market in India may result in weeding out the inefficient players and the credit market may become more efficient in future.

Robust economic growth has increased the demand for credit. Proper functioning of credit institutions in general and banks in particular is key to sustained economic growth. In the current situation of high credit expansion, banks have been unwinding their surplus investments in SLR securities, over and above the prescribed minimum. This unwinding would soon reach a limit. Therefore, banks need to make sustained efforts for mobilising stable retail deposits by extending banking facilities and wide-spreading their deposit base. In particular, banks would need to devise imaginative ways to mop up the resources in rural areas to balance their deposit mobilisation and credit expansion.

REFERENCES

1. Bernanke, Ben, and A. Blinder. (1988). "Credit, Money and Aggregate Demand." *American Economic Review* 135-139, May.
2. Bernanke, Ben, and M. Gertler. (1995). "Inside the Black Box: The Credit Channel of Monetary Policy Transmission."
3. Pandit, B.L., Ajit Mittal, Mohua Roy and Saibal Ghosh. 2006. "Transmission of Monetary Policy, and the Bank Lending Channel: Analysis and Evidence for India." *Journal of Economic Perspectives*, Vol. 9: 27-48. DRG Study No. 25, Reserve Bank of India.

Pages 202-209

POVERTY ALLEVIATION THROUGH MICROFINANCE
Edited by : Dr. B. Ramachandra Reddy
Edition : 2017
ISBN : 978-93-5056-865-1
Published by : Discovery Publishing House Pvt. Ltd., New Delhi (India)

26

Microfinance
Current Status and Growing Concerns in India

Dr. K. Rajaiah

INTRODUCTION

"Microfinance is the provision of financial services to low-income clients or solidarity lending groups including consumers and the self-employed, who traditionally lack access to banking and related services." Microfinance is not just about giving micro credit to the poor rather it is an economic development tool whose objective is to assist poor to work their way out of poverty. It covers a wide range of services like: credit, savings, insurance, remittance and also non-financial services like: training, counseling etc.

Salient Features of Microfinance

- Borrowers are from the low income group.
- Loans are of small amount – micro loans.
- Short duration loans.
- Loans are offered without collaterals.
- High frequency of repayment.
- Loans are generally taken for income generation purpose.

Gaps in Financial System and Need for Microfinance

According to the latest research done by the World Bank, India is home to almost one third of the world's poor (surviving on an equivalent of one

Academic Consultant, Department of Commerce, V.S.U.P.G. Centre, Kavali.

dollar a day). Though many central government and state government poverty alleviation programmes are currently active in India, microfinance plays a major contributor to financial inclusion. In the past few decades it has helped out remarkably in eradicating poverty. Reports show that people who have taken microfinance have been able to increase their income and hence the standard of living.

About half of the Indian population still doesn't have a savings bank account and they are deprived of all banking services. Poor also need financial services to fulfill their needs like consumption, building of assets and protection against risk. Microfinance institutions serve as a supplement to banks and in some sense a better one too. These institutions not only offer micro credit but they also provide other financial services like: savings, insurance, remittance and non-financial services like: individual counseling, training and support to start own business and the most importantly in a convenient way. The borrower receives all these services at her/his door step and in most cases with a repayment schedule of borrower's convenience. But all this comes at a cost and the interest rates charged by these institutions are higher than commercial banks and vary widely from 10 to 30 per cent. Some claim that the interest rates charged by some of these institutions are very high while others feel that considering the cost of capital and the cost incurred in giving the service, the high interest rates are justified.

Channels of Microfinance

In India microfinance operates through two channels:

1. SHG – Bank Linkage Programme (SBLP).
2. Microfinance Institutions (MFIs).

1. SHG – Bank Linkage Programme

This is the bank-led microfinance channel which was initiated by NABARD in 1992. Under the SHG model the members, usually women in villages are encouraged to form groups of around 10-15. The members contribute their savings in the group periodically and from these savings small loans are provided to the members. In the later period these SHGs are provided with bank loans generally for income-generation purpose. The group's members meet periodically when the new savings come in, recovery of past loans are made from the members and also new loans are disbursed. This model has been very much successful in the past and with time it is becoming more popular. The SHGs are self-sustaining and once the group becomes stable it starts working on its own with some support from NGOs.

2. *Microfinance Institutions*

Poverty is the main cause of concern in improving the economic status of developing countries. A microfinance institution is an organization that offers financial services to low income populations. Almost all give loans to their members, and many offer insurance, deposit and other services. A great scale of organizations is regarded as microfinance institutes. They are those that offer credits and other financial services to the representatives of poor strata of population. Microfinance is increasingly being considered as one of the most effective tools of reducing poverty. Microfinance has a significant role in bridging the gap between the formal financial institutions and the rural poor. The Microfinance Institutions (MFIs) accesses financial resources from the Banks and other mainstream Financial Institutions and provide financial and support services to the poor.

MFIs are the pivotal overseas organizations in each country that make individual microcredit loans directly to villagers, micro entrepreneurs, impoverished women and poor families. An overseas MFI is like a small bank with the same challenges and capital needs confronting any expanding small venture but with the added responsibility of serving economically-marginalized populations. Many MFIs are creditworthy and well-run with proven records of success, many are operationally self-sufficient.

Various types of institutions offer microfinance: credit unions, commercial banks, NGOs (Non-governmental Organizations), co-operatives, and sectors of government banks. The emergence of 'for-profit' MFIs is growing. In India, these 'for-profit' MFIs are referred to as Non-Banking Financial Companies (NBFC). NGOs mainly work in remote rural areas thereby providing financial services to the persons with no access to banking services.

The microfinance sector consistently focuses on understanding the needs of the poor and on devising better ways of delivering services in line with their requirements, developing the most efficient and effective mechanisms to deliver finance to the poor. Continuous efforts towards automation of operations are steady improving in efficiency. The automated systems have also helped accelerate the growth rate of the microfinance sector.

The goal for MFIs should be:

- To improve the quality of life of the poor by providing access to financial and support services.
- To be a viable financial institution developing sustainable communities.

- To mobilize resources in order to provide financial and support services to the poor, particularly women, for viable productive income-generation enterprises enabling them to reduce their poverty;
- Learn and evaluate what helps people to move out of poverty faster.
- To create opportunities for self-employment for the under privileged.
- To train rural poor in simple skills and enable them to utilise the available resources and contribute to employment and income-generation in rural areas.

Those institutions which have microfinance as their main operation are known as micro finance institutions. A number of organizations with varied size and legal forms offer microfinance service. These institutions lend through the concept of Joint Liability Group (JLG). A JLG is an informal group comprising of 5 to 10 individual members who come together for the purpose of availing bank loans either individually or through the group mechanism against a mutual guarantee. The reason for existence of separate institutions *i.e.* MFIs for offering microfinance are as follows:

- High transaction cost - generally micro credits fall below the break-even point of providing loans by banks.
- Absence of collaterals - the poor usually are not in a state to offer collaterals to secure the credit.
- Loans are generally taken for very short duration periods.
- Higher frequency of repayment of installments and higher rate of Default.

Legal Structure and Regulation

Although the SHG-Bank linkage model is well managed in India by NABARD, currently there is no proper regulatory body for the supervision of MFIs. The presence of institutions with a variety of legal forms makes it difficult for the regulation of all such institutions by a single regulatory body in the current Indian legal structure. Though NBFCs, which cover the major part of the outstanding loan portfolio by the microfinance channel, are regulated by Reserve Bank of India, other MFIs like: societies, trusts, Section-25 companies and cooperative societies fall outside the purview of RBI's regulation.

1. *Financial Illiteracy*

One of the major hindrances in the growth of the microfinance sector is the financial illiteracy of the people. This makes it difficult in creating awareness of microfinance and even more difficult to serve them as microfinance clients. Though most of the microfinance institutions claim to have educational trainings and programmes for the benefit of the people, according to some of the experts the first thing these SHG and JLG members are taught is to do their own signature. The worst part is that many MFIs think that this is what financial literacy means. We all know how dangerous it can be when one doesn't know how to read but he/she knows how to accept or approve it.

2. Inability to Generate Sufficient Funds

Inability of MFIs to raise sufficient fund remains one of the important concern in the microfinance sector. Though NBFCs are able to raise funds through private equity investments because of the for-profit motive, such MFIs are restricted from taking public deposits. Not-for-profit companies which constitute a major chunk of the MFI sector have to primarily rely on donations and grants from Government and apex institutions like NABARD and SIDBI. In absence of adequate funding from the equity market, the major source of funds for MFIs are the bank loans, which is the reason for high Debt to Equity ratio of most MFIs.

3. Dropouts and Migration of Group Members

Majority of the microfinance loans are disbursed on group lending concept and a past record of the group plays an important role in getting new loans either through SHG-Bank linkage or through MFIs. The two major problems with the group concept are dropouts (when one or more members leave the group) and migration (when one or more members move to another group). Most MFIs lend on the basis of the past record of the group *i.e.* SHG or JLG and also on the individuals repayment performance. In absence of a decent past record, members are deprived of getting bigger loan amounts and additional services.

4. Transparent Pricing

Though the concern about the transparent pricing in the microfinance sector has been an older one, it is gaining significance with the growing size and the increasing competition in the sector. Non-transparent pricing by MFIs confines the bargaining power of the borrowers and their ability to compare different loan products, because they don't know the actual price. In absence of the proper understanding of the pricing, clients end up borrowing more than their ability to payback which results in over-indebtedness of the borrower.

5. Cluster Formation - Fight to Grab Established Market

MFIs' drive to grab an established market and reduce their costs is resulting in formation of clusters in some areas leaving the others out of the microfinance outreach. By getting an established microfinance market, MFIs reduce their initial cost in group formation of clients, educating them and creating awareness about microfinance. This is one of the reasons for the dominance of the microfinance sector in the southern states. Now the problem is that a similar trend is being followed in the northern states as well. We have already seen what happened in A.P and it seems that most of the MFIs have not taken a lesson from the Andhra crisis.

6. Multiple Lending and Over-Indebtedness

Both of these are outcome of the competition among the MFIs. Microfinance is one such sector where the Neo-liberal theory of free market operation fails, at least to some extent. Though competition is good for many sectors but in this case it is going against both the parties. In order to eat away each others' market share, MFIs are ending up giving multiple loans to same borrowers which in some cases is leading to over-indebtedness (a situation where the borrower has taken loans more than her/his repaying capacity) of the borrower. MFIs are getting affected because borrowers are failing to make payments and hence their recovery rates are falling, while over-indebtedness is making the borrower go to depression and in some cases forcing them to commit suicide.

Recommendations

1. *Proper Regulation:* The regulation was not a major concern when the microfinance was in its nascent stage and individual institutions were free to bring in innovative operational models. However, as the sector completes almost two decades of age with a high growth trajectory, an enabling regulatory environment that protects interest of stake-holders as well as promotes growth, is needed.
2. *Field Supervision*: In addition to proper regulation of the microfinance sector, field visits can be adopted as a medium for monitoring the conditions on ground and initiating corrective action if needed. This will keep a check on the performance of ground staff of various MFIs and their recovery practices. This will also encourage MFIs to abide by proper code of conduct and work more efficiently. However, the problem of feasibility and cost involved in physical monitoring of this vast sector remains an issue in this regard.

3. *Encourage Rural Penetration*: It has been seen that in lieu of reducing the initial cost, MFIs are opening their branches in places which already have a few MFIs operating. Encouraging MFIs for opening new branches in areas of low microfinance penetration by providing financial assistance will increase the outreach of the microfinance in the state and check multiple lending. This will also increase rural penetration of microfinance in the state.
4. *Complete Range of Products*: MFIs should provide complete range of products including: credit, savings, remittance, financial advice and also non-financial services like: training and support. As MFIs are acting as a substitute to banks in areas where people don't have access to banks, providing a complete range of products will enable the poor to avail all services.
5. *Transparency of Interest Rates*: As it has been observed that, MFIs are employing different patterns of charging interest rates and a few are also charging additional charges and interest free deposits (a part of the loan amount is kept as deposit on which no interest is paid). All this make the pricing very confusing and hence the borrower feels incompetent in terms of bargaining power. So a common practice for charging interest should be followed by all MFIs so that it makes the sector more competitive and the beneficiary gets the freedom to compare different financial products before buying.
6. *Technology to Reduce Operating Cost:* MFIs should use new technologies and IT tools and applications to reduce their operating costs. Though most NBFCs are adopting such cost cutting measures, which is clearly evident from the low cost per unit money lent (9%-10%) of such institutions. NGOs and Section 25 companies are having a very high value of cost per unit money lent *i.e.* 15-35 per cent and hence such institutions should be encouraged to adopt cost-cutting measures to reduce their operating costs. Also initiatives like development of common MIS and other software for all MFIs can be taken to make the operation more transparent and efficient.
7. *Alternative Sources of Fund:* In absence of adequate funds the growth and the reach of MFIs become restricted and to overcome this problem MFIs should look for other sources for funding their loan portfolio.

Conclusion

I conclude that Microfinance sector has grown rapidly over the past few decades. Nobel Laureate Muhammad Yunus is credited with laying the foundation of the modern MFIs with establishment of Grameen Bank, Bangladesh in 1976. Today it has evolved into a vibrant industry exhibiting a variety of business models. Microfinance Institutions (MFIs) in India exist as NGOs (registered as societies or trusts), Section 25 companies and Non-Banking Financial Companies (NBFCs). Commercial Banks, Regional Rural Banks (RRBs), co-operative societies and other large lenders have played an important role in providing refinance facility to MFIs. Banks have also leveraged the Self-Help Group (SHGs) channel to provide direct credit to group borrowers.

REFERENCES

1. Barry, N. (1995). "The Missing Links: Financial System that Works for the Majority," Women's World Banking, New York.
2. Barry, Nancy, Armacost, Nicola and Kawas Celina (1996). "Putting Poor People's Economics at the Center of Urban Strategies," Women's World Banking, New York.
3. Churchill, C.F. (1996). "An Introduction to Key Issues in Microfinance: Supervision and Regulation, Financing Sources, Expansion of Microfinance Institutions," Microfinance Network, Washington, D.C. February.
4. Ghate, P. *et al*. (1992). Informal Finance: Some Findings from Asia, Oxford University Press, Hong Kong.
5. Grameen Trust (1995). Grameen Dialogue No. 24, Dhaka, October.

Pages 210-217

POVERTY ALLEVIATION THROUGH MICROFINANCE
Edited by : Dr. B. Ramachandra Reddy
Edition : 2017
ISBN : 978-93-5056-865-1
Published by : Discovery Publishing House Pvt. Ltd., New Delhi (India)

27 Significance of Microfinance Institutions in Rural Development of India

Dr. D. Subramanyam[1]
Dr. D. Yuvaraju[2]
Prof. Devarajulu[3]

ABSTRACT

Microfinance is to supply micro credit to people living in utter poverty and has no reach to the conservative and formal financial products. It is an aid to engage them in productive activities and grow their tiny businesses. Microfinance focused on availing the credit in a standard manner. Microfinancial schemes plays vital role in increasing women's participation in economic activities and decision-making. In this research paper an effort is made to investigate the role of microfinance in rural development especially through Microfinancial schemes. This study is an empirical study which aims to find out the role and responsibilities of microfinance in rural development. Our experience while doing this study suggests that microfinance provides key lessons for development in terms of what mechanism and best practices should be adopted and how to make small change that creates a big difference. It is concluded that poor people in rural areas especially in under developing countries, are in immense need of credits so microfinance programmes must make available this credit needs and motivate the poor people to increase their standard of living.

Keywords: Microfinance, Rural Development, Economy, Financial Services etc.

1. Teaching Assistant, Department of Economics, S.V. University, Tirupati.
2. Department of Business Management Studies, S.V. University, Tirupati.
3. Registrar, S.V. University, Tirupati.

INTRODUCTION

With a huge segment of the world's under privileged, India is likely to have a large possible demand for microfinance. For this reason, it makes sense to consider the changing face of microfinance for rural development in India. Microfinance refers offering exceptionally small loans to very poor families with the purpose of engaging them into productive activities. Microfinance bank is an institution that extends small loan or microfinance, to applicant who typically belongs to the lowest group of society. Loans are extended to borrower to allow them to initiate a business, repair their homes and improve the general living condition of their families and the community. Microfinance is considered as a tool for socio-economic development, and can be clearly differentiated from donations. When it comes to rural development, with the growth of the credit infrastructure, credit flow to the poor and especially to poor women, remained near to the ground. As a result National Bank for Agriculture and Rural Development (NABARD) was set up with the objective of framing appropriate policy for rural credit, provision of technical assistance backed liquidity support to banks, supervision of rural credit institutions and other development initiatives. After a time it was experienced that the existing banking policies, systems and procedures, and deposit and loan products were possibly not well matched to meet the instant needs of the poor. It was experienced that the poor desired improved access to these services and products, more willingly than cheap financed credit. If a person observes an institution to be unfriendly or uncaring to them, they hesitate to move toward it. Thus a requirement has been experienced for alternative policies, systems and procedures, savings and loan products, other matching services, and new delivery mechanisms, which would fulfill the requirements of the poorest, especially of the women members of such families. This has given beginning to an increasing emphasis on Microfinance for improving the access to credit for the poor. A large number of NGOs have started their own microfinance programmes in an attempt to develop the people in their respective areas. Micro credit has become a major tool of development.

The most current succession in this area is savings and credit groups or Self-Help Groups (SHGs) as they are known in India, as well as a variety of specialized Microfinance Institutions (MFIs). To assist and encourage the activities of these groups, significant institutional structures have emerged. A major portion of such support in India has come from non-profit NGOs. These organizations originally initiated the concept of

Microfinance and continue to work towards the delivery of Microfinance projects in India especially for rural development.

Existence of Microfinance in India

The term microfinance came into existence in 1970s when organizations, such as: Grameen Bank of Bangladesh with the microfinance pioneer Muhammad Yunus, were starting and shaping the modern industry of microfinancing. Even Microfinance in India can map out its origins back to the early 1970s when the Self-Employed Women's Association ('SEWA') of the state of Gujarat formed an urban cooperative bank, called the Shri Mahila SEWA Sahakari Bank, with the objective of providing banking services to poor women employed in the unorganized sector in Ahmadabad City, Gujarat. The microfinance sector went on to evolve in the 1980s around the concept of SHGs, informal bodies that would provide their clients with much-needed savings and credit services.

Due to large size and population of around 1000 million, India's GDP ranks among the top 20 economies of the world. However, around 400 million people or about 60 million households, are living under the poverty line. It is further predictable that of these households, only about 20 per cent have access to credit from the formal sector. As well, the segment of the rural population has no good access to the recognized financial intermediary services, including savings services. Credit on rational terms to the poor can bring about a significant fall in poverty. Hence micro credit assumes significance in the Indian context. With about 60 million households below or just above the strictly defined poverty line and with more than 80 per cent unable to access credit at reasonable rates, it is obvious that there are certain issues and problems, which have banned the reach of microfinance to the needy. With globalization and liberalization of the economy, opportunities for the unskilled and the illiterate people are not increasing fast enough, as compared to the rest of the economy. In this context, the institutions involved in microfinance have a significant role in reducing inequality and contribution in rural development for overall growth.

Microfinanace and Poverty Reduction for Rural Development in India

India consists over a quarter of its population below to poverty line. The World Bank reports that India is a home around some 260 to 290 million poor, numbers that rise to around 390 million if poverty is measured by the international standard of those living on less than 1US$ dollar a day. Almost half of India's poor, more or less 133 million, are found in three states: Uttar Pradesh, Bihar, and Madhya Pradesh. Rural area in India is the home of three quarters of India's poor which is supported by the increasing urban and rural disparities. The Indian government's poverty reduction strategy focuses on infrastructure, social development (especially education and health), and rural livelihoods. The improvement of rural livelihoods is the aspect of poverty reduction that Microfinance Institutions concentrate on. Most poor people manage resources to develop their enterprises and their home over a time. Financial services could enable the poor to force their initiative, accelerating the process of assembling incomes, assets and economic safety.

Traditional finance institutions rarely lend money to serve the needs of low-income families and women-headed households. However, the income of many self-employed households is not stable, regardless of its size. A large number of small loans are needed to serve the poor, but lenders prefer dealing with large loans in small numbers to minimize administration costs. They also look for guarantee which many low-income households do not have in hand. Over the last ten years, however, successful experiences in providing finance to small entrepreneur and producers demonstrate that poor people, when given access to responsive and timely financial services at market rates, pay back their loans and use the profits to increase their income and assets. This is not shocking since the only realistic alternative for them is to borrow the money from informal market. Community banks, NGOs and credit groups around the world have shown that these micro enterprise loans can be profitable for borrowers and for the lenders, making microfinance one of the most effective poverty reducing strategies.

Microfinance and Self-Help Groups (SGHs) for Rural Develpoment

There are two common approaches of Microfinance India - The Self-help groups method and the Grameen system. An SHG is an unofficial group of approximately 10-20 members. The members of the SHG are joined for the specific purpose of facilitating saving and credit services for its members. This is made possible through members pooling their resources to create a common fund. The process and social involvement of SHGs are intended to be instruments of empowerment, building the capacity of members to eventually conduct and manage SHGs for themselves, and enabling them to have greater autonomy in financial decision-making as well as wider social participation. SHG meetings are set to take place at regular intervals and at a designated time. Group members are drawn from the same social economic layer and work on the basis of equal participation and contribution from all members.

The groups are chaired by one lead member at a time; this role is usually rotated to allow capacity building for all members. Meetings are structured and accurate and up to date records of all financial transactions, group decisions and actions are compiled. Once established, SHGs are encouraged to make links with other SHGs and eventually with financial institutions to allow access to further financial assistance.

Microfinance and Women Empowerment for Rural Development

Women are essential part of the society. The role of women in economic activities and decision-making is very low. Microfinancial schemes plays vital role in increasing women's participation in economic activities and decision-making. There has been huge growth of organizations, known as Microfinance Institutions (MFIs) in this field to deal with the microfinancial activities. With increasing demand for rural finance, and the shortages of formal sources, the MFIs have tremendous challenges and opportunities in microfinance in India. In India self-help groups (SHGs) constitutes of 85-95 per cent women. The reasons for this is that women are familiar with finances responsibility; making them trustworthy, reliable and prompt savers. Empowerment of women also occupies central place to wide development goals.

Women empowerment is critical factor in the eradication of poverty, as the women are the key contributors to the economic and to fighting with poverty through both remunerative and unremunerative work at home, in the community and in the workplace. SHGs have been recognized as one efficient means of empowering women.

Critical Issues for Microfinance Institutions

This is not a point of consideration that Microfinancial services have capability to offer better services than conventional banking services and carry out the needs of the underprivileged people. The significant factor is that external Microfinancial services should join hand to the running system of lending and/or borrowing money in rural areas instead of throwing them out. In this way the poor people especially women who require the fund to run their business and family activities in a well-organized manner will get benefitted more. Some critical issues for microfinance organizations are as follows:

Sustainability

The primary issue is related to sustainability. It has been reported in much news that the Microfinancial institutions are comparatively costlier in terms of delivery of financial services. This is partially explained by the fact that the cost of supervision of credit is high, while the loan quantity and loan volume is low. Therefore it is necessary for MFIs to develop strategies for increasing the range and volume of their financial services.

Lack of Capital

The next part of concern for MFIs, which is on the expansion path, is that they face a scarcity of owned funds. This is a critical constraint in their being able to scale up. Many of the MFIs are socially oriented institutions and do not have adequate access to financial capital. As a result they have high debt equity ratios.

Borrowings

In comparison with earlier years, MFIs are now finding it relatively easier to raise loan funds from banks. This change came after the year 2000, when RBI allowed banks to lend to MFIs and treat such lending as part of their priority sector funding obligations. Private sector banks have designed innovative products such as: the Bank Partnership Model to fund MFIs and have started viewing the sector as a good business proposition. But banks need to be most careful when they feel most confident about MFIs. Bank should find the right technologies to assess the risk of funding MFIs.

Capacity of MFIs

It is now accepted that MFIs has both social and commercial dimensions. Since the sustainability of MFIs and their clients complement each other, it follows that building up the capacities of the MFIs and their primary stakeholders. These are preconditions for the successful delivery of flexible, client responsive and innovative microfinance services to the poor.

Conclusion

The MFI is leaving enormous economic and social impact. Microfinance provide both savings and loan facilities An MFI is likely to provide the much needed funds to the potential entrepreneurs of the rural India. Also it is anticipated that the people would become socially more advanced as they come into touch with the outside world. In order to be sustainable, microfinance lending should be fixed on market principles because large scale lending cannot be completed through financial support.

A core conclusion of this paper is that microfinance can contribute into solving the problem of insufficient housing and rural services as an integral part of poverty alleviation programmes and empower women to play a vital role in the society. Eventually it would be ideal to improve the creditworthiness of the poor and to make them more bankable to financial institutions and allow them to meet the criteria for long-term credit from the formal sector. Microfinance institutions have a lot to contribute to this by building financial discipline and educating borrowers about compensation requirements.

REFERENCES

1. Bhatt Nitin, Tang Shui (2001). "Delivering Microfinance in Developing Countries: Controversies and Policy Perspectives Policy Studies", *Policy Studies Journal,* 29(2); 3-9.
2. Brau, James C. Woller, Gary M. (2004). "Microfinance a Comprehensive Review of the Existing Literature", *Journal of Entrepreneurial Finance,* 9(1); 1-26.
3. Chaves Rodrigo A., Claudio Gonzalez-Vega (1996). 'The Design of Successful Rural Financial Intermediaries: Evidence from Indonesia", *World Development,* 24(1); 65-78.
4. Dichter Thomas W. (1996). "Questioning the Future of NGOs in Microfinance", *Journal of International Development,* 8(2); 259-269.
5. Havers M. (1996). "Financial Sustainability in Savings and Credit Programmes", *Journals of Economics,* 6(2); 144-150.
6. Iqubal Farukh (1988). "The Determinants of Money Lender Interest Rates: Evidence from Rural India", *The Journal of Development Studies,* 3; 364-378.
7. James C. Brau, Gary M. Woller (2004). "Microfinance: A Comprehensive Review of the Existing Literature", *Journal of Entrepreneurial Finance and Business Ventures,* 9(1) 1- 26. International Letters of Social and Humanistic Sciences Vol. 21 89.
8. Kumar Manish, Bohra Narendra, Singh Johari Amar (2010). "Microfinance as an Anti Poverty Vaccine for Rural India" *International Review of Business and Finance,* 2(1); 29-35.
9. McIntosh Craig, Bruce Wydick (2005). "Competition and Microfinance", *Journal of Development Economics,* 78(2); 271-298.
10. Pitt Mark M., Shahidur R. Khandker (1998). "The Impact of Group-based Credit Programmes on Poor Households in Bangladesh: Does the Gender of the Participants Matter?", *Journal of Political Economy,* 106(5); 958-996.
11. Rajakutty S. (1997). "Development of Women and Children in Rural Areas: Are we in the Right Course?", *Journal of Rural Development,* 16(1); pp. 85-11.

12. Robert Cull, Asli Demiguc Kunt, Jonathan Morduch (2007): "Financial performance and outreach: A Global Analysis of Leading Microbanks", *Economic Journal*, 3; 107-133.

13. Robert Cull, Asli Demirguc-Kunt, Jonathan Morduch (2009). "Microfinance Meets the Market", *Journal of Economic Perspectives*, 23(1); 167-192.

Index

*****